War Crimes Tribunals and Transitional Justice

Advocates of the 'Nuremberg legacy' emphasize the positive impact of the individualization of responsibility and the establishment of an historical record through judicial procedures for 'war crimes'. This legacy has been cited in the context of the establishment and operation of the UN ad hoc international criminal tribunals in the 1990s, as well as for the International Criminal Court.

The problem with this legacy, however, is that it is based solely on the experience of West Germany. Furthermore, the long-term effect of the procedure on post-conflict society has not been empirically examined. This book does this by analysing the Tokyo Trial, the other International Military Tribunal established after the Second World War, and its impact on post-war Japan.

This book examines the short- and long-term impact of the International Military Tribunal for the Far East (the Tokyo Trial) on post-war Japan, in order to improve the understanding of what international criminal justice can necessarily achieve to transform a war-torn society and promote reconciliation and thus strategy for ongoing international war crimes tribunals.

This book will be of much interest to students of war crimes, international law, transitional justice and international relations in general.

Madoka Futamura teaches International Relations at Doshisha University, Japan and is a Visiting Research Fellow with the War Crimes Research Group at King's College, London.

Contemporary security studies

NATO's Secret Armies
Operation Gladio and terrorism in Western Europe
Daniele Ganser

The US, NATO and Military Burden-Sharing
Peter Kent Forster and Stephen J. Cimbala

Russian Governance in the Twenty-First Century
Geo-strategy, geopolitics and new governance
Irina Isakova

The Foreign Office and Finland 1938–1940
Diplomatic sideshow
Craig Gerrard

Rethinking the Nature of War
Edited by Isabelle Duyvesteyn and Jan Angstrom

Perception and Reality in the Modern Yugoslav Conflict
Myth, falsehood and deceit 1991–1995
Brendan O'Shea

The Political Economy of Peacebuilding in Post-Dayton Bosnia
Tim Donais

The Distracted Eagle
The rift between America and Old Europe
Peter H. Merkl

The Iraq War
European perspectives on politics, strategy, and operations
Edited by Jan Hallenberg and Håkan Karlsson

Strategic Contest
Weapons proliferation and war in the greater Middle East
Richard L. Russell

Propaganda, the Press and Conflict
The Gulf War and Kosovo
David R. Willcox

Missile Defence
International, regional and national implications
Edited by Bertel Heurlin and Sten Rynning

Globalising Justice for Mass Atrocities
A revolution in accountability
Chandra Lekha Sriram

Ethnic Conflict and Terrorism
The origins and dynamics of civil wars
Joseph L. Soeters

Globalisation and the Future of Terrorism
Patterns and predictions
Brynjar Lia

Nuclear Weapons and Strategy
The evolution of American nuclear policy
Stephen J. Cimbala

Nasser and the Missile Age in the Middle East
Owen L. Sirrs

War as Risk Management
Strategy and conflict in an age of globalised risks
Yee-Kuang Heng

Military Nanotechnology
Potential applications and preventive arms control
Jurgen Altmann

NATO and Weapons of Mass Destruction
Regional alliance, global threats
Eric R. Terzuolo

Europeanisation of National Security Identity
The EU and the changing security identities of the Nordic states
Pernille Rieker

International Conflict Prevention and Peace-building
Sustaining the peace in post conflict societies
Edited by T. David Mason and James D. Meernik

Controlling the Weapons of War
Politics, persuasion, and the prohibition of inhumanity
Brian Rappert

Changing Transatlantic Security Relations
Do the US, the EU and Russia form a new strategic triangle?
Edited by Jan Hallenberg and Håkan Karlsson

Theoretical Roots of US Foreign Policy
Machiavelli and American unilateralism
Thomas M. Kane

Corporate Soldiers and International Security
The rise of private military companies
Christopher Kinsey

Transforming European Militaries
Coalition operations and the technology gap
Gordon Adams and Guy Ben-Ari

Globalization and Conflict
National security in a 'new' strategic era
Edited by Robert G. Patman

Military Forces in 21st Century Peace Operations
No job for a soldier?
James V. Arbuckle

The Political Road to War with Iraq
Bush, 9/11 and the drive to overthrow Saddam
Nick Ritchie and Paul Rogers

Bosnian Security after Dayton
New perspectives
Edited by Michael A. Innes

Kennedy, Johnson and NATO
Britain, America and the dynamics of alliance, 1962–68
Andrew Priest

Small Arms and Security
New emerging international norms
Denise Garcia

The United States and Europe
Beyond the neo-conservative divide?
Edited by John Baylis and Jon Roper

Russia, NATO and Cooperative Security
Bridging the gap
Lionel Ponsard

International Law and International Relations
Bridging theory and practice
Edited by Tom Bierstecker, Peter Spiro, Chandra Lekha Sriram and Veronica Raffo

Deterring International Terrorism and Rogue States
US national security policy after 9/11
James H. Lebovic

Vietnam in Iraq
Tactics, lessons, legacies and ghosts
Edited by John Dumbrell and David Ryan

Understanding Victory and Defeat in Contemporary War
Edited by Jan Angstrom and Isabelle Duyvesteyn

Propaganda and Information Warfare in the Twenty-First Century
Altered images and deception operations
Scot Macdonald

Governance in Post-Conflict Societies
Rebuilding fragile states
Edited by Derick W. Brinkerhoff

European Security in the Twenty-First Century
The challenge of multipolarity
Adrian Hyde-Price

Ethics, Technology and the American Way of War
Cruise missiles and US security policy
Reuben E. Brigety II

International Law and the Use of Armed Force
The UN charter and the major powers
Joel H. Westra

Disease and Security
Natural plagues and biological weapons in East Asia
Christian Enermark

Explaining War and Peace
Case studies and necessary condition counterfactuals
Jack Levy and Gary Goertz

War, Image and Legitimacy
Viewing contemporary conflict
James Gow and Milena Michalski

Information Strategy and Warfare
A guide to theory and practice
John Arquilla and Douglas A. Borer

War Crimes Tribunals and Transitional Justice
The Tokyo Trial and the Nuremberg legacy
Madoka Futamura

War Crimes Tribunals and Transitional Justice

The Tokyo Trial and the Nuremberg legacy

Madoka Futamura

Routledge
Taylor & Francis Group
LONDON AND NEW YORK

First published 2008
by Routledge
2 Park Square, Milton Park, Abingdon, Oxon OX14 4RN

Simultaneously published in the USA and Canada
by Routledge
270 Madison Ave, New York, NY 10016

Routledge is an imprint of the Taylor & Francis Group, an informa business

Typeset in Times by Wearset Ltd, Boldon, Tyne and Wear
Printed and bound in Great Britain by TJI Digital, Padstow, Cornwall

British Library Cataloguing in Publication Data
A catalogue record for this book is available from the British Library

Library of Congress Cataloging in Publication Data
A catalog record for this book has been requested

ISBN10: 0-415-42673-1 (hbk)
ISBN10: 0-203-94592-1 (ebk)

ISBN13: 978-0-415-42673-2 (hbk)
ISBN13: 978-0-203-94592-6 (ebk)

Contents

Preface and acknowledgements

This study of war crimes tribunals and transitional justice is interdisciplinary in its theoretical framework, content and methodology. The theoretical framework is set in the context of post-Cold War international peace and security and the creation and operation of ad hoc international criminal tribunals. The analysis of the main body of the book is focused on the Japanese reaction to and perception of the Tokyo Trial from 1946 to 2006, in order to elucidate the trial's impact on post-war Japan. The aim of this study is to re-examine, through the impact of the Tokyo Trial, the so-called 'Nuremberg legacy', which has been strongly influencing ongoing international war crimes tribunals.

Analysis of the Japanese reaction and perception is based on historical, cultural and social research conducted through a range of sources, including newspapers, books and articles written by Japanese authors, and public discourse. In order to get hold of people's subtle and nuanced attitudes towards and perceptions of the Tokyo Trial, I conducted a number of semi-structured intensive interviews with people from a range of backgrounds, ages, experience and social group. Interviews were conducted with 21 individuals, ages ranging from 24 (born in 1979) to 68 (born in 1935) at the time of interviews. I also conducted five focus groups to examine the interaction of different opinions, points of consensus and divergence. Both forms of interview, conducted during the autumn and winter of 2003, are an important source to clarify the complex and delicate perception and, thus, impact of the international war crimes trial on contemporary Japan. Furthermore, comments of these interviewees encouraged me to work on this controversial and difficult topic for the Japanese, assuring me of its importance to present-day Japan. They also helped me minimize my preconceptions that I have as a Japanese person, which I was highly aware of on analysing Japanese perceptions. Most of the interviewees were happy to have their name quoted in the book, but the author felt that because of the sensitivity of the topic and the fact that some requested anonymity, the identity of all interviewees would be kept confidential. Details of each interview and focus group are noted in the Appendix, Tables A.1 and A.2.

The multidisciplinary nature of this study exactly reflects my academic background of law, international history, international relations and war studies. I owe a debt of gratitude to all those people who supported and inspired me during my course of study. In particular, I could never have incorporated these multidisciplinary backgrounds into one piece of work without Professor James Gow, who inspired and encouraged me to take on this interesting but challenging topic. I am enormously grateful to him. I am also grateful to Dr Rachel Kerr for her constructive and inspiring instruction, which helped me develop, clarify and sharpen the argument. My thanks also go to Professor Sir Adam Roberts and Professor Ian Nish for their scrupulous and thoughtful comments on a previous version of this study. They have helped improve this version very much. I would also like to thank Professor Nisuke Andō who gave me feedback on early drafts of this work, helped me gain access to useful research materials and participated in an intensive interview. Professor Sadao Asada participated in an intensive interview and helped organize a focus group with his students. I am grateful to him. I am also grateful to Professor Mats Berdal, Professor Lawrence Douglas, Professor John Horne, Professor Yasuaki Ōnuma and Dr Ryō Ikeda, who have inspired me pointing out various important issues that I had not realized. I would also like to thank members of the War Crimes Research Group in the Department of War Studies at King's College London, especially Dr Tony Millett and Dr Ivan Zverzhanovski. I would also like to express my thanks to all those who participated in intensive interviews and focus groups whom I cannot name here. James Zobel at MacArthur Archives helped me with some primary sources. Andrew and Penny Johnson and Hilary Parker helped me with proofreading. This study could never be in this current form without all these people. However, of course, I am solely responsible for any errors found in this work.

On a personal level, I would like to thank Yoshiki for his love, patience and humour, which enabled me to survive this long and lonely journey. I owe my thanks also to Ai for her belief in me during the hardest time of the research. My thanks, of course, go to my parents and my brother, Atsushi, who never lost interest in my work and always supported, encouraged and comforted me with their love and wisdom.

I gratefully acknowledge the support of the Department of War Studies and the School of Social Science and Public Policy at King's College London for providing financial support for my fieldwork through the Student Research Fund and the Small Grants Fund for Postgraduate Research. I also acknowledge Cambridge University Press for permission to reproduce my work in 'Individual and Collective Guilt: Post-war Japan and the Tokyo War Crimes Tribunal', *European Review*, Vol. 14, No. 4 (2006); and Carnegie Endowment for International Peace for permission to reprint a table from 'The Tokyo Trial', in *International Conciliations*, by Solis Horwitz (New York; Carnegie Endowment for International Peace, 1950).

In this study, the translations of quotations from Japanese-written primary and secondary sources and comments made by interviewees and participants of focus groups were done by myself. The translations of the title of Japanese-written sources are noted in the bibliography. In the main body, the Japanese names are cited with the family name first, then the first name, following Japanese convention.

Madoka Futamura
November, 2006

Abbreviations

GHQ	General Headquarters, Supreme Commander for the Allied Powers
ICC	International Criminal Court
ICTR	International Criminal Tribunal for Rwanda
ICTs	ICTR and ICTY
ICTY	International Criminal Tribunal for former Yugoslavia
ILC	International Law Commission
IMT	International Military Tribunal
IMTFE	International Military Tribunal for the Far East
NGO	Non-governmental Organization
SCAP	Supreme Commander for the Allied Powers

Introduction

In 1945, the Allies, on the initiative of the United States, established the International Military Tribunal for the Trial of Major German War Criminals (the Nuremberg Tribunal) to prosecute and punish top leaders of Nazi Germany for war crimes conducted during the Second World War. Almost half a century later, the United Nations, with the United States again playing a leading role, created the ad hoc international criminal tribunals for the former Yugoslavia and Rwanda (ICTs). The ICTs, both in their creation and operation, are strongly based on and influenced by the experience of the Nuremberg Tribunal and post-war Germany and 'lessons' learned from it. The historical, legal and political precedent of the 'Nuremberg legacy' was explicitly invoked with the creation of the ICTs and subsequent discourse surrounding their expected impacts. At the opening of the commemoration of '50 years after Nuremberg' in October 1995, US President Bill Clinton declared: 'We have an obligation to carry forward the lessons of Nuremberg. That is why we strongly support the United Nations War Crimes Tribunals for the former Yugoslavia and for Rwanda'.[1]

However, Nuremberg is not the only precedent to which the ICTs can refer. The International Military Tribunal for the Far East (the Tokyo Trial) was also created in the aftermath of the Second World War to prosecute major Japanese war criminals. This tribunal is often neglected in the literature on war crimes tribunals and some argue that it 'achieved nothing whatever, as far as Japan was directly concerned'.[2] This comment, while not based on extensive research, nonetheless reflects a commonly shared view of the Tokyo Trial. The aim of this book is to interrogate this claim; to ascertain the experience and legacy of the Tokyo Trial and its impact on post-war Japan. Crucially, it addresses the extent to which the Japanese experience challenges or strengthens the 'Nuremberg legacy', and thus our current understanding of the utility of international war crimes trials.

In order to do so, it is necessary first to consider the purpose, strategy and impact of international war crimes prosecutions as understood by those who supported the establishment of the ICTs. The International Criminal Tribunal for the former Yugoslavia (ICTY) was established on 25 May 1993 by the United Nations Security Council. It was established on an ad hoc basis with a mandate to prosecute those responsible for serious violations of international humanitarian law committed during the war in the former Yugoslavia from 1991 onwards. The following year, in November 1994, the Security Council established a second ad hoc international criminal tribunal for Rwanda (ICTR). As of October 2006, the ICTY had indicted 161 persons, out of whom six accused were at large. Of the 98 persons who had concluded their proceedings, 46 were sentenced.[3] Although his case has been closed with his death, Slobodan Milosevic, the former President of the Federal Republic of Yugoslavia, was indicted while he was still in office and brought to The Hague. The ICTR has completed 21 cases including that of the former Prime Minister of Rwanda, Jean Kambanda, who was sentenced to life imprisonment. As of September 2006, there were 65 detainees, including several former senior cabinet ministers in the interim government of Rwanda of 1994, former military commanders, political leaders, journalists and senior businessmen. Thirty-one accused had completed their cases and 26 were on trial.[4]

The impact of the ICTs is not limited to the individuals on trial, nor indeed to the two regions. Their creation has had a slow but steady normative impact on international relations by reinforcing a norm of accountability for serious violations of international humanitarian law and the principle of 'universal jurisdiction' over such crimes. Subsequent developments appeared to reinforce these trends, including the British government's decision in 1998 to allow extradition hearings to proceed with regard to the former Chilean President Augusto Pinochet, who was indicted by a Spanish judge for crimes against humanity and crimes of torture committed while in office, and the establishment of a Special Court for Sierra Leone on the basis of an agreement between the United Nations and the government of Sierra Leone and other 'internationalized' mechanisms, involving international and domestic law and personnel in Kosovo, East Timor and Cambodia.[5] Meanwhile, already in 2002, the United States, while opposed to the form of international criminal justice espoused by the International Criminal Court (ICC), appeared to favour prosecuting Saddam Hussein over summary execution.[6] Although the Iraqi Special tribunal eventually took the form of a domestic court, there were elements of international involvement in the process. Finally, of course, the ICTs were a direct driving force for the establishment of the ICC with the adoption of the Rome Statute in July 1998 and its coming into force four years later.[7]

It seems that, since the creation of the ICTY, some form of international, or internationalized, criminal justice mechanism is seen by the United Nations and the international community as an important prerequisite to tackling the aftermath of armed conflicts and violence. At the same time, these developments and the effectiveness of the ICTs are enthusiastically discussed and studied both by practitioners and scholars specializing in international law, human rights, international politics and regional studies.[8] What needs more attention in existing research and arguments on the effectiveness and success of international war crimes tribunals, however, is thorough examination of *what exactly is achieved by prosecuting individuals suspected of committing war crimes in an international tribunal*. This is a critical question that requires examination of political as well as legal, domestic as well as international, issues. The debate over the success of the ICTs remains unproductive without a common understanding of the expected purposes; that is, what the tribunal is actually for. The success of the ICTs matters not only in their own terms but also within the broader context of international criminal justice, in which the experience of the ICTs has been given significant weight.

The strategic purposes of the ICTs and transitional justice

The ICTY, as well as the ICTR, was created as UN Security Council Chapter VII enforcement measures. The effect of this was that all member states had a binding obligation to cooperate with the tribunals. The legal basis for invoking Chapter VII to establish an international criminal tribunal was that the serious and widespread violence occurring in the former Yugoslavia was regarded as 'threats to international peace and security'. Security Council Resolution 827 (1993), which established the ICTY, set out the 'sole purpose' of the tribunal as 'prosecuting persons responsible for serious violations of international humanitarian law committed in the territory of the former Yugoslavia'.[9] Yet, prosecution *per se* was not the aim for which the tribunal was established; it was a means to achieve broader aims. The creation of the ICTY was a measure taken by the Security Council to fulfil its 'primary responsibility for the maintenance of international peace and security'.[10] Resolution 827 states that the tribunal would contribute to 'the restoration and maintenance of peace'.[11] Resolution 955, establishing the ICTR, echoed this by also declaring that the tribunal would contribute to 'the restoration and maintenance of peace'.[12] The key to assessing the work of the ICTs, therefore, is whether the creation and operation of the tribunal are 'appropriate and effective for the purpose of the restoration and maintenance of international peace and security'.[13] The understanding of this broader aim, the *strategic purposes* of war crimes prosecution, is indispensable in assessing the ICTs. What is furthermore necessary is a theoretical and conceptual framework within which to assess the effectiveness of international war crimes prosecutions based on their strategic purposes.

In order further to clarify the strategic purposes of the ICTs, it is necessary to go one step further and examine what the 'restoration' and 'maintenance' of peace means. Within the United Nations security system, Article 1 of the UN Charter declares that 'the maintenance of international peace and security' is the purpose of the United Nations. It does not refer to 'the restoration of peace' in this context. The Charter seems to assume the existence of international peace and security to start with. If there is no peace, it is not possible to maintain it. 'To "maintain" international peace means to prevent a breach of the peace', argues Hans Kelsen: 'If the peace has been broken, it cannot be maintained, but only restored'.[14] The United Nations was established in the aftermath of the Second World War in order to protect the peace regained and 'to save succeeding generations from the scourge of war, which twice in our lifetime has brought untold sorrow to mankind'.[15] The Charter reflects the assumption, and hope, of the founders of the organization that the post-Second World War international system would be essentially static.[16] The primary goal of the United Nations, therefore, is the 'maintenance' of a status quo, and when it is disturbed by 'aggressors', then a measure of 'restoration' is required. This point is reinforced in Article 39 of the Charter, which states that measures taken by the Security Council are 'to maintain or restore', not 'to restore or maintain'.

The phrase 'maintain *or* restore international peace and security' signifies that the two measures are regarded as independent or different from each other. The act of 'restoring' peace implies the non-existence of peace and relates to the removal of an immediate threat, or the achievement of a ceasefire; thus it is a short-term and consequence-oriented approach to a threat. Maintenance, on the other hand, is a long-term and process-oriented project to create long-lasting peace and, in a general sense, an action that follows restoration, as noted above. In other words, restoration is strongly related to the pursuit of 'peace', traditionally understood in terms of order among states and the absence of armed hostilities, and maintenance to the pursuit of 'justice', which tends to be related to the remedy for the non-military sources of instability.[17] In the past, measures taken by the Security Council under Chapter VII had been merely assigned either to 'restore', 'maintain' or 'restore or maintain', international peace and security. However, the phrasing of Resolution 827 signified that the ICTY, a Chapter VII enforcement measure, was formally expected to contribute both to 'restoration' *and* 'maintenance' of peace. This was the first such case in the history of the Security Council. The phrase reappeared in Resolution 955 (1994) on the establishment of the ICTR.[18]

It is here that the ICTs came to acquire muddled or seemingly conflicting strategic purposes; there exists no shared understanding of precisely in what ways international war crimes prosecution contributes to the restoration and maintenance of international peace and security. On the one hand, the ICTs are burdened with all possible 'good' – many and too diverse roles, some of which are not even asked of domestic criminal justice. These overly diverse roles bring about confusion in analysis and a tendency to lump together means, ends and impacts, each of which should be examined at a different level.[19]

On the other hand, the pros and cons of the ICTs, and of other approaches to post-conflict justice, continue to be debated and discussed from various different perspectives of the goal.[20] It is in this context that a conventional 'peace-vs-justice' argument was raised with regard to the ICTs, especially the ICTY. The incompatibility of 'restoration' and 'maintenance', or peace and justice, was discussed in terms of theory, practice, timing and moral implications. The pursuit of peace in the conflicts in the former Yugoslavia was to achieve a ceasefire and implement a peace process. Having been created in the midst of the conflict, the ICTY, in its first stages, was expected to contribute, through its existence and procedures, to the deterrence of further violence on the ground.[21] Critics of the ICTY argued that indictments and prosecutions were not only ineffective but were also counterproductive for restoring peace in the region.[22] It was claimed that in order to stop the fighting, it was necessary to negotiate with political and military leaders with supreme responsibility for the conduct of war, and, thus the prime targets presumably of the tribunal. 'Is it realistic', Anthony D'Amato asked, 'to expect them to agree to a peace settlement in Bosnia if, directly following the agreement, they may find themselves in the dock?'[23] There was a concern that the attempt to prosecute war criminals might prolong the war. An anonymous contributor to *Human Rights Quarterly* argued in 1996 from a peace negotiator's point of view that the pursuit of criminals was incompatible with the pursuit of peace and that it was the latter that needed to be prioritized: 'The quest for justice for yesterday's victims of atrocities should not be pursued in such a manner that it makes today's living the dead of tomorrow'.[24] In D'Amato's words, the situation was 'the apparently novel dilemma' of attempting to achieve peace and justice at the same time.[25]

In contrast, some pointed out the tribunal's contribution to the peace, emphasizing the significance of the elimination of Radovan Karadzic and Ratko Mladic from the Dayton Peace Process as a result of their indictment in July 1995. The Peace Agreement, it was argued, could not have been concluded if these two figures had been at the table.[26]

The incompatibility of peace and justice has been argued also from a moral viewpoint. Oliver Schuett argues that peace superseded justice under the Dayton Agreement, pointing out the direct involvement of Slobodan Milosevic and the President of Croatia, Franjo Tudjman, in concluding the Peace Agreement in December 1995, in spite of the fact that both of them were the potential indictees at the time: 'Bringing peace to the region through the [General Framework Agreement], and doing justice through the tribunal, are therefore contradictory'.[27] The argument of 'peace versus accountability',[28] although in itself is important, has gradually lost significance since the ceasefire in 1995; instead, the long-term contribution of the ICTY to the region came to be the focus of attention.

Some commentators raise a more fundamental objection to the ICTs, arguing that their creation was contrary to the structure of the international legal and political order based on state sovereignty.[29] International criminal tribunals do challenge state sovereignty by 'intrud[ing] on one of the most sacred areas of state sovereignty: criminal jurisdiction'.[30] This is even more so because both the ICTY and ICTR were given primacy over domestic courts regarding prosecution of war crimes.[31] In that sense, the ICTs, as some rightly put, constitute a form of intervention.[32] What makes some academics and practitioners worried is the possibility that justice might be pursued at the expense of peace, understood in terms of order among states based on the mutual respect of sovereignty.

Regarding the tension between peace and justice noted above, it is important to go back to Resolution 827 (1993) to examine the expected role of the ICTY in international peace and justice. What does 'the restoration *and* maintenance of peace' mean in this context? Aurélien Colson sees in the creation of the ICTs 'an intention to transcend traditional notions of peace and justice'.[33] This is well reflected in the words of Carl August Fleischhauer, United Nations Under-Secretary-General for Legal Affairs, who regarded the fundamental goals of the ICTY as 'ending war crimes, bringing the perpetrators to justice and breaking an endless cycle of ethnic violence and retribution'.[34] In other words, the tribunal was expected to restore peace, achieve justice and maintain long-term peace, all of which were regarded as neither independent nor conflicting, but mutually supportive within the overall project of 'the restoration and maintenance of peace'. The vital question in the context of the former Yugoslavia and Rwanda was not merely 'how war ends' but also 'how peace starts'. It is for this 'critical juncture' of the transition from war to peace that peace needs to be both 'restored' and 'maintained'; in other words, 'a long-lasting peace needs to be established' by deterring the recurrence of violence. Here, the logic of peace and the logic of justice are both needed to be followed.[35] The point about the ICTs is that *justice is endorsed for the sake of peace by justice as a means*. It is the idea of 'peace through justice' that has been strongly embedded in the strategic purposes of the ICTs, which is expected to play a significant role in the region and thus to contribute, in turn, to overall international peace and security.[36]

As indicated above, the ICTs hold, or are expected to hold, several strategic purposes such as: short- and long-term deterrence, the end of the culture of impunity, the development of international law, a purely victim-centred approach to bring justice to victims, strengthening of the rule of law and so on. The ICTY itself raises the following five points as its core achievements: spearheading the shift from impunity to accountability; establishing the facts; bringing justice to thousands of victims and giving them a voice; the accomplishments in international law; and strengthening the Rule of Law.[37] Although some of them are purely international or normative in their nature, not necessarily targeting the situation in the former Yugoslavia and Rwanda, many others are efforts to pursue 'justice' in the context of post-conflict social transition. Supporters of the 'peace through justice' project emphasized the tribunals' role in the transformation of war-torn societies and reconciliation in it.[38] The ICTY Annual Report of 1994 clearly stated that 'it is a tool for promoting reconciliation and restoring true peace'.[39] This study, therefore, regards post-conflict social transformation and reconciliation, in other words, the pursuit of the so-called 'transitional justice', as the most prominent strategic purpose of the ICTY, as well as ICTR, and develops the following analysis based on this understanding.[40]

Assessment of the ICTs and the 'Nuremberg legacy'

In a number of significant respects, the ICTs drew on an essential historical, legal and judiciary basis from one of their predecessors: the Nuremberg Tribunal, the first public international war crimes tribunal to be created in the aftermath of the Second World War. The creation of the ICTs, especially the ICTY, has been largely viewed through the prism of 'Nuremberg'.[41] On the assessment of the tribunals, Virginia Morris and Michael Scharf noted early on in the life of the ICTY: 'As the first international criminal jurisdiction, the Nuremberg Tribunal provides *the benchmark for assessing the International tribunal and its prospects for success*'.[42]

On the expected impact of war crimes prosecution, although the Nuremberg Tribunal itself held several strategic purposes,[43] it was its impact on post-war Germany that attracted considerable attention in the context of the creation and operation of the ICTs. Nuremberg was seen to have demonstrated that war crimes prosecutions can achieve the broader ends of promoting the transformation of a society: from Nazi-led to denazified Germany. In addition, it was seen to have proved that international prosecution was both feasible and desirable for such ends. It is this aspect of the experience of Nuremberg – the Nuremberg legacy – that the international community in the 1990s came to appreciate as a positive model within the context of post-conflict social transformation and reconciliation.[44] Regarded as the universal model for transforming war-torn societies, the Nuremberg legacy became the basis for the operation and assessment of the ICTY and ICTR. Just as Nuremberg had been seen as 'the last act of the war and first act of the peace',[45] the ICTs were created for their potential contribution at a critical juncture, the transition from war to peace. In this context, the idea of 'peace through justice' surely has a root in Nuremberg.

The Nuremberg legacy re-examined

Several factors, however, make universalization of the Nuremberg legacy problematic. The legacy is based solely on the experience of Nuremberg and post-war Germany. The Nuremberg Trial was conducted in the context of the Allies' occupation policy to promote denazification of post-war Germany, which is a different context from the transformation of post-conflict ethnically divided societies. The 'decontextualized' application of the Nuremberg experience is problematic; the legacy cannot be imported wholesale into a wholly different set of circumstances. Furthermore, rather than stressing domestic impact, the proponents of the Nuremberg Trial originally stressed the tribunal's contribution to establishing post-Second World War *international* peace by creating a legal order based on the deterrent effect of international law. It should also be noted that the Nuremberg legacy itself is not necessarily positive with regard to *jus ad bellum*; Nuremberg, which was to be the trial to end all wars, did not have such a deterrent impact on post-Second World War international relations.[46] Finally, Nuremberg was a military trial and the ICTs are criminal trials. The former pursue military justice, which gives more limited rights to the defendant.

In spite of these problems, however, the Nuremberg legacy is taken as a universal model for post-conflict social transformation and reconciliation, and is strongly connected to the strategic purposes of the ICTs. Re-examination of the Nuremberg legacy, therefore, is vital for the assessment of the strategy and success of the ICTs, as well as the project of international war crimes prosecution.

There are several options open for re-examining the Nuremberg legacy. We could look at the Nuremberg experience itself, by empirically studying the impact of the International Military Tribunal on post-war German social transformation. Research of this kind has already been conducted by various scholars.[47] However, what matters here is not whether the assumed German experience is authentic or not; what matters is the fact that the legacy is currently interpreted in a certain way to support international war crimes prosecutions and the idea of 'peace through justice'. Another way to tackle the Nuremberg legacy is to examine directly the impact of the ICTs on societies in the former Yugoslavia and Rwanda. However, such research will necessarily be limited in scope because the work of the ICTs is not yet complete. It is difficult, if not impossible, at this point to make an assessment of the long-term impact and effect of the tribunal on social transformation and reconciliation of societies in the former Yugoslavia and Rwanda, as well as on international peace and security as a whole.

The approach taken in this study is to re-examine the Nuremberg legacy as a notion, and the idea of 'peace through justice', based on a different case: the Tokyo Trial. The Tokyo Trial was created at around the same time, for the same aims, as Nuremberg: to prosecute and punish the vanquished of the Second World War for having conducted 'crimes against peace', war crimes and 'crimes against humanity'. This study will re-examine the Nuremberg legacy by analysing the Tokyo Trial and its impact on post-war Japan. Has the Tokyo Trial contributed to the transformation and reconciliation of post-war Japan? If so then does it operate in the manner that the Nuremberg legacy claims? These questions are addressed through empirical research on the Japanese perception of the Tokyo Trial: how the Japanese themselves recognized and discussed the Tokyo Trial since its establishment in 1946.[48]

The Tokyo Trial as a 'forgotten' trial

Compared to the Nuremberg Trial, there is a general lack of interest in the Tokyo Trial, even among those who study war crimes prosecutions and international criminal justice. This is a curious but serious defect when the Nuremberg experience is regarded as the legacy of war crimes tribunals in general. What is important, but often ignored, is the fact that Tokyo is the only *international* tribunal, other than Nuremberg, prior to the creation of the ICTY, and it is one of the four 'pure' international tribunals that have actually conducted the prosecution and punishment of individual war criminals. This signifies the importance of Tokyo as a precedent for international war crimes tribunals.

John Pritchard states: 'In scope and in implications for the post-war world, the Tokyo Trial may exceed the importance of its Nuremberg counterpart'.[49] However, compared with the Nuremberg Trial, there is very little written in English on the Tokyo Trial. Some of the exceptions are Richard Minear's *Victors' Justice* and B. V. A. Röling and Antonio Cassese's *The Tokyo Trial and Beyond*.[50] Even among those who conduct research on war crimes prosecutions, the Tokyo Trial is generally lumped together with the Nuremberg Trial, but by simply focusing on the latter.[51] In the worst cases, the 'Tokyo Tribunal' or 'International Military Tribunal for the Far East' are altogether absent from the indexes of literatures on war crimes tribunals.

There are several reasons for the scarcity of research on the Tokyo Trial. First, there is a general belief that Nuremberg and Tokyo are identical in their appearance, procedure and, therefore, effects. Tokyo is a sister institution, nothing more. Second, for many, the atrocities perpetrated by Nazis appear to overshadow the inhumane campaigns conducted by the Japanese army towards POWs and civilians. Gerry Simpson states:

> The metaphorical equation of war crimes with Nazis is inscribed on the culture. Most of the war crimes trials held since 1945 has been a restatement of this relationship. The Nazi regime remains the epitome of absolute evil in Western culture and each successive war crimes trial owes as much to this doctrine as to the tenacious efforts of Nazi hunters Beate Klarsfeld and Simon Weisenthal.[52]

Third, there is the fact that the participants at Nuremberg, both the prosecutor and judges, and the defendant, were far better known to the world than those at Tokyo. Fourth, some degrade the Tokyo Trial's value as 'an historical example of international justice', pointing out that several key figures and war crimes were exempted from the trial.[53] Fifth, linguistic barriers cannot be ignored. More researchers can read both German and English than can work in Japanese and English; yet knowledge of both languages are indispensable to gaining a full picture of the trial. In addition, while German publications can easily be introduced, with or without translation, to the English-speaking academic world, research conducted in Japanese cannot be introduced without translation, which does not happen very often.[54] Furthermore, the scarcity of research can be attributed simply to a lack of general interest within English-speaking academia regarding the trial in the 'Far East'. Whatever the reason, as early as in 1950, Telford Taylor wrote:

> Nuremberg has become a synonym for war crimes trials and has received the lion's share of attention from both journalists and jurists. Unhappily, public indifference to the Tokyo Trial has been matched by an apparent lack of interest on the part of the sponsoring governments themselves.[55]

From a practical point of view, the scarcity of research on the Tokyo Trial is also a result of the unavailability of the trial records.[56] In the case of Nuremberg, stenographic records were published soon after the trial in four different languages, and the proceedings of the trials and all documentation given in evidence were published in 1947 in 42 volumes together with detailed indexes. However, in the case of Tokyo, there was little effort to publish, or even to preserve, the records of the trial. An enormous amount of the record relating to the Tokyo Trial was removed from Japan by the Foreign Documents branch of the Central Intelligence Agency. However, the US government did not attempt to publish the record soon after the trial and to make it available to a larger public, as they had done for Nuremberg: 'The documentation and records of the "Trial of the Major War Criminals" remained in the hectographed form in which they had been circulated during the trial'.[57] Donald Watt depicts the situation:

> The various sets of papers, records, indexes, transcripts, and so forth were scattered over the globe, disappearing into archives and repositories to surface years later in imperfect form in the public and university collections of some of the eleven participating countries. The complete files of the prosecution, comprising working papers, minutes, secretarial papers, and so on, and of its national components, if any such existed (and it is difficult to believe they did not exist in some form or other), seem to have disappeared from sight entirely.[58]

In 1957, the Centre for Japanese Studies at the University of Michigan published an index to the proceedings of the Tokyo Trial.[59] This index, according to Watt, is 'very limited [in scale] compared with the two volumes of indexes to the Nuremberg [*sic*] documents, and the references were confined to the pages of the transcripts'.[60] It was not until 1975 that the US National Archives and Records Administration opened many of the classified documents from the International Prosecution Section. According to Awaya Kentarō, a Japanese scholar of the Tokyo Trial, most of those documents were left unexamined until around the mid-1980s.[61] It was not until 1977 that the judgment of the tribunal, the separate, dissenting and concurring opinions, and the majority judgment, were first published *in toto* by the University of Amsterdam;[62] and the stenographic record of the trial in English was not published until 1981. On publishing *The Tokyo War Crimes Trial: The Complete Transcripts of the Proceedings of the International Military Tribunal for the Far East in Twenty-two volumes* in 1981, John Pritchard stated: 'To the best of my knowledge, this is the first time anyone has tried to assemble a comprehensive collection of [the] records [of the Proceedings in Chambers of the Tokyo Trial]'.[63]

The unavailability of primary source material is not very different for documents written in Japanese. The Tokyo Tribunal published the stenographic record of the trial in Japanese; however this record seems to have been not widely circulated. It is the reproduction of this record, which was published in 1968, that can be more easily accessed now.[64] At the time of the trial, there was no official publication of the record. Instead, it was the court staff of the *Asahi Shimbun* newspaper who reported a full picture of the trial and published nine volumes of records between 1946 and 1948 as the trial took place. According to the press corps, it was very difficult to take any printed matter or written papers out of the court. And it was not known whether this was due to the court's policy or the Military Police.[65] In 1962, the press corps of the *Asahi* republished its nine volumes of trial report, pointing out that those volumes had been the only record, except for the stenographic records, that depicted the whole trial but that they were now impossible to get even at second-hand bookstores.[66]

When asked about the unavailability of the trial record, the Dutch justice of the Tokyo Tribunal, Bernard Röling, answered:

> I suppose that [the British and the Americans] were perhaps a bit ashamed of what happened there ... I suspect that they didn't want the Tokyo Trial to become very well known. But I have no evidence for that. It's just a strange thing that the 'biggest trial in recorded history', as it has been called, was so over-looked.[67]

John Dower takes the view that the fact that the Tokyo Tribunal did not officially publish its record as symbolizing the cynicism of the tribunal staff, who by 1948, because of changes in the world, especially the development of the Cold War, did not believe that Tokyo, as well as Nuremberg, could contribute to a post-war peace based on international law and justice.[68] Awaya acknowledged that the materials of the Tokyo Trial were 'an historical treasure house', but argued in 1983: 'The fact that these documents have not yet been exploited is related closely to the manner in which the trial was concluded'.[69] These comments suggest that Nuremberg and Tokyo were not identical but have several differences in their structure and procedures, and thus probable impacts afterwards.

The significance of the Tokyo Trial and its impact on post-war Japan

Considering the currently limited literature written in English on the Tokyo Trial, this study will be beneficial to those who are interested in the Tokyo Trial. More importantly, this work focuses not only on the trial itself but also on its short- and long-term impact on post-war Japanese society. In addition, the Tokyo Trial's impact will be analysed through the Japanese perception of the trial. An analysis of the Tokyo Trial and the Japanese perception, of course, is important in its own terms. However, the study emphasizes its significance for re-examining and questioning current understanding of the impact of international war crimes trials on post-conflict societies: the universal validity of the Nuremberg legacy. The significance of the Tokyo Trial thus goes beyond historical and regional context and expands into contemporary and international context.

Whilst in Germany, Nuremberg and the crimes for which their leaders were punished have been widely debated, Japanese attitudes towards the Tokyo Trial are often characterized in terms of passivity and apathy. In Japan, until the late 1970s, academic research on the Tokyo Trial had not been enthusiastically conducted, and the trial had rarely appeared in public discourse until the 1980s.[70] In 1998, the Ministry of Foreign Affairs disclosed all material it possessed on the Tokyo Trial, but the Ministry of Justice, which collected the material from the Tokyo Trial, as well as other minor war crimes trials and created a catalogue, still does not make these collections open to the public.[71] Perceptions of and attitudes towards the trial are one set of barometer, which is especially important when the trial's impact on post-war society is examined. In that sense, the difference in the general attitude of the Japanese and the Germans towards the Tokyo and Nuremberg Trials indicates the possible different impact of international trials, probably the flaws in 'universalizing' the Nuremberg experience. A question then will be raised: to what extent can the Japanese attitude towards the Tokyo Trial be explained by the impact of the trial itself?

Some scholars attributed a passive Japanese attitude towards the Tokyo Trial to Japanese culture. For example, Judith Shklar stated: 'it is doubtful whether a trial as a legal drama could have had any great political effect in a non-European country so lacking in legalistic traditions'.[72] Röling pointed out the uniqueness of Japanese culture – and its influence from Zen Buddhism – which he had sensed from the attitude of the defendants at the tribunal.[73] Certainly, cultural and philosophical backgrounds are important and cannot be ignored in assessing Japanese perceptions of the Tokyo Trial. However, this research seeks to avoid the conclusion that the 'international tribunal worked differently – or did not work at all – *because of* the Japanese non-Western, or unique, cultural background'; a conclusion that has been raised by some to excuse their not taking the Tokyo Trial seriously.[74] It will be argued here that the experience of the Tokyo Trial, the only international tribunal other than Nuremberg that actually operated and completed all its procedure, is too important to be dismissed in this way, because the Japanese attitude towards the Tokyo Trial indicates other possible impacts that an international tribunal might have on society, which may not correspond to the perceived Nuremberg legacy. What is more, the Tokyo Trial becomes even more important if we are concerned about the impact of international war crimes tribunals on non-Western societies, given the fact that international or internationalized courts are currently operating for societies such as Rwanda, Sierra Leone, East Timor or Cambodia.

Ian Buruma argues that the ambivalence in the Japanese attitude towards the Tokyo Trial 'has less to do with the lack of a legal tradition, or with nationalist bloody-mindedness, than with the nature of the trial itself'.[75] The nature of the trial derives partly from the nature of international military tribunals in general and partly from the nature of the Tokyo Trial in particular, which was strongly influenced by a different geopolitical context from that of post-war Germany. It is often argued that the Tokyo Trial was far more politicized or unfair than Nuremberg; the Japanese attitude can be attributed to such a defect per se. In this study, I would not wish to ignore the unique nature of the Tokyo Trial and the context in which it operated. However, the aim here is to go beyond emphasizing the 'uniqueness' of the case and investigate whether there is any general lesson to be learned from Japan's experience with the international war crimes tribunal. For this reason, the study analyses the Japanese perception in relation to two devices of international war crimes prosecution: the individualization of responsibility and the creation of an historical record, the positive impacts of which have been emphasized by the advocates of the Nuremberg legacy.[76] Through the examination of Japanese perceptions and attitudes, the present study analyses the short- and long-term impact of these two devices. In this way, general lessons of the Tokyo Trial can be inferred and the core of the

Nuremberg legacy – the utility of the two devices in a different context – can be critically examined.

A number of scholars downgraded the impact of the Tokyo Trial on post-war Japan.[77] They may have been right when we consider 'positive' or 'visible' effects. However, no positive effect does not mean no effect at all, and no visible impact does not deny a subtle impact buried deep. On the contrary, the passive attitude of the Japanese towards their past and the Tokyo Trial itself illustrates different, potentially negative effects that international tribunals can have on society, especially when it comes to social transformation and reconciliation. The silence of the Japanese people about the Tokyo Trial and the war crimes legacy is vocal in its own sense.

The Tokyo Trial has not been erased from Japanese national memory; rather it persistently haunts society whenever people try to face the past, war, defeat and the issues of war responsibility and reconciliation. This is stark in relations between Japan and its neighbouring countries in Asia, where tension is continuously raised, even 60 years after the end of the war, over issues of war crimes, history textbooks and government officials visiting the controversial Yasukuni shrine, the origin of which can be all traced back to who was prosecuted for what and how the war was depicted in the trial.[78] The Tokyo Trial, in this sense, clouds Japanese reconciliation with the victims of its war, as well as with its own past. This potentially negative aspect of the impact of the Tokyo Trial is as important as its positive aspects for analysing the impact of international war crimes trials on post-conflict society.

Compared to English language literature, there has been more academic work done on the Tokyo Trial in Japanese.[79] However, most of it analysed the trial in historical context or focused on legal aspects of the trial. Not many of these texts examined, academically, its significance from contemporary and interdisciplinary points of view.[80] Even those who sought to identify its significance from a contemporary standpoint mostly did so within a national context and did not extract general lessons. This book will also contribute to research on the Tokyo Trial in Japan by presenting the wider and deeper significance of the trial to contemporary international peace and security.

Before examining the Nuremberg legacy in the light of the experience of the Tokyo Trial, Chapter 1 discusses the significance of international war crimes tribunals in post-Cold War international peace and security, through examining how the creation of the ICTs became both 'possible' and 'necessary' in the new security environment. The chapter illustrates the interaction of law and politics and the coexistence of the logic of peace and justice in the creation and operation of the ICTs, and argues that to understand the ICTs' strategic purposes, an interdisciplinary approach and non-static theoretical framework are necessary. It will be argued that war crimes tribunals and the issue of transitional justice have implications not only for international lawyers and human rights theorists but also for theorists of international politics and security studies. The chapter also focuses on the Nuremberg and Holocaust analogy made by the international community in the context of war crimes in the former Yugoslavia and illustrates how a Nuremberg-like institution came to be established for that conflict.

Chapter 2 examines the meaning of the 'Nuremberg legacy' and analyses why that legacy was revived in the form of the ad hoc international criminal tribunals nearly half a century after the Nuremberg judgment. The legacy is often mentioned but its meaning has never been coherent, changing from time to time, context to context. The first part of the chapter examines how the Nuremberg legacy was understood during the Cold War, focusing on the development of international law since Nuremberg, the claim of 'victor's justice', and post-Second World War international relations and state practices. It clarifies the background to international reluctance to follow the Nuremberg precedent during this period. It also shows that in spite of this international reluctance, the Nuremberg legacy started to acquire broader significance through human rights movements and the pursuit of 'transitional justice' from the 1980s onwards. The second part of the chapter demonstrates that the post-Cold War understanding of the Nuremberg legacy is different from that in the previous period because of the new international security environment. The chapter argues that two points – the pursuit of individual responsibility and the creation of an historical record – are the lessons that the promoters of the ICTs specifically derived from Nuremberg, and illustrates how they have been adopted in the context of post-Cold War international war crimes prosecutions. Examination, in the following chapters, of the Nuremberg legacy through the Tokyo Trial will be based on the impact of these two devices of war crimes prosecution.

In Chapter 3, an overview of the Tokyo Trial is offered. After a brief examination of the structure and procedures of the Tokyo Trial, the chapter analyses the Allies' strategic purpose, in the context of post-war Japan, of holding the trial and the intention of both pursuing individual responsibility and creating an historical record. Despite this strategic purpose and the two devices, which are identical to the Nuremberg Trial, the chapter points to several significant differences between the two trials, which derive from the different degree of initiative taken by the United States.

Chapter 4 analyses the general character of Japanese perceptions of the Tokyo Trial from 1946 to 2006 chronologically. Research is based on examination of Japanese publications, both academic and non-academic, on the trial, focusing both on quality (the nature of the arguments) and quantity (the fluctuating research output in each decade). The chapter also looks at events related to the Tokyo Trial, for example, the release of two films in 1983 and 1998, the so-called 'textbook row', the issue of 'comfort women', politicians' words and deeds regarding the trial, and how society has reacted to each of these. From these *public* discussions of the trial, the chapter examines whether, and in what way, the Japanese are passive and ignorant regarding the Tokyo Trial, and whether there has been a change and/or greater coherence in Japanese attitudes, values and beliefs.

In the following two chapters, the general Japanese perception illustrated in Chapter 4 will be examined in more detail through the two devices of war crimes prosecution identified: the individualization of responsibility and an historical record created by the tribunal. In addition to sources used in Chapter 4, examination and analysis in these two chapters are also based on intensive interviews and focus groups, which explore people's nuanced and subtle attitude and get hold of contemporary and private Japanese perceptions. The aim of Chapters 5 and 6 is to analyse the short- and long-term impact and effects on post-war Japan of the two devices of the international tribunal.

Chapter 5 focuses on the impact of the Tokyo Tribunal's historical record. The tribunal's record of the war has become the focus of strong criticism by nationalists and some revisionists, and of neo-nationalism in the 1990s. The chapter analyses the nationalist frustration with the 'Tokyo Trial view of history', together with the general reaction of the Japanese to the tribunal's historical record. The chapter also explores, through interviews, 'knowledge' and 'image' that people hold regarding the Tokyo Trial: what the current generation knows about the trial and its account of war, how they perceive the Tokyo Trial and how they regard the revisionist and neo-nationalist views of history and the Tokyo Trial. The chapter further investigates the nature of the Japanese 'silence' over the Tokyo Trial and analyses whether the 'silence' has something to do with the tribunal's historical record. Based on these, the chapter examines whether, and to what extent, Japanese historical perceptions of the war and the awareness of war crimes are influenced by the Tokyo Trial's judgment and its historical record, and how they have affected Japanese attempts at reconciliation with its Asian neighbours as well as with its past.

Chapter 6 focuses on the impact of the Tokyo Trial's pursuit of individual criminal responsibility of Japan's wartime leaders. The chapter analyses the impact of and limits to the individualization of responsibility by examining how people at the time understood the individual responsibility of their leaders, on the one hand, and perceived their own war responsibility, on the other. The chapter also looks at the view of 'victor's justice' held by the Japanese and examines whether and how this view clouds the legacy of the Tokyo Trial. Given the inseparable relationship between the international trial and 'victor's justice', the feasibility and desirability of holding domestic trials soon after the war are also examined. The aim is to see whether, and to what extent, people's sense of war guilt and responsibility has been influenced by their leaders having been prosecuted by means of the Tokyo Trial. The chapter concludes with an analysis of how the current Japanese sense of war guilt and responsibility, observed from their perception of the Tokyo Trial, influences Japan's reconciliation with its neighbouring countries as well as its own past.

Based on empirical research about the Tokyo Trial and its impact on post-war Japan, this study critically examines the Nuremberg legacy, and relates this examination to analysis of the strategic purpose of international tribunals. It suggests a need to question the role of war crimes tribunals in transitional justice and the understanding held by advocates of international tribunals regarding what international criminal justice can necessarily achieve, and what outsiders can and cannot do to transform a war-torn society and promote reconciliation within it.

The study of the Tokyo Trial may seem, at first glance, irrelevant to the examination of strategic purposes of the ICTs, as the contexts in which the Tokyo Trial and the ICTs were established are very different, much more so than Nuremberg and the ICTs.[81] However, as this research attempts to show, it enhances understanding of the strategy and impact of the ICTs because they are expected to produce a positive impact on a post-conflict society through the devices of the individualization of responsibility and the creation of an historical record, which were also applied to the Tokyo Trial and may have caused a different impact from what is assumed by the 'Nuremberg legacy'. The experience of the Tokyo Trial and post-war Japan, I conclude, demonstrates that the impact and effect of international war crimes tribunals and their two principal devices are not necessarily wholly positive, nor are they straightforward.

The Tokyo Trial is an important case with which to test the 'Nuremberg legacy'. Whether vindicating or criticizing the Nuremberg idea of international war crimes prosecution, examination of the Tokyo experience is indispensable in order to understand more thoroughly the multifaceted impact of international war crimes tribunals on post-conflict societies. This 'forgotten' trial offers significant lessons, which need to be examined in the field of transitional justice and international criminal justice.

1 The international criminal tribunals and international peace and security

Theory and practice

In spite of the amount of research on the ad hoc international criminal tribunals (ICTs) undertaken in the past decade, little has been focused on the ICTs' *strategic purposes* regarding international peace and security.[1] This is because of a disciplinary boundary between international politics and international law and a philosophical boundary between Realism and Liberalism that exist in studies of international affairs. This chapter illustrates the importance of breaking these boundaries for understanding the significance of the ICTs in international peace and security. The aim is to show the role of international war crimes tribunals in post-Cold War international relations by examining a new understanding of international peace and security, and the relationship between law and politics, and peace and justice there. The chapter also illustrates how the international reaction to the conflict in the former Yugoslavia led to the establishment of a Nuremberg-like institution.

Law and politics in the international criminal tribunals

That the strategic purposes of the ICTs are not fully examined in existing research is related to the fact that the ICTs, as well as international war crimes prosecution, have been studied, until very recently, mostly by international lawyers who are more interested in procedural aspect of the tribunals than in the relations between the means and ends of international criminal justice. The question 'what do the ICTs aim to achieve?' is highly political in nature, the significance of which is traditionally either ignored or dismissed by legal scholars. For international political theorists or the scholars of international security, on the other hand, the ICTs and international criminal justice are regarded as not in their sphere of interest. It is this disciplinary boundary between international politics and international law, not only in terms of their interest but also in their methodology, that has been an obstacle to understanding the significance of the ICTs in international peace and security.[2]

International political theorists had shown relatively little interest in the creation of the ICTs at least until the late 1990s. International political scholars are traditionally cynical about or indifferent to the role of law in international relations due to the influence of the Hobbesian view of the world: with no super-ordinate authority over states, international politics is a self-help arena, in which '[e]ach state pursues its own interests, however defined, in ways it judges best'.[3] In such an arena, there is little place for international law to play a significant role. While accepting its existence, Hans Morgenthau argues that international law is 'a primitive type of law' because of the absence of central government and law-enforcement institutions:

> Wherever an attempt has been made to give international law the effectiveness of a centralized legal system, reservations, qualifications, and the general political conditions under which nations must act in the modern state system have nullified the legal obligations entered into for the purpose of establishing centralized functions.[4]

Some international political theorists, especially neo-liberals, take into account international rules and norms, namely 'international institutions', for theorizing states' cooperation and the problem of cheating.[5] However, even in their cases, international law is merely given supplemental and instrumental roles. States care about international law for the sake of maximizing their interests, and institutions and regimes cease to exist when states see no utility in maintaining them: 'Treaties are inherently temporary, and their observance is inherently conditional on their continuing to serve the vital interests of the state'.[6] Norms, rules or laws are seen as mere reflections of state interests and power, and as such they have little significance at least in comparison to the domestic arena.

Reflecting such views on international law, many diplomats and international political theorists viewed the establishment of the International Criminal Tribunal for the former Yugoslavia (ICTY) cynically as no more than a 'fig leaf' to cover up failure to have taken immediate and decisive action for atrocities in Bosnia.[7] The great powers, especially the United States, were reluctant militarily to intervene in the situation. At the same time, even reluctant government leaders could no longer ignore the public moral pressure to 'do something' in response to the worst atrocities occurring in Europe since the Holocaust.[8] 'It was in this vacuum' between the public pressure to intervene and state leaders' reluctance to do so, Aryeh Neier argued, 'that the proposal for a tribunal advanced until its establishment was formally approved'.[9] The ICTY's creation was seen to be based on the dubious political calculations of political leaders to give the impression of doing something against humanitarian disasters, while avoiding direct and costly intervention. The same thing was argued for the International Criminal Tribunal for Rwanda (ICTR), which, unlike the ICTY, was created *after* the international community had failed to prevent 800,000 to one million people from becoming the victims of genocide.[10] To their eyes, the ICTs appear very unlikely to operate successfully because the critical aspect of their work, the arrest and detention of war criminals, is heavily reliant on states' commitment, even with military force, which states were reluctant to make in the first place. For those cynics, the strategic purposes of the ICTs may not be of interest.

On the other hand, many international lawyers welcomed the ICTs as the development of international law under an anarchical international society.[11] Anne-Marie Slaughter *et al.* argue that 'numerous IL scholars have shown that demystification of sovereignty has been a part of the culture of international law for decades'.[12] For many of them, the ICTs were the first step towards universal jurisdiction and towards the creation of a permanent international criminal court.[13] Several lawyers saw that the key to the success of the ICTs is whether trials are conducted fairly and efficiently.[14] This, for them, can be achieved by protecting the legal process of the trial from 'being poisoned' by political elements.[15]

Because many international political theorists take little interest in international war crimes trials on the one hand, and analysis of the ICTs has been conducted enthusiastically by international legal scholars, on the other, existing works have been heavily based on the legal and procedural aspects of the tribunal; rarely touched on, until quite recently, has been what it is the ICTs aim to achieve through war crimes prosecution and what the implications are for international peace and security.

The ICTs as judicial bodies were created by the UN Security Council as its enforcement measures for the sake of international peace and security. It is here, as Rachel Kerr identifies, 'an explicit linkage' between law and politics exists in their creation.[16] The ICTY, Kerr argues, is a judicial body that is expected to function in 'a highly politicized context', and it is exactly because of this that law and politics are both vital elements in the operation of the ICTs:

> in order to be successful, the tribunal must perform a delicate balancing act at the interface of law and politics, so that it is able to manipulate the political environment in order to serve the judicial function, without the judicial process becoming politicized.[17]

This suggests that the ICTs are a research topic not only for international lawyers and human rights scholars but also for scholars of international politics and international security. At the same time, either of these alone cannot grasp the whole significance of international war crimes prosecution in the setting of post-Cold War international peace and security. This gradually came to be recognized by scholars in the field. Entering into the twenty-first century, there has been a number of researches conducted by political theorists on the significance of war crimes tribunals on the one hand, and by legal scholars on the political context of international war crimes prosecution, on the other.[18]

The application of both political and legal approaches to international affairs, which are representatively seen in the case of the ICTs, is not merely an academic exercise. Post-Cold War international peace and security itself demonstrates that international law and international politics together 'comprise the rules and the reality of "the international system"'.[19] The new security environment has come to be discussed in terms not only of politics and national interests but also of norms, ethics and justice. It is such a new reality that requires the application of both political and legal approaches to the study of international peace and security.

Peace and justice in the international criminal tribunals

Being Security Council enforcement measures, the ICTs are not irrelevant to international peace and security, especially to changes in the post-Cold War international security environment. Indeed, it is these changes that made the creation of the ICTs 'possible'. What is more, the new security environment made international war crimes tribunals 'necessary' within the context of ethnic conflicts accompanying mass atrocities and the gross violations of human rights. The ICTs came to be understood as an important tool for the restoration and maintenance of international peace and security.

While the possibility of nuclear war between the great powers decreased with the end of the Cold War, the impact of intrastate conflicts on international affairs increased. Accordingly, the focus of states has changed. The change can be seen from cases that have been determined by the Security Council as 'a threat to the peace', 'a breach of the peace' or 'an act of aggression'.[20] During the Cold War, a 'threat to the peace' was understood primarily as a *military* threat caused by one *state* against another. At the time the UN Charter was drafted in the early 1940s, the Second World War was still under way; this fact surely had an impact on the Charter and the structure of the United Nations. The primary target of the organization was war, and peace was regarded as *international* peace, which is the order among states, not *within* a state.[21] There are a few cases in the 1960s and 1970s, in which domestic situations were determined as a threat to the peace.[22] However, the major understanding was that it was 'not the purpose of the United Nations to maintain or restore *internal* peace by interfering in a civil war within a state'.[23] After all, mutual respect of state sovereignty was the basis of international peace. With the end of the Cold War, however, situations that were not necessarily a 'threat to the peace' previously came to be regarded as constituting such a threat: a threat posed by *non-international* and *non-military* incidents.

New interventionism: non-international threat to the peace

Since the Iraqi invasion of Kuwait in 1990 up to 11 September 2001, most of the cases determined as a threat to the peace by the Security Council were civil wars or conflicts of a non-international nature in strict terms.[24] Conflicts and instability *within* a state have become a matter of international concern because the international impact of those incidents has increased. As in the case of the Kurdish minority in Iraq, Somalia or Bosnia, mass violence and gross violations of human rights within a state's borders ceased to remain domestic issues when they came to endanger the security of the neighbouring states through the expansion of conflicts and the flow of refugees. What is more, 'ethnic conflicts' in a region tend to have a 'domino effect' on neighbouring countries, which also have similar ethnic compositions within society. This is exactly the case with the conflicts in the Balkans and Rwanda; accordingly they became a serious concern of the international community at the time. Furthermore, globalization and the development of communication technology promote the 'internationalization' of foreign domestic threats in psychological terms. Now one becomes a witness of the incident, on the one hand, via the media, and a potential victim, on the other hand, because of the cross-border effects of the threat.

When domestic issues become internationalized and threaten the international community, the concept of international peace and security changes. As James Gow states: 'International peace and security have become not a matter of protecting the internal order of states from external intrusion, but a matter of protecting the state's external environment from threats of internal extrusion'.[25] Under a new security environment, the principle of non-intervention ceased to be a guarantor of peace but became an obstacle to restoring and maintaining peace. Regarding the success of the operation in northern Iraq to aid Kurdish refugees, the then UN Secretary-General Pérez de Cuéllar declared: 'It is now increasingly felt that the principle of non-interference with the essential domestic jurisdiction of States cannot be regarded as a protective barrier behind which human rights could be massively or systematically violated with impunity'.[26] Boutros Boutros-Ghali, while in office, also emphasized the need for governments to understand that sovereignty is not absolute: 'The time of absolute and exclusive sovereignty … has passed; its theory was never matched by reality'.[27] In sum, the international community came to discredit the absolute nature of state sovereignty as the basis of international peace and security. This opened the door for international intervention.

The early 1990s saw the proliferation of 'New Interventionism': intervention in domestic affairs was understood no longer as a threat to but as a remedy for international peace and security.[28] This international expectation of intervention was backed by the revival of the Security Council, which, after the end of the ideological confrontation of the Cold War, could respond to crises collectively and thus more effectively. It was in such an international climate that the ICTY was established in 1993, half a century after its predecessors: the International Military Tribunals (IMTs). The new interventionist international atmosphere of the early 1990s is an important element that made the creation of the tribunal 'possible'. The ICTY, created as a Security Council enforcement measure to pursue criminal responsibility of individuals, including state leaders, clearly was an 'international judicial intervention'.[29]

Mass atrocities and humanitarian crises: non-military threat to the peace

As domestic issues came to be seen as a threat to peace, non-military dimensions of international peace and security also became a matter of concern. On the Kurdish crisis, Resolution 688 (1991) interpreted Chapter VII of the UN Charter in a more expansive way to include situations of extremely aggravated civil oppression. On 31 January 1992, the heads of government of the Security Council members declared:

> The absence of war and military conflicts amongst States does not in itself ensure international peace and security. The non-military sources of

> instability in the economic, social, humanitarian and ecological fields have become threats to peace and security. The United Nations membership as a whole, working through the appropriate bodies, needs to give the highest priority to the solution of these matters.[30]

The 'economic, social, humanitarian and ecological fields', raised in the declaration, had been regarded in the previous period as being of secondary importance, or the sphere of 'justice', which often clashed, or was seen to clash, with the pursuit of international peace and security.[31] However, the declaration expressed the understanding that injustice and a sense of injustice existing in a society are the seeds of threats to international peace and security. In other words, the Security Council recognized that the issue of justice needed to be sorted out in order to fulfil its principal aim: to maintain international peace and security.

It was humanitarian and human rights issues that especially caught the eye of the international community in the early 1990s. In the armed conflict in Bosnia and Herzegovina, systematic and widespread massacres and rapes repeatedly occurred as a result of propagated historical hatred between different social groups. There was a situation in which war crimes and crimes against humanity committed by one group brought about the others' vengeful act of further war crimes, leading to the escalation of conflict. Facing such a state of affairs, the Security Council, despite having already regarded the situation in the former Yugoslavia as constituting 'a threat to international peace and security' in Resolution 713 (1991), once more specifically determined, in Resolution 808 (1993), 'widespread violations of international humanitarian law occurring within the territory' as constituting a threat.[32] This signifies the recognition by the Security Council that they should take some action against gross violations of international humanitarian law and the strong hatred existing among the victims of war crimes, which accompanied those violations. It is for such a 'threat' that the Security Council established the ICTY, as an enforcement measure to maintain international peace and security. Following the precedent of the ICTY, the Security Council established the International Criminal Tribunals for Rwanda (ICTR) through Resolution 955 (1994), stating that 'genocide and other systematic, widespread and flagrant violations of international humanitarian law … committed in Rwanda' are 'a threat to international peace and security'. The achievement of justice by prosecuting those who have violated international humanitarian law was seen as 'necessary' for international peace and security.

Peace and justice in the ICTs

In the cases of the former Yugoslavia and Rwanda, mass atrocities and 'ethnic cleansing' were not merely a consequence of war but also an instrument of war;[33] and one 'ethnic cleansing' became the seeds for future 'ethnic cleansing'. When 'threats to international peace' are of such a nature, a ceasefire is not enough for the achievement of peace; long-term stability without any prospect of the revival of violence has to be ensured. In other words, the *quality* of peace that follows the war comes to matter. To ensure this quality, legacies of large-scale violence need to be addressed and the voice for 'justice', demanding remedies for gross violation of human rights, needs to be heard. '[P]eace without justice is an illusion', Richard Goldstone maintained:

> If you have peace without justice in countries where millions of people have suffered, where hundreds of thousands of people have been murdered and tens of thousands of women have been raped, do you really expect that by brushing the atrocities committed under the carpet and allowing collective guilt to take hold one will achieve lasting peace? I do not believe so.[34]

Peace that is unjust or seen as unjust in societies in transition would become a hotbed for future violence and private revenge. Regarding the long-term, Payam Akhavan claimed, 'punishing the perpetrators of ethnic cleansing is *the only realistic option for achieving peace*'.[35] It is here that peace and justice, traditionally seen as an antinomy in international relations, face a common task under the operation of the ICTs: to promote the transformation of war-torn societies. The two as complementary concepts led to the idea of 'peace through justice'.[36]

The idea of 'peace through justice' is strongly related to the strategic purposes of the ICTs. However, the idea cannot be understood through the conventional Realism/Liberalism (or Idealism) dichotomy. Realism and Liberalism each holds a different view of the world, thus prioritize different values to be pursued in international life: peace and justice.[37] What is more, each tends to pose a question from a different philosophical level: 'what can be done?' and 'what should be done?'. The discourse between the two, therefore, rarely reaches agreement.[38]

'Contemporary' Liberalism, unlike classical Liberalism focusing on free market principles, takes a normative approach to reality. Liberals believe that human rights and democracy, for example, are universal values and thus they need to be promoted internationally. The gross violations of human rights in other countries are taken seriously and the justice of the victim is regarded as necessary to be met for its own sake. Some see a strong link between the Liberal's stance and a legalistic approach to the punishment of war criminals.[39] Realism, on the other hand, not only disregards the legalistic approach to international politics, as seen above, but also regards state interests, the maximization of power in a material sense, as being of primary importance. The pursuit of human rights tends to mean little for Realists both in terms of practice and values; it is even regarded as harming international peace, based on the mutual respect of state sovereignty.

International security environments in the 1990s, however, clearly showed the limitation in such a dichotomized approach to peace and justice. The logic of justice came to be regarded as important not only in itself but in its potential contribution to peace. US President Bill Clinton expressed his sympathy for this idea: 'Some people are concerned that pursuing peace in Bosnia and prosecuting war criminals are incompatible goals. But I believe they are wrong. There must be peace for justice to prevail, but there must be justice when peace prevails'.[40] This is a pragmatic, or more *realistic*, understanding of justice in the context of post-Cold War international peace and security. The ICTs, therefore, cannot be easily dismissed as 'liberalist' or 'legalist' because they were originally embedded in the pursuit of international peace and security, the core agenda of Realism, which itself has been facing various challenges since the end of the Cold War.[41] At the same time, Liberalism also needs to take into account the fact that without peace, justice cannot be fully pursued.

Crossing boundaries: Constructivism and international war crimes tribunals

What is required in research of international war crimes tribunals is a *non-static* approach to international peace and security. During the 1990s, the international community witnessed that normative discourse affected the interests and behaviour of states. The growing significance of human rights claims, debates over humanitarian intervention and the limitations on the use of certain weapons, all raise normative as well as empirical interests to explain 'how the "ought" becomes the "is" ... how people's ideas about what is good and what "should be" in the world become translated into political reality'.[42] The ICTY, in spite of cynics' views, certainly created the momentum for further international war crimes prosecutions, paving the way for the creation of the International Criminal Court and other international criminal justice mechanisms in Rwanda, Sierra Leone and so on. The ICTs certainly reflect a delicate intersection of a traditional norm – the non-intervention principle – and an evolving idea – the principle of 'universal jurisdiction' over serious violations of international humanitarian law.

Regarding the necessity of crossing the Realist/Liberalist boundary, Constructivism provides a potential approach for analysing the role and impact of the ICTs in international peace and security. The strength of Constructivism is its incorporation of ideas and values to theorize about state interests, which is traditionally understood only in terms of material elements. Rather than regarding state interests and identities as exogenously given and thus static, Constructivism argues that they are constructed, as well as constrained, by the structure and culture of international politics, which themselves consist of the ideas and behaviour of states. Regarding state identity and interests as being not only produced but also reproduced in this way, or even transformed through interaction among states, Constructivism understands and explains changes in the structure and culture of international politics.[43]

It is this process-oriented theorization that explains changes that can potentially bridge gaps between Realism and Liberalism because it 'applies equally to Realism, Idealism and any other school of thought, or practice'.[44] Unlike Alexander Wendt, the original advocate of Constructivism in international studies, James Gow argues that Constructivism is neither a uniquely Liberal nor counter-Realism approach; rather it enhances Realism by 'permitting it greater variety and flexibility, as well as allowing legitimate scope to values and other elements than power'.[45] 'Constructivist Realism', Gow identifies, has true value and utility in understanding the complex and fluctuating nature of threat and thus tackling 'the real security problems in the contemporary world'.[46] This suggests that Constructivism as a methodology and approach, rather than as a theoretical school of thought, adds 'realistic' perspectives, which is sometimes absent in Realism and Liberalism and, thus, is necessary for examining the operation and impact of the ICTs.

In addition to crossing the Realist/Liberalist boundary, a Constructivist approach also has the potential to promote the collaboration of the two disciplines of international law and international politics. The approach focuses not merely on the regulative function of rules, laws and norms but also their constitutive function. In other words, it can theorize that rules and norms matter even if they fail to regulate state behaviour in the short term. Through the constitutive function focusing on long-term process, the significance of international law with regard to a normative impact on international politics can be understood. This is an important point considering the fact many international political theorists dismiss international law from the standpoint that it is unable to constrain state behaviour effectively.

What is more, such an approach to international law can be commonly held by international legal scholars, which is important when the true collaboration of the two disciplines is sought.[47] International legal scholars have been interested in the 'compliance question', an issue that is both legal and political in nature. Harold Hongju Koh argues that it is through the repeated cycle of *interaction* among states, *interpretation* of international norms and *internalization* of new interpretations of the norms into the other party's internal normative system that 'international law acquires its "stickiness," that nation-states acquire their identity, and that nations come to "obey" international law out of perceived self-interest'.[48] This 'transnational legal process', Koh argues, will explain well why states obey international law in, for example, the human rights area, 'where enforcement mechanisms are weak, but core customary norms are clearly defined and often peremptory (*jus cogens*)'.[49] For Constructivism, how international law is institutionalized in the international system is the important part of its theorization.[50] Through its process-oriented approach, Constructivism incorporates international politics and international law, showing that law/politics is a false dichotomy: 'no political society can exist without law, and … law cannot exist except in a political society', states E. H. Carr, who sought to be 'realistic' rather than 'idealistic' about reality.[51]

The Nuremberg analogy and the establishment of the ICTY

Along with the new security challenges inherent in post-Cold War international peace and security that enabled and required international war crimes tribunals, the NGOs and the media played a vital catalytic role in the birth of the ICTs, through their discourses applying the Nuremberg and Holocaust analogy to the conflict in the former Yugoslavia.

The proposal for a 'new Nuremberg court' for crimes committed during the war in the former Yugoslavia was made as early as May 1991 by a Yugoslav reporter, Mirko Klarin. In his article in the Yugoslav newspaper *Borba*, he claimed:

> Not *when* 'this is all over', but *instead of* whatever might soon befall us. Precisely because of what has already happened and what is happening now, all of which can quite easily be shown to be punishable under the terms of the Nuremberg judgement and other legal documents just as valid here at home as in the rest of the world [*sic*].[52]

'All the more reason', Klarin emphasized, 'to ask for an objective assessment by impartial foreign experts in international laws of war. *A tribunal, in other words, similar to the one at Nuremberg* [*sic*].'[53]

Internationally, it was the Helsinki Watch Committee of Human Rights Watch that first called on the United Nations 'to establish such a tribunal and to prosecute, adjudicate and punish those responsible for war crimes starting with those with the highest level of responsibility for the most egregious crimes'.[54] Its report in July 1992 on war crimes in Bosnia and Herzegovina claimed: 'The principle of universal jurisdiction to try war crimes was recognized in the establishment of the Nuremberg Tribunal'.[55]

In August that year, ITN's coverage showed the world pictures of Omarska, a Serb detention centre for Muslim prisoners. The image of prisoners behind barbed wire reminded viewers around the world of Nazi concentration camps and the Holocaust, 'reinforcing powerfully the analogy to Nazi practices made by reports of ethnic cleansing'.[56] Considering the atrocities in Bosnia, David Owen stated on 4 August 1992:

> This is a moral issue. History really is repeating itself in Europe. And this time we can see it on television. The annexation of territory, the concentration camps, even the jargon is the same with racial purity being replaced by the even more odious 'ethnic cleansing'. We have been spared the gas chambers, but tales of death and brutality make it no exaggeration to warn of a *holocaust*.[57]

The media, NGOs and practitioners started to talk about the atrocities in Bosnia in terms of the Holocaust and Nazism, and state leaders were criticized for having turned their backs 'in the style of Neville Chamberlain, on a modern holocaust'.[58]

Facing Nazi-like crimes, it is natural that the idea of establishing a Nuremberg-like institution eventually emerged. David Scheffer, the first US Ambassador at Large for War Crimes Issues, says the response of the international community towards atrocities in Bosnia and Croatia was reminiscent of the Allies' response to Nazi atrocities during the Second World War: 'Government officials and scholars have debated theories of law and prosecution just as their predecessors did in the 1940s. US federal agencies have had to struggle to coordinate their war-crimes work just as they did during the Second World War'.[59] This can be observed from the initiative of the United States, which had made great efforts 50 years earlier to establish the IMTs, to create an international tribunal for the situation in the former Yugoslavia. According to M. Cherif Bassiouni, on establishing the Commission of Experts to investigate violations of international humanitarian law in the region, the United States wanted to have the words 'war crimes' as part of the name of the commission, 'which would have been reminiscent of the 1943 [United Nations War Crimes Commission] and the Nuremberg proceedings'. Bassiouni stated: 'The US position was based on its expectation that the Commission would pave the way for an eventual tribunal'.[60] It might not be a coincidence that one of the strongest advocates of the tribunal, Madeleine Albright, 'the mother of all the tribunals' according to Richard Goldstone, was herself a refugee from the Nazis in Czechoslovakia.

On adopting Resolution 808 (1993), which decided the establishment of an international tribunal for the conflict in the former Yugoslavia, Albright, as American Ambassador to the United Nations, stated at the Security Council:

> There is an echo in this chamber today. *The Nuremberg principles* have been reaffirmed. We have preserved the long-neglected compact made by the community of civilized nations 48 years ago in San Francisco to create the United Nations and enforce *the Nuremberg Principles*.[61]

She continued:

> It is worthwhile recalling that the Nuremberg Principles on war crimes, crimes against the peace, and crimes against humanity were adopted by the General Assembly in 1948. By its action today, with resolution 808 (1993) the Security Council has shown that the will of this Organization can be exercised, even if it has taken nearly half a century for the wisdom of our earliest principles to take hold.[62]

The ICTY was valued for having formulated and given credibility to principles set out by Nuremberg. Furthermore, it was appreciated also for having modified Nuremberg's legal procedures and its structural shortcomings. The Statute of Nuremberg was carefully examined and revised into the ICTY Statute in such a way as to ensure the fairness of the trial and to avoid being criticized as 'victor's justice'.[63] The drafters of the statute for the ICTY were especially concerned about the nature of the jurisdiction to avoid *ex post facto* legislation.[64] They were also very sensitive to the rights of the accused being respected.[65] Above all, it was hailed that the ICTY, unlike its predecessor, was a true international tribunal established by international society.[66] On analysing the Tadic trial, the first case of the ICTY, Michael Scharf stated: 'Just as the Nuremberg Trials following the Second World War launched the era of human rights promulgation fifty years ago, the Tadic trial has inaugurated a new age of human rights enforcement'.[67]

Some others saw 'the revival of Nuremberg' cynically, arguing that Nuremberg was 'unique' and thus could not be taken as a model.[68] One feature of such uniqueness was 'unconditional surrender'. It was argued that, in order for an international tribunal to work effectively and successfully, it had to meet this condition, which enabled outside powers to occupy the territory, guaranteeing the arrest of the indicted and the seizure of evidence and documents.[69] Without such a condition, the ICTY has to depend on the cooperation of states, including the state whose nationals it is indicting, for crucial aspects of its work: the arrest and detention of the accused within their territories. However, in practice, there is no guarantor for compelling such cooperation; unlike Nuremberg, it is not guaranteed that anyone, let alone 'big fish', would be seen in the dock. For example, at the time of writing, the Bosnian Serb leader, Radovan Karadzic, and commander of the Bosnian Serb military forces, Ratoko Mladic, have been at large ever since they were indicted by the tribunal in 1995.

Sharing this cynicism, Timothy Mak nonetheless stated: 'Perhaps the most remarkable feature of the [Nuremberg and Tokyo] Trials was not the fact that they occurred, but the fact that they have subsequently been universally accepted by the international community as indicative of international norms'.[70] It is true that since their creation, Nuremberg, as well as Tokyo, has been regarded as synonymous with war crimes trials in general.[71] What is more, the Nuremberg Trial has been treated as the quasi-norm not only for its significance as an event, i.e. its establishment, but also for its promising process, the achievement of long-lasting peace.

Conclusion

The ICTs were established in response to the new security environment that emerged after the end of the Cold War. The creation of the ICTs was based on a delicate balance between rational calculation and the normative concerns of states. Their procedures were and are based on the delicate interaction between the function of politics and law. They aim to contribute to international security through a delicately balanced logic of peace and justice. And, the impact of war crimes prosecutions is clearly legal as well as political. It is here that the ICTs and their success, and war crimes tribunals and their role in transitional justice, have become an important topic not only for international lawyers but also for international political theorists, not only for human rights scholars but also for the scholars of international peace and security.

What is more significant about the ICTY is that an international tribunal was created to prosecute war crimes half a century after the Nuremberg Tribunal, and the Tokyo Tribunal, which were created in the aftermath of the Second World War. The establishment of the ICTY, the first tribunal since the IMTs, was discussed, considered and put into practice with the experience of its predecessors, especially the Nuremberg Tribunal, borne closely in mind. It is within the context of the ICTs and post-Cold War international peace and security that the experience of the Nuremberg Trial came to be focused. Among those theorists and practitioners of international tribunals, the phrase the 'Nuremberg legacy' became a mantra, accompanying certain assumptions about the impact of Nuremberg on the subsequent peace and security.

However, the exact content and significance of the 'Nuremberg legacy' is not necessarily clear nor is its usage coherent. Before re-examining the Nuremberg legacy through the experience of the Tokyo Trial and post-war Japan, the next chapter examines and analyses what the Nuremberg legacy exactly is.

2 The Nuremberg legacy

Ideas and practices

The International Military Tribunal for the trial of Major German War Criminals, the so-called Nuremberg Trial, has been treated as a synecdoche for war crimes tribunals. As the titles of articles and books on this subject show, examination and assessment of the international war crimes tribunals have been strongly coloured by the experience of the Nuremberg Tribunal: *the Nuremberg legacy*.[1] In spite of the casual usage of the phrase, the meaning of the Nuremberg legacy is neither clear nor coherent. Telford Taylor suggests that the name *Nuremberg* 'conjures up the moral and legal issues raised by applying judicial methods and decisions to challenged wartime acts'.[2] David Luban puts 'the *legacy* of Nuremberg' as

> the potential of [Nuremberg] principles for growth and development, for extension and precedent-setting, for adaptability to changed political circumstances, for underlying moral commitments that are not so much the logical implications of the principles as they are their deep structure.[3]

Defined as such, the Nuremberg legacy takes various forms. On the one hand, the legacy is legal and can be observed through the development of international law, especially international humanitarian law and human rights law, or the actual trial and punishment of crimes dealt with under Nuremberg. The legacy in this sense takes a concrete form.

On the other hand, the Nuremberg legacy can be political, moral or normative, taking more abstract forms such as culture, norm or 'lesson'. The impact of Nuremberg derives both from Nuremberg as an event and as a process. 'This process', Richard Falk states, 'is often *interpreted teleologically* as containing an assumed promise of future justice'.[4] The content of the Nuremberg legacy in this sense depends strongly on the understanding of what the Nuremberg Trial aimed at and achieved. However, as one prosecutor at Nuremberg stated, the trial itself had various faces:

> The trial turned out to be many things: a court of justice; an historical inquest; a forum in which Nazi leaders could state their motivations and their rationalizations; a condemnation of tyranny and of racial prejudice;

> and a precedent in moving toward international means for bringing to justice modern day perpetrators of gross evils wherever they may be found.[5]

It is here that a question arises: do people who talk about the Nuremberg legacy look at the same aspects of the trial in the same way? Was the Nuremberg legacy mentioned in the past in the same way as it is now?

This chapter first examines how the Nuremberg legacy was seen and understood during the Cold War. The examination of the legacy as it was perceived in this period clarifies the background of the international community's reluctance to set up any international war crimes tribunal for nearly half a century. This is important for highlighting why it took 50 years for the legacy to be revived in the form of ad hoc international criminal tribunals (ICTs), in other words, what is significant about the experience of Nuremberg in the context of post-Cold War international relations. The point is strongly related to the theme of this study: the strategic purposes of international war crimes prosecutions and their significance to international peace and security. The chapter then moves on to examine the significance of the Nuremberg legacy in the context of ongoing international criminal tribunals.

The Nuremberg legacy and post-Second World War international peace and security

In his final report to the President on 7 October 1946, Robert H. Jackson, US chief prosecutor at the Nuremberg Tribunal, insisted: 'The importance of the trial lies in the principles to which the Four Powers became committed by the Agreement, by their participation in the prosecution, and by the judgment rendered by the tribunal'.[6] Jackson expected that the principles set out by Nuremberg would become 'a basic charter in the international law of the future'. Those principles did become a milestone for the development of international humanitarian law and human rights law that followed after the trial. However, the experience of Nuremberg as a whole had been regarded cynically or had been ignored during the Cold War. This can be attributed partly to the defects of the Nuremberg Trial. It is, however, more to do with the international security environment during the Cold War, as examined below. Unlike the early 1940s, what was lacking in post-Second World War international relations was not law but political will: states were reluctant to prosecute individuals for conducting war crimes.

Legal aspects of the Nuremberg legacy

The Nuremberg Trial, which prosecuted 24 major German war criminals for 'crimes against peace', war crimes and 'crimes against humanity', contributed significantly to the development of international law after the Second World War.[7] The United Nations General Assembly on 11 December 1946 unanimously adopted Resolution 95 (I): Affirmation of the Principles of International Law recognized by the Charter of the Nuremberg Tribunal.[8] In 1950, the principles of the Nuremberg Tribunal together with its judgment were formulated into seven principles by the International Law Commission (ILC). In addition to the statement that 'crimes against peace', war crimes and 'crimes against humanity' are crimes under international law (Principle VI), the Commission set out individual criminal responsibility under international law: 'Any person who commits an act which constitutes a crime under international law is responsible therefore and liable to punishment' (I), whether or not international law imposes a penalty for such an act (II).[9] The four Geneva Conventions of 1949 and their two protocols of 1977 further endorsed the concept of individual criminal responsibility for war crimes, requiring the party states to 'enact any legislation necessary to provide effective penal sanctions for persons committing, or ordering to be committed, any of the grave breaches of the present Convention'.[10]

Theodor Meron regards the definition of 'crimes against humanity' as the most revolutionary contribution made by the Nuremberg Charter to international law: 'it established, for the first time, direct international criminal responsibility under international law for atrocities committed in one country, even as between its citizens'.[11] The concept of 'crimes against humanity' was developed into various international laws: the Convention on the Prevention and Punishment of the Crime of Genocide came into force in 1951, the International Convention on the Suppression and Punishment of the Crime of Apartheid came into force in 1976, and the Convention against Torture and other Cruel, Inhuman or Degrading Treatment or Punishment came into force in 1987. Crimes against humanity also became the basis of the development of the post-Second World War human rights regime. In 1948, the UN General Assembly adopted the Universal Declaration of Human Rights, which was followed by the two Covenants of Economic, Social and Cultural Rights, and of Civil and Political Rights, which came into force in 1976. These developments, as Yves Beigbeder pointed out, were promoted by clear evidence of the Holocaust and other crimes presented at the Nuremberg Tribunal, which had shocked, horrified and thus motivated the international community to create a human rights regime through the United Nations.[12] War crimes are thus codified and the concept of individual responsibility has penetrated international law.

In spite of this remarkable development of international law, however, the 'Nuremberg Principles' were rarely implemented during the Cold War. This relates to the fact that the international community, though affirming the Charter and judgment of Nuremberg, was cynical and critical about the trial per se. This is attributed to the 'original sin' of Nuremberg: retroactive justice and 'victor's justice'.

The original sin of Nuremberg

The Nuremberg judgment claimed that the Charter of the International Military Tribunal (IMT), annexed to the London Agreement in 1945 for the Establishment of the tribunal, was 'not an arbitrary exercise of power on the part of the victorious nations, but in the view of the tribunal ... it is the expression of international law existing at the time of its creation'.[13] However, many international legal scholars then and now argue that the defendants at Nuremberg were prosecuted and punished retroactively, charged for acts that were not crimes at the time they were conducted.[14] *Ex post facto* law raises a serious question on the fairness and legality of the trial because *Nullum crimen, nulla poena sine lege* – no crime without law, no punishment without law – is an important legal principle to guarantee the fair application of law.

The defence counsel argued that 'crimes against peace', or wars of aggression, were not clearly codified at the time the alleged acts were committed. Even if, as the prosecutor insisted, Germany's act was 'illegal' because of the violation of the Kellogg–Briand Pact of 1928 that renounced war as an instrument of national policy in states' relations with one another, it does not automatically mean that her conduct was 'a crime', leading to punishment.[15] It may also be possible to argue that the pact did not completely outlaw the conduct of war because there was no provision for sanctions and it implicitly acknowledged the state's right of self-defence.[16] In the case of the violation of those interwar treaties that renounced war, Hans Kelsen argued, the sanction provided by general international law – authorization to resort to reprisals or counterwar against the violator – would have applied, but not the pursuit of individual criminal responsibility under an international court.[17]

As for 'crimes against humanity', it was a totally new 'legal' category introduced by the IMT Charter.[18] Under the name of 'crimes against humanity', atrocities conducted by a state against its own citizens before or during the war were criminalized. Traditionally, a state's acts against its citizens and acts before the war did not constitute war crimes; they had simply been ignored under international law.[19]

War crimes, that is violations of the laws or customs of war, was a less problematic concept, as the origin of the development of the laws of war can be traced back to the Middle Age of Europe.[20] By the early part of the twentieth century, the restriction on the conduct of war, *jus in bello*, was codified through the 1899 and 1907 Hague Conventions and the 1929 Geneva Convention, which recognized constraints on the method of warfare and certain duties towards enemy civilians and soldiers not engaging in battle. However, international law had not established individual criminal responsibility under international law. Individual criminal responsibility was not an international matter dealt with under an international trial, but was a matter for states, who were in charge of judging violators under *national* jurisdiction by introducing the category of war crimes into their penal or military codes.[21] The Nuremberg Tribunal broke this tradition by prosecuting and punishing individuals directly under an international tribunal. 'That international law imposes duties and liabilities upon individuals as well as upon States has long been recognised', the judgment stated: 'Crimes against international law are committed by men, not by abstract entities, and only by punishing individuals who commit such crimes can the provisions of international law be enforced'.[22]

Along with the affirmation of individual responsibility under international law, the Nuremberg Charter denied the official position of defendants of immunity from prosecution. By prosecuting state leaders, the tribunal departed from the traditional doctrine of 'act of state'.[23] The denial of the notion of superior orders, which had protected individual soldiers following their superiors, was also a departure from the traditional mentality and practice of the military.[24] The judgment at the tribunal stated: 'the very essence of the Charter [of the IMT] is that individuals have international duties which transcend the national obligations of obedience imposed by the individual State'.[25]

In spite of international support for principles recognized by the Nuremberg Charter, the legality of the application of such principles to the Nazi leaders has been fiercely argued. The Allies themselves were well aware of defects of the trial right from the beginning.[26] However, it was felt absolutely necessary to judge the crimes even through *ex post facto* legislation. There was a common understanding that the crimes committed by the Nazis were unprecedented both in scale and character and thus could not be treated with the then existing law: 'Novel problems may require novel wrenchings of normal legal practice'.[27] The tribunal did violate the principle of legality but '[b]y violating this principle for the first time', Kriangsak Kittichaisaree argues, 'the Nuremberg Tribunal set precedents for future criminal prosecution of individuals before an international tribunal' applying the concept of crimes against peace, war crimes and crimes against humanity.[28] However, what makes this *ex post facto* law even more problematic is the fact that only the German and the Japanese, the vanquished, were prosecuted and punished under those new principles. It is here that the tribunal was given the notorious name: 'victor's justice'.

Whether the Nuremberg Tribunal was purely a legal product or not has been argued, and the tribunal is often regarded as a political trial that 'pursues a very specific policy – the destruction, or at least the disgrace and disrepute, of a political opponent'.[29] The Nuremberg Trial was a one-sided trial: no alleged crimes committed by the Allies, the victors, were examined. Examining the concept of crimes against peace, war crimes and crimes against humanity, for which the Nazi officers were prosecuted, the tribunal could also have prosecuted some of Allies' war conduct: the British and American strategic air bombing against Hamburg, Dresden and other German cities; the American use of atomic bombs on Hiroshima and Nagasaki; Russia's aggression against Finland and its invasion of its other Baltic neighbours in 1940; and Russia's participation in Germany's seizure of Poland. However, all these were outside the terms of the Nuremberg Charter: beyond its mandate.

From a practical point of view, this was related to the setting up of the tribunal, which was established 'for the just and prompt trial and punishment of the major war criminals of the European Axis' and consisted of judges exclusively from the Allied states: the United States, the United Kingdom, France and the Soviet Union.[30] In the absence of judges from neutral states and other parts of the world, some question whether it really was an 'international' tribunal, as the Allies wanted it to be seen.[31] From a moral point of view, prosecuting Allies leaders such as Truman and Churchill for the above alleged crimes together with Nazi leaders, would have lessened the moral appeal that the tribunal was eager to convey to the world.[32]

Through the creation of the tribunal and the application of law instead of summary execution, the victors declared to the world their moral stance on the issue. Barrie Paskins and Michael Dockrill argued: 'They are thus subject to judgment in moral terms which they themselves espoused'.[33] However, the partial application of the Charter did only partial justice, which undermined the normative weight of the trial. The only way to justify 'victor's justice', as well as retroactive justice, is to show that victors themselves have been committed to institutionalizing, through laws and practices, the 'justice' created at the Nuremberg Trial. However, the view that Nuremberg was 'victor's justice' was further strengthened by the poor record, in the post-Nuremberg era, of states' commitment to the idea and principles they themselves established.

War crimes, crimes against humanity and state sovereignty

The post-Second World War international climate was hardly favourable to the implementation of the international humanitarian law and human rights law developed after Nuremberg. Accordingly, there was no international war crimes tribunal to follow Nuremberg and Tokyo. Some argue that this is because there had been, since the Second World War, 'no recurrence of the unique circumstances that made the Nuremberg and Tokyo Tribunals possible': unconditional surrender of an obvious aggressor and violator of international law.[34] What is more significant was the lack of will to resort to the Nuremberg precedent. The international community as a whole was reluctant to prosecute and punish individuals for war crimes or crimes against humanity because of the concern that such conduct would infringe states' interests.

Nuremberg was revolutionary in introducing individual criminal responsibility into international law, which is claimed to have altered 'some state-to-state aspects of international humanitarian law'.[35] However, it is important to differentiate between two levels of responsibility emerging from this: individual criminal responsibility for the crime one has committed, and state responsibility to prosecute and punish those individuals. Under international society, which, unlike domestic society, lacks a central authority to conduct enforcement and punishment 'vertically', the pursuit of individual criminal responsibility had been heavily based on state responsibility.[36] International humanitarian law is implemented within a 'horizontal' relationship between states, respecting and relying on the action and policy of the individual state.[37] However, states do not always fulfil this responsibility.

States are not always enthusiastic about prosecuting and punishing their own soldiers for alleged crimes committed during war, the pursuit of national interests. The United States faced this problem in the case of the massacre at My Lai during the Vietnam War, in which the American troops allegedly killed about 350 village residents including women, children and the aged who showed no resistance. The Army's Criminal Investigation Division conducted an inquiry and determined that Lieutenant William Calley and 12 men under his command were chiefly responsible for the 1968 massacre. Of the 13 men charged, it was only Calley that was convicted. Several officers were also accused of covering up the atrocity but only Calley's immediate superior, Captain Ernest Medina, and his brigade commander, Colonel Oran Henderson, were court-martialled. Both were acquitted. Although Calley was originally sentenced to life imprisonment in 1971, the case subsequently went through several reviews; his sentence was finally reduced to ten years. After having served for a while in jail, he was paroled in 1974.[38] Some see the case as evidence of the reluctance of the United States, the principal sponsor, organizer and executant of the International Military Tribunal, to apply the 'Nuremberg Principles' strictly to its own side.

Nuclear strategy also was one of the reasons why states were reluctant during the Cold War to implement the Nuremberg Principles. Nuclear weapons together with massive bombing against cities, Donald Wells pointed out, would imply that '[t]he crime against humanity had now become conventional war strategy'.[39] Strict pursuit of the responsibility for 'crimes against humanity', therefore, would question the usage of nuclear weapons, which would have shaken the then international order based on a delicate balance of nuclear deterrence.

Considering the fact that 'crimes against humanity' are often carried out by a state against its own people during civil wars or under dictatorships, it is unlikely that the state concerned would conduct trials to prosecute crimes against humanity by itself. In such a case, other states were also reluctant to prosecute leaders of the state concerned, as the strict pursuit of the crime may lead to the infringement of state sovereignty. The pursuit of responsibility for crimes against humanity faced difficulties under international relations where the non-intervention principle was the basis of the order among states. As Adam Roberts states, 'Where there seemed to be a conflict between the morality of states and the morality of individual justice, the morality of states generally prevailed'.[40] When India's intervention in Pakistan brought to an end the latter's massacre of over one million Bengalis, members of the Security Council and General Assembly, except the Soviet Union, did not support India's justification of its use of force based on humanitarian grounds. Vietnam's intervention in Cambodia was heavily sanctioned for breaking the principle of non-intervention, in spite of the fact that the intervention ended the murderous Pol Pot regime.[41] Richard Falk warns 'an overestimation of the willingness and capacity of governments operating in a realist mode to adhere to Nuremberg constraints if doing so runs counter to their perceptions of vital national interest'.[42] It was difficult during this period of time to expect states to implement the Nuremberg Principles by themselves.

One way of resolving this dilemma was to create a permanent international criminal court with a jurisdiction to prosecute individuals directly, regardless of nationality. Such a court, however, was not established during the Cold War. One reason for this is the failure of the international community after Nuremberg to codify 'crimes against peace'.

'Crimes against peace' and aggression in the Cold War period

Criminalization of aggression was emphasized by the organizers and participants of Nuremberg as one of the main aims of the trial. For those who pressed for a trial instead of summary execution, Nuremberg was a means to criminalize aggressive war and create post-war international peace and order. Robert Jackson declared in his Opening Statement at the trial:

> This trial is part of the great effort to make the peace more secure. One step in this direction is the United Nations organization, which may take joint political action to prevent war if possible, and joint military action to insure that any nation which starts a war will lose it. This Charter and this Trial implementing the Kellogg–Briand Pact, constitute another step in the same direction – juridical action of a kind to ensure that those who start a war will pay for it personally.[43]

Jackson was determined to establish a precedent for punishing individuals who committed aggressive war, expecting a deterrent effect: 'while this law is first applied against German aggressors, the law includes, and if it is to serve a useful purpose it must condemn aggression by any other nations, including those which sit here now in judgment'.[44] At the same time, by enforcing international law directly on individuals rather than states, the tribunal sought to lessen the possibility of warfare, 'the most practicable method of coercing a state'.[45] In sum, Nuremberg was anticipated as 'the trial to end all wars'.[46]

However, 'crimes against peace', unlike 'crimes against humanity', was not codified or institutionalized thereafter. Having received an instruction from the UN General Assembly in 1947, the ILC prepared in 1954 the Draft Code of Offences against the Peace and Security of Mankind. While laying down that acts of aggression 'are crimes under international law, for which the responsible individuals shall be punished', the draft could not reach an agreed definition of 'aggression'.[47] Within the context of the Cold War and ideological confrontation, it was almost impossible to reach a consensus on the use of word 'aggression'. In 1974 the General Assembly adopted a consensus Definition of Aggression.[48] Yoram Dinstein points out that although it is 'the most recent and the most widely … accepted', the Definition of Aggression is less useful for actual international prosecution and punishment because 'the General Assembly largely deemphasized the criminal aspect of its formulation, and brought to the fore the political dimension'.[49]

The lack of codification of aggression had an effect on the creation of the permanent court. The attempt to create a permanent international criminal court started soon after Nuremberg. The General Assembly established a Special Committee, which prepared the Draft Statute for an International Criminal Court in 1951, which was then revised in 1953. The General Assembly, however, found it necessary to consider first the codification of international crimes: the Draft Code of Offences. Accordingly, the Draft Statute had been tabled until the definition of 'aggression' was formulated in 1974. However, it took until 1991 to finalize the text, which took another five years to be revised and adapted by the ILC in 1996. The Rome Statute of the International Criminal Court was finally adopted in 1998.[50] M. Cherif Bassiouni pinpoints the scepticism and reluctance among the major powers to establish an international criminal court as the reason for the failure to synchronize the codification of international crimes and the elaboration of a draft statute for an international court: 'it was the result of a political will to delay the establishment of an international criminal court because that was a time when the world was sharply divided and frequently at risk of war'.[51] After all, aggression and war crimes are too political and ideological as matters to be put under the jurisdiction of an institution that is entitled to prosecute even heads of states, and therefore to override the sovereignty of states.

While 'aggressive war' was not formally codified, there have been a number of alleged 'crimes against peace' in a Nuremberg sense. Wells, for example, claimed: 'The major elements of a crime against the peace and the crime of aggressive war were to be found in the American role in Vietnam'.[52] Eugene Davidson pointed to the limitation of the Nuremberg Principles in preventing wars of aggression:

> Despite these sweeping declarations of a new legal world order, we have lived since the Nuremberg Trial in a time of unremitting international tension in which more than eighty wars or revolutions have been fought: armed conflicts of all.... kinds waged with the full range of modern weapons (aside from the nuclear ones).[53]

The idea that 'Nuremberg was to be the Trial to End All Wars' was seen as naive. Davidson cynically concluded:

> it may be argued that the uneasy peace that has endured between the major powers since the Second World War has been kept not because of, but despite, Nuremberg. Had the Nuremberg principles of the illegality of aggressive war been maintained as rigorously as many of their proponents would have liked, a world war could have started in Hungary, in the Middle East, in the Far East – in fact, anywhere at all... it is by ignoring the doctrines of Nuremberg rather than by trying to enforce them that the post-war world has lived through the cold war and then peaceful coexistence, which is another stage of the same process.[54]

'Crimes against peace' having been one of the main foci of the trial, it may be natural that the Nuremberg legacy was perceived rather cynically by the post-Second World War international community, because the record of the legacy in this aspect was very poor.

Nuremberg, as Theodor Meron argues, contributed to changing the emphasis of international humanitarian law from the interest of states to the rights of individuals. He argues that the trend of human rights law influencing the formation of international humanitarian law began in Nuremberg.[55] However, the foundation of international humanitarian law, the laws of war, is not humanity; it has 'consisted principally of a set of internationally-approved national professional military standards'.[56] What is more, international humanitarian law was from the beginning 'paradigmatically interstate law, driven by reciprocity',[57] which does not protect people from their own government. Furthermore, although the UN General Assembly unanimously affirmed the Charter and judgment of Nuremberg, it in fact could not affirm the Nuremberg Principles formulated by the ILC because of several 'observations' made by member states.[58] As Roberts states, 'A questionable part of the legacy of Nuremberg is *the creation of expectations* that, in general, trials are an appropriate way to handle war crimes issues'.[59] A further interesting aspect of the Nuremberg legacy, moreover, is the fact that such expectations were created in spite of the poor record of the 'Nuremberg Principles' being implemented.

Human rights, transitional justice and the Nuremberg legacy

While they had not been implemented internationally, principles derived from the Nuremberg Trial surely had some *normative* impact on post-Second World War international relations. Barrie Paskins points out that the Nuremberg Trial provided 'a common vocabulary of moral discourse' with which states' foreign and military policy could be discussed and examined.[60] This can be seen in the context of the Vietnam War, in which many of the opponents of American policy cited Nuremberg. One American commented: 'Our actions in Vietnam fall within the prohibited classifications of warfare set down at Nuremberg ... the United States is clearly guilty of "War Crimes," "Crimes against Peace" and "Crimes against Humanity," crimes for which the top German leaders were either imprisoned or executed'.[61]

The normative and moral aspects of Nuremberg remained even after the conclusion of the Vietnam War. 'Once having entered the discourse', Jonathan Bush argues, 'talk of war crimes spread from the Vietnam War to become a typical part of the public response to any number of brutal foreign wars and regimes'.[62] According to Bush, 'By the mid-1970s, activists pressed to extend Nuremberg from the context of war to that of domestic human rights violations as well ... the new, exciting feature seemed to be the use of Nuremberg in domestic human rights settings'.[63] The human rights movement embraces the idea that universal values and morality exist in human life and thus that 'it is not reasonable to allow this value to be diluted by the mere boundaries which human beings happen to have constructed against each other'.[64] This idea is strongly tied to 'crimes against humanity'. Geoffrey Robertson regards crimes against humanity as the vital legal legacy of Nuremberg, and expects it to 'become the key to unlocking the closed door of state sovereignty'.[65] For human rights advocates, Steven Ratner and Jason Abram, Nuremberg presents 'an opportunity to enforce human rights in the most direct way possible – by assigning responsibility to those who abuse human rights in the belief that they do so with impunity'.[66] The important point here is that the Nuremberg legacy started to be discussed within the context not only of the relations between states but also of the relations between a state and its citizens.

Together with the increasing interest in accountability for human rights violations, the late 1970s to 1980s saw a wave of transition in Latin American countries from military dictatorship to democracy. What those post-totalitarian societies had to tackle along with the democratization process was the state's traumatic past, in which former authoritarian regimes perpetrated, or permitted, gross human rights abuses.[67] Anguished demands for apology, retribution or reparation for past suffering were raised by victims and their families. In addition, increasing international awareness of human rights also pressured new governments to respond to those voices.[68] Addressing legacies of past human rights abuses, in other words pursuing so-called 'transitional justice', became vital for new governments in order to achieve national unity and reconciliation and prevent the recurrent violence that threatened order within society.[69] The question, however, was how to achieve transitional justice. It is in this context that 'the Nuremberg ethos' was revived.[70]

On analysing the concept of transitional justice, Ruti Teitel wrote: 'How justice was done at Nuremberg ... has become virtually synonymous with successor justice'.[71] And this successor justice came to be 'generalized beyond its post-war uses to other transitions in which its central normative force appears to be condemnatory of past political violence'.[72] Punishment and trials are regarded as being necessary for the transition to democracy not only to achieve justice per se. These are taken as a ritual to draw a clear line between the old and new regimes, delegitimize the past 'evil' governments and thus facilitate the transition and legitimization of the new government.[73] Some commentators further emphasize that prosecution and punishment are indispensable to preserving collective memory or to deter the recurrence of future human rights abuses.

Transition in Latin American countries was haunted by the Nuremberg legacy. In practice, however, government confronted a serious dilemma. Under the government of President Alfonsin, Argentina once decided to prosecute the leaders of guerrilla organizations, who had been involved in thousands of 'disappearances' and arbitrary imprisonment and torture under the previous military regime. Facing military disobedience, the government gradually realized that some degree of clemency and forgiveness was needed in order to achieve national reconciliation and social order. In the end, the government decided not to proceed with new prosecutions. José Zalaquett, examining the case in Argentina, points out that prosecution and punishment causes several practical problems when perpetrators of human rights abuse still possess considerable power within the new government, which was often the case with transition in Latin America.[74] This is a significant difference from the case in post-war Germany and Japan, where unconditional surrender made it impossible to negotiate or hinder the process of war crimes prosecution. The ultimate goal of transitional justice is social reconciliation and the transformation of society into democracy. Whether prosecution and punishment contribute to this end, in other words, whether Nuremberg is an appropriate model for achieving that goal, remains the main focus of the debate on the issue of transitional justice.[75]

There are other points that question the applicability of the Nuremberg experience to achieve transitional justice. The context of post-war Germany is different from the contexts of Latin American countries: the former was concerned with the transition from war to peace within an international context, and the latter was concerned with the transition from one regime to another, a process mostly confined to a domestic setting. In this sense, the Nuremberg legacy is interpreted in the case of Latin America in 'decontextualized' ways. As the pursuit of transitional justice depended on 'what the transition is *from*' and 'what the transition is *to*', there, in theory, should be no universal approach to the issue.[76] Nonetheless, the experience of Nuremberg influenced a wave of transition not only in Latin America but also in Eastern and Central Europe.[77]

What needs to be pointed out in terms of the present research is that, in spite of these practical and theoretical problems, the Nuremberg precedent 'has shaped the pervasive understanding of transitional criminal justice'.[78] What is even more important is that, with the decontextualized application of the Nuremberg legacy, that legacy acquired a different significance and nuance from that which it had originally possessed. Being connected to the concept of transitional justice, war crimes prosecutions acquired the role to prosecute not only the violation of international humanitarian law but also gross violations of human rights conducted by state leaders against their people. In other words, war crimes trials came to be discussed in the context not only of states' relations but also of relations between a state and its people. And, it is along with this process that the focus of the Nuremberg legacy shifted from 'crimes against peace', the crime committed against other states, to 'crimes against humanity', the crime committed against people. The perceived aim of war crimes prosecutions also shifted from the deterrence of war to the pursuit of victim's justice and the promotion of transition from the old regime.

In sum, within the context of transitional justice activity, the Nuremberg legacy acquired significance beyond the original emphasis of its own advocates. And it is with the end of the Cold War that there emerged a space for such Nuremberg legacy to prevail in international contexts.

The Nuremberg legacy in the post-Cold War context

The revival of the Nuremberg legacy in the 1990s in the form of ad hoc International Criminal Tribunals for the former Yugoslavia and for Rwanda (ICTs) is strongly related to the growth of international interest in gross violations of human rights. However, as seen above, the idea of and movements for universal human rights alone could not lead to the setting up of international war crimes tribunals during the Cold War. State leaders mostly ignored human rights violations, which were still marginalized issues in international relations. What is more, state leaders had little incentive to prevent and stop the gross violations of human rights by risking the mutual respect for sovereignty.

The new international security environment that emerged after the end of the Cold War more or less eliminated elements – the absoluteness of state sovereignty and the marginalization of human rights issues in international relations – that had been preventing the Nuremberg precedent from being followed during the Cold War. As examined in the previous chapter, the ICTs were created against the backdrop of changes in the international security environment. The creation of the ICTs was the result of the political will of states to take action against humanitarian disasters, even through intervention in another state's domestic matters, which were regarded as 'threats to international peace'. As the understanding of 'who or what is being secured, from what threats' changed, so did the understanding of 'by what means' to tackle threats.[79] An ad hoc international criminal tribunal, inspired by the experience of Nuremberg, was regarded as a new option in response to post-Cold War international peace and security. This means that the Nuremberg legacy was revived in the form of the ICTs not for its own sake but as a solution to new problems the international community faced. In that sense, the legacy was to be interpreted 'teleologically'.

As argued in previous chapters, what is vital in cases of armed conflicts in the former Yugoslavia and Rwanda was not only a ceasefire but also long-lasting stability in the post-conflict society. It is the transition from war to a long-lasting peace that the ICTs and a 'peace through justice' project are tackling.[80] The project overlaps with the Nuremberg Trial, which was also meant to be 'the last act of the war and first act of the peace'.[81] Nuremberg came to be understood in the 1990s as a model for post-conflict peace building, promoting the transformation of war-torn society. In this context, one aspect of the aims of the Nuremberg Trial stood out: the promotion of the democratization and denazification process in post-war West German society.[82] In order to examine further exactly in what way war crimes prosecutions promote post-conflict social transformation, the following examines this aspect of the Allies' strategic purposes – the political and social policy towards post-war Germany – and compares to the strategic purposes of war crimes prosecution raised by those who supported the ICTs.

Nuremberg and the Allies' policy on post-war German transformation

The immediate aim of the International Military Tribunal for Major German War Criminals was to prosecute and punish Nazi leaders. In addition to the consideration for post-Second World War international peace and security, prosecution and punishment were also placed within wide-ranging social and political reform policies towards post-war Germany, which were laid down at Potsdam in August 1945 and can be summarized as four 'd's: *denazification*, *demilitarization*, *decentralization* and *decartelization*.[83] It was the United States who took the lead in planning and establishing an international tribunal. In *Law and War: An American Story*, Peter Maguire illustrates the background of the American war crimes policy towards Germany: 'It was not enough for American leaders to simply defeat and destroy the Third Reich; they also insisted on *reforming* their vanquished foes'.[84] Punishment, in this sense, completes only half of the project;

making the Germans accept the criminality of their own leader was also crucial. The trial was expected to achieve this *strategic purpose* through two interrelated devices: *the pursuit of individual responsibility* and *the creation of an historical record of Nazi crimes*.

The pursuit of individual responsibility

The US chief prosecutor at the Nuremberg Tribunal emphasized in the Opening Statement that the trial had 'no purpose to incriminate the whole German people'[85] but to target 'the brains and authority back of all the crimes'.[86] By pursuing individual responsibility of the Nazi leaders through judicial procedure, the trial avoided assigning the burden of 'collective responsibility' to the whole German nation and people.[87] This was based on three strategic concerns.

First, a war crimes tribunal was one way of normalizing relations between the victor and the vanquished. There was a lesson from the victor's treatment of the vanquished in the aftermath of the First World War. On seeing Germany re-emerge as an enemy of the Allies in the interwar period, the Washington planners believed that they 'had not done a sufficiently thorough job of purging the country after the First World War'.[88] As the German defeat became certain in the autumn of 1944 and the report of the atrocities committed by the Nazis became public, there emerged within Washington a plan for 'punitive peace', led by the Secretary of the Treasury Henry Morgenthau, Jr. Morgenthau's main idea was complete economic oppression through 'de-industrialization' of the country. Secretary of War, Henry L. Stimson, however, saw that such an excessively bitter approach would produce dangerous resentment within Germany: 'Such methods, in my opinion, do not prevent war, they tend to breed war'.[89] Indeed, the interwar international community had witnessed how an excessive burden through heavy reparations on the German nation had raised serious frustration and hatred on the part of the vanquished. This negative emotion, together with poverty, became the seedbed for the rise of Nazism, and paved the way for the Second World War.[90] As the alternative to the Morgenthau Plan, Stimson saw, Bradley Smith points out, 'a comprehensive war criminal trial system, systematically punishing Nazi leaders and organizations, as the best means of settling the Allies' score with the Third Reich and securing the future peace of the world'.[91] The failure of the post-First World War attempt to prosecute and punish German leaders in the German courts also made American leaders believe that national trials would not be feasible for these ends. In this sense, the Allies' policy on war crimes prosecution was based on realist considerations of post-war Germany and international peace and security. Stimson in the end succeeded in making President Roosevelt take the issue of war crimes trials seriously.

Second, the pursuit of individual responsibility, especially of those most responsible for the grave crimes, was to respond to the victims' outcry for revenge in a way that would stop the cycle of hatred.[92] As the details of the Holocaust became clear, there was an angry and violent reaction on the part of the victims, which could very likely have led to post-war arbitrary 'lynch mob' justice against the Germans in Europe. In the case of large-scale violence, the whole society from which the victimizer comes is, to some extent, involved in the crimes, and there was a possibility that the victims tend to demonize everyone and pursue collective responsibility. One side's collective revenge for collective responsibility leads to future collective revenge from the other side: the mechanism of the cycle of hatred, which is the source of future conflict and an obstacle for long-lasting peace. Individual criminal punishment was aimed at diverting the victim's hatred from the whole nation to a handful of leaders.

What is significant about the judicial procedure is that it is an example of pursuing justice, an alternative to raw revenge. While diverting the direction of the victim's hatred, Judith Shklar argues that the Nuremberg Trial 'replaced private, uncontrolled vengeance with a measured process of fixing guilt in each case, and taking the power to punish out of the hands of those directly injured'.[93] A society infested with private revenge faces serious disorder. 'The political function of criminal law', Shklar states, 'is here shown to be clearly not just a matter of protecting society against its deviant members, but of protecting all the members of society against themselves, against the corrosive effects of their own passion for vengeance'.[94] A trial is a way to pursue justice for the victim and thus plays an important role in reducing the tension between the victim and the victimizer, which is an indispensable step towards post-war reconciliation. Instant summary execution alone would not achieve this.

Third, and most important, the strategy of the tribunal focusing on individual responsibility was based on an agenda to isolate Nazi leaders from the German population and thus comprised an important part of the denazification policy.[95] Jackson emphasized at the International Military Tribunal that Nazi aggression had ruined not only neighbouring countries but also Germany itself: 'The German, no less than the non-German world, has accounts to settle with these defendants'.[96] There was a clear intention on the part of the trial advocates to demarcate the German people from the Nazi regime and its crimes. Detachment from the past 'evil' regime is necessary for re-educating people and rehabilitating society destroyed by war.

The trial was also able to promote denazification through the rule of law, which is normally absent in society under totalitarianism. The tribunal, the embodiment of the rule of law, was expected to 'prove to the German people that under an American-inspired system of justice, due process of law was extended to even the guiltiest'.[97] In spite of several defects, the trial's judicial procedure was generally regarded as fair to the accused.[98] Compared to some alternatives, such as summary execution and the show trials said to have been proposed by Churchill and Stalin, the form of judicial trial itself is fair. 'To free them without a trial would mock the dead and make cynics of the living', Jackson wrote in his report to the President: 'But undiscriminating executions or punishments without definite findings of guilt, fairly arrived at, would violate pledges repeatedly given, and would not set easily on the American conscience or be remembered by our children with pride'.[99] Jackson also recorded in his opening statement: 'If these men are the first war leaders of a defeated nation to be prosecuted in the name of the law, they are also the first to be given a chance to plead for their lives in the name of the law'.[100] What mattered was that justice was *seen to be* done. The promoter of the trial was convinced that it was 'an expression of civilization's condemnation of the Nazi philosophy'.[101]

The creation of an historical record

The denazification and political and social reform of Germany were expected to be promoted even more directly through the second device of the tribunal: the creation of an historical record of German war crimes.

Discrediting Nazism in the eyes not only of the international community but also of the German population was indispensable in order to prevent the martyrdom of the Nazi leaders and the repetition of the atrocities at a later date. Summary execution would not achieve this but would, instead, glorify Nazism and its leaders. Re-education of the German people, advocates of the war crimes trial believed, would be promoted by revealing through legal procedure the record of aggressive war and brutal atrocities conducted by the Nazi regime. Stimson claimed: 'we can demonstrate the abhorrence which the world has for such a system and bring home to the German people our determination to expiate it and all its fruits forever'.[102] This idea can also be found behind the reason why the Anglo-American legal concept of conspiracy was brought into the IMT Charter.[103] Stimson believed that prosecuting Nazism for conspiracy 'with all of the actors brought in from the top to the bottom would be the best way to try it and would give us a record and also a trial which would certainly persuade any onlooker of the evil of the Nazi system'.[104] In the words of Shklar, Nuremberg was 'a legalistic means of eliminating the Nazi leaders in such a way that their contemporaries, on whom the immediate future of Germany depended, might *learn exactly what had occurred in recent history*'.[105] The presentation of evidence of the Nazis' crimes was expected to make Germans acknowledge the criminality of their leaders.[106]

Establishing the record of Nazi crimes was also necessary for the Allies and their people. The trial's comprehensive account of Nazi crimes was expected to vindicate the just cause of the Allies' battle against the Axis powers, and convince people that their sacrifices had been worthwhile.[107] Stimson believed that prosecution of Nazi criminals 'will afford the most effective way of making a record of the Nazi system of terrorism and of the effort of the Allies to terminate the system and prevent its recurrence'.[108]

The staff at the Nuremberg Tribunal were well aware that their judgment would inevitably be seen as '*making* history'.[109] Sir Hartley Shawcross, Britain's chief prosecutor, stated at Nuremberg: 'we believe that this tribunal, acting ... with complete and judicial objectivity, will provide a contemporary touchstone and *an authoritative and impartial record* to which future historians may turn for truth, and future politicians for warning'.[110]

By pursuing individual responsibility – avoiding collectivization of guilt – and presenting an authoritative record of atrocities, the Nuremberg Trial was expected not only to contribute to international peace and security but also to endorse the transformation of German society and Germany's reconciliation within its society as well as with its neighbouring countries. It is widely seen from outside that the Nuremberg Trial did help German society to rehabilitate from Nazism, re-educate its people and promote reconciliation within and with other nations. Otto Kranzbuehler saw the International Military Tribunal as 'the painful starting point for building the relations that exist today [1965] between Germany and her Western Allies'.[111] This view of Nuremberg surely inspired those who worked and are working for the International Criminal Tribunal for the former Yugoslavia (ICTY), the first international tribunal since the two post-Second World War international military tribunals.

The lesson of Nuremberg learned by the ICTs

Armed conflict in the former Yugoslavia, which was characterized by systematic murder, rape and torture and mass violence among the different social and ethnic groups, threatened international peace and security in the 1990s.[112] What has been crucial for international as well as regional peace is the long-lasting stability of post-conflict society with no future prospect of a recurrence of violence deriving from hatred and vengeance. This, the proponents of the ICTY believe, is impossible if the culprits are allowed to go unpunished: 'Those who have suffered, directly or indirectly, from their crimes are unlikely to forgive or set aside their deep resentment'.[113] The ICTY Annual Report of 1994 stated:

> The only civilized alternative to this desire for revenge is to render justice: to conduct a fair trial by a truly independent and impartial tribunal and to punish those found guilty. If no fair trial is held, feelings of hatred and resentment seething below the surface will, sooner or later, erupt and lead to renewed violence.[114]

Prosecution and punishment themselves are not the goal of the ICTY. The ICTY itself noted that it would work as 'a tool for promoting reconciliation and restoring true peace'.[115] The most prominent goal of the tribunals, therefore, was transformation of war-torn society and reconciliation within it. It is here, as Paul Van Zyl argues, close relations between post-conflict peace building and transitional justice can be observed. [116]

As the transformation and reconciliation of war-torn society became an important issue,[117] the Allies' political and social agenda behind the Nuremberg Trial and its strategy became the major lesson to be learned by the ICTs. The two devices of war crimes prosecution – the pursuit of individual responsibility and the creation of an authoritative historical records of events – came to be seen by academics and practitioners supporting war crimes tribunals as the necessary tools for transformation and reconciliation of post-conflict society.

The pursuit of individual responsibility

The Nuremberg Tribunal's attempt to individualize responsibility is one of the most important points reiterated within the discourse on the ICTs. '[The] purpose of an impartial tribunal', Antonio Cassese, first President of the ICTs, stated, 'is to determine *individual* criminal responsibility of *individual* offenders, *collective* guilt ... is replaced with *individual* guilt'.[118] For many of those who support the ICTs, the Nuremberg Trial proved the feasibility of ascribing individual guilt by assigning responsibility to individual offenders. Richard Goldstone, first Chief Prosecutor of the ICTs, recognized Nuremberg as 'a meaningful instrument for avoiding the guilt of the Nazis being ascribed to the whole German people'.[119]

The importance of the individualization of responsibility has been argued from several perspectives, the logic of which were also found in the Allies' policy on Nuremberg examined above. First, it was strongly emphasized that the victims of violence in the former Yugoslavia and Rwanda should see justice done in order to discourage their desire for private vengeance.[120] At the same time, just as in the case of Nuremberg, it was strongly claimed that justice should be rendered in such a way as to avoid collectivization of responsibility. De-collectivization of responsibility is especially important in cases like the former Yugoslavia and Rwanda, in which systematic violence was based on the demonization of all the adversarial groups. The ICTY Annual Report stated: 'The history of the region [in the former Yugoslavia] clearly shows that clinging to feelings of "collective responsibility" easily degenerates into resentment, hatred and frustration and inevitably leads to further violence and new crimes'.[121] To promote reconciliation and long-lasting peace in regions that are torn apart by mass violence based on ethnic hatred, breaking the cycle of hatred by pursuing individual responsibility is regarded as indispensable.[122]

Second, the pursuit of individual responsibility aims to remove, from post-conflict peace building, political and military leaders who have played significant roles in mass atrocities conducted because of ethnic hatred. Payam Akhavan highlighted the importance in the Yugoslav conflict of 'the role played by élites in transforming ethnic consciousness from a legitimate communal identity into a legitimization of mass violence against rival groups'.[123] It is regarded as indispensable to undermine the influence as well as the legitimacy of such leaders and eliminate them from post-conflict rehabilitation processes and domestic politics.[124] *Stigmatization* of war criminals through indictment and actual prosecution are expected to achieve this. Stigmatization also isolates those indicted internationally. Being indicted by the ICTs, those political and military leaders, once beyond their national borders, will face possible arrest by international forces. 'They will become international pariahs', stated Madeleine Albright at the Security Council: 'While these individuals may be able to hide within the borders of Serbia or in parts of Bosnia or Croatia, they will be imprisoned for the rest of their lives within their own land'.[125]

What the stigmatization and delegitimization of guilty leaders, together with de-collectivization of responsibility, is expected to do is to demarcate clearly, both practically and psychologically, war criminals and others 'dragged into' terrible crimes. The ritual of demarcation provides post-conflict society an opportunity to transform itself from conflict to peace. It is here that the criminality of those responsible needs to be clearly illustrated in the eyes of people in the war-torn society. This is expected to be further promoted by another device of the tribunal: creating an authoritative record of events.

The creation of an historical record

The ICTs, like Nuremberg, are expected to reveal what happened during a given conflict and to build an impartial and objective record of events. Recognition of what happened in what way is claimed as necessary for preventing a recurrence of mass violence. Akhavan, emphasizing the elites' role in the Yugoslav conflict, claimed the importance of revealing the mechanisms of mass violence to the people in the region in order to counter distorted ethnic hatred instigated by their political leaders: 'The truth will demonstrate that there was nothing inevitable or irreversible about the eruption of ethnic violence and that interethnic harmony is both possible and desirable'.[126] The pivotal role played in genocide not by inevitable ethnic hatred but by state leaders and the media is also pointed out in the case of Rwanda.[127]

In addition to preventing future violence, constructing a record of events is also regarded as important to promote the coexistence of former rival groups in post-conflict society. '[The] record of an international tribunal', Cassese stated, 'is of crucial value as an historical account of events, a public acknowledgement of their existence for *collective memory*'.[128] Cultivation of collective memory has been argued as important for restoring national identity, or the collective, which is lost in a society torn apart by large-scale violence. The collective is vital in order that former enemies, or victims and victimizers, can coexist. Indeed, attempts have often been made to shape this collective memory through legal process.[129] José Alvarez examined this idea and stated: 'The goal of using … trials to preserve an accurate collective memory is also based on the model of closure', which he suggested has been inspired by Nuremberg.[130]

The key to the work of the ICTs, it has been emphasized, is to satisfy the victims of conflicts, that is to achieve 'victim's justice'. From the victim's perspective, it is strongly argued that the victims and their families first of all need to be told what has happened during mass violence: they have a 'right to know'. Albright stated: 'it is only the truth that can cleanse the ethnic and religious hatreds and begin the healing process'.[131] At the same time, the victims needed their suffering to be officially recognized, which is important for restoring their dignity. Some pointed out that a trial has a potentially therapeutic effect by providing victims with 'an official public forum for the acknowledgement and vindication of the suffering of the victims'.[132] Akhavan referred to the Holocaust and argued: 'the recognition of the truth through testimony is an irreplaceable remedy and a powerful catharsis that will contribute to deterrence by discouraging acts of vengeance and retaliation'.[133] It is here that putting the procedures of the ICTs under the scrutiny of the international community is regarded as important.

There are various mechanisms for 'truth-telling' and constructing an historical record of events. A truth commission, attempted during the transitional period in Latin America and South Africa, is one popular forum, which provides both victims and victimizer opportunities to tell their story and to reveal the 'truth' but mostly not accompanied by criminal punishment.[134] Not surprisingly, however, the promoter of the ICTs emphasized the desirability of trials for the truth-telling process. Michael Scharf maintained that 'the most authoritative rendering is possible only through the crucible of a trial that accords full due process'.[135] On analysing the first case of the ICTY, he stated: 'By carefully establishing these facts one witness at a time in the face of vigilant cross-examination by distinguished defense counsel, the Tadic trial produced a definitive account that can endure the test of time and resist the forces of revisionism'.[136] Albright stated at the Security Council: 'Truth is the cornerstone of the rule of law, and it will point towards individuals, not peoples, as perpetrators of war crimes'.[137] The idea of an international trial as an appropriate forum for creating a record of events is strongly influenced by the legacy of Nuremberg. On analysing the Milosevic trial, Geoffrey Robertson referred to Nuremberg and argued that the Nuremberg Trial succeeded for the reason that 'it provided *an imperishable factual record* to confound future Holocaust denials'.[138]

The positive impact of the ICTs is also claimed, based on their educational effect. A culture of impunity, the promoters of the ICTs believe, is a source of recurring war crimes and crimes against humanity. The tribunal is seen as playing an indispensable role in establishing a culture of law and order, which not only promotes the transformation of post-conflict society but also contributes to international peace and security by sending a warning to dictators and potential war criminals around the world.[139]

Although supporters of the ICTs refer very often to Nuremberg with regard to their expectation of international trials having a positive impact, their discourse is different from those at Nuremberg in one important point: the focus on victim's justice. Strictly speaking, Nuremberg was not necessarily a victim-conscious trial,[140] while the ICTs are strongly aware of the victims of violence. James O'Brien stated:

> Ultimately, it is not who is accountable that matters the most, but to whom the international community is accountable. The people who have been victimized by atrocities in the former Yugoslavia – and those elsewhere who will benefit from strong international humanitarian law – deserve to see that justice is sought. They should be allowed to turn their attention to building the future, not to seeking vengeance for the past.[141]

In this sense, the ICTs were influenced more by the experience of Latin America and elsewhere with regard to the pursuit of transitional justice than by Nuremberg per se. This can be seen from the fact that Richard Goldstone, first chief prosecutor of the ICTs, has a great record in pursuing justice for post-apartheid South Africa as chairperson of the Commission of Inquiry Regarding Public Violence and Intimidation.[142] The ICTs, in sum, received the Nuremberg legacy via the experience of transitional justice, which has interpreted and adopted Nuremberg more 'normatively' than the creators of Nuremberg intended.

Conclusion

The legacy of Nuremberg during the Cold War was rather ambiguous and ambivalent. While international humanitarian law and human rights law developed immensely based on principles set out by the Nuremberg Tribunal, states were reluctant to resort to the Nuremberg precedent; there was no international war crimes tribunal established thereafter to prosecute war crimes and crimes against humanity. The international community also failed to institutionalize crimes against peace, which the Nuremberg Trial called 'the supreme international crime'. The underlying belief was that strictly following the Nuremberg precedent would threaten state sovereignty and the non-intervention principle, on which international peace and security rested. What was fatally lacking during the Cold War was the political will of states to revive the experience of Nuremberg. States are always cautious about any step that might challenge their sovereignty. They also had little incentive to remedy injustice done to people in other parts of the world that were irrelevant to their own interests. Nonetheless, as Falk rightly pointed out, the Nuremberg legacy survived the Cold War due to 'the unexpected, yet vital, role that civil society has played in keeping the Nuremberg idea alive'.[143] Furthermore, within this half century, the Nuremberg legacy has been given new impetus.

The ICTs are expected to promote reconciliation and the transformation of a society that has experienced mass atrocities conducted among rival groups under the influence of mutual hatred. The key devices are to pursue only those who are the most responsible and thus to avoid the collectivization of responsibility; and to create an authoritative account of what has actually happened during such conflicts. Supporters of the ICTs repeatedly emphasize the importance of the individualization of responsibility and an historical record, referring to the experience of Nuremberg. What is more, the experience of Nuremberg is seen as having proved the necessity of rendering justice through criminal procedure as well as the feasibility of a fair trial under an international tribunal.[144]

The extent to which the Nuremberg Trial itself promoted transformation and reconciliation in post-war German society is still debated.[145] Nonetheless, for those who talk about the Nuremberg legacy in the context of post-Cold War international war crimes tribunals, the aspects of the Nuremberg experience discussed above are regarded as a positive model, which can be applied to the former Yugoslavia, Rwanda and elsewhere universally.

However, to regard the Nuremberg legacy as a universal model is problematic because this universality is based only on the experience of post-war

Germany. This is a serious point because an international military tribunal was established not only for Germany but also for another Second World War vanquished state: Japan. The International Military Tribunal for the Far East (the Tokyo Tribunal) was created on the heels of the Nuremberg Tribunal, based on the Nuremberg Charter and for the same objective: prosecuting the major war criminals conducting 'crimes against peace', war crimes and 'crimes against humanity'. The key questions, therefore, are the following: What does the Tokyo Trial tell us about the validity of the Nuremberg legacy? Has the Tokyo Trial promoted the transformation and reconciliation of Japanese society, as the Nuremberg Trial is claimed to have done for German society? Did the individualization of responsibility and the record of events provided by the tribunal contribute to post-war Japan in some ways? If so, the Nuremberg legacy, though still based only on two cases, becomes more credible and profound. If not, the current attempts at international war crimes prosecution may require some theoretical and practical reconsideration. It is the aim of the remainder of this study to re-examine the Nuremberg legacy as understood in the post-Cold War context by examining the Tokyo Trial and its impact on post-war Japan.

3 The Tokyo Trial

An overview and purposes of the trial

This chapter begins by setting out the key features of the Tokyo Trial, formally named the International Military Tribunal for the Far East (IMTFE), its purposes and the impact expected by the Allies. Based on an examination of documents and the discourse of those who organized and participated in the Tokyo Trial, the chapter illustrates that the trial was expected to create identical effects to those expected at the Nuremberg Trial: the transformation of post-war society through demilitarization and democratization, using as devices the pursuit of individual responsibility and the creation of an authoritative record of the war.

The Tokyo Tribunal and the Nuremberg Tribunal are often regarded as twin institutions. However, in spite of the fact that Tokyo and Nuremberg both took the form of an international military tribunal prosecuting the Second World War vanquished, close examination of the two cases reveals that there are several important differences between them. The latter half of the chapter analyses those differences, linking them to the different degree of initiative taken by the United States in the Tokyo Trial.

The Tokyo Trial

The Allies' intention to 'retain and punish the aggression of Japan' was announced as early as 1 December 1943, in the form of the Cairo Declaration released by the leaders of the United States, Great Britain and China. However, the basic policy to *punish by trying individual Japanese war criminals* was publicized for the first time in the Potsdam Declaration of 26 July 1945, which stated, in its Article 10, that 'stern justice shall be meted out to all war criminals, including those who have visited cruelties upon our prisoners'.[1] The terms of the declaration were accepted by the Japanese government through the Instrument of Surrender on 2 September 1945, and became the legal basis for the trials of Japanese war criminals. At the same time, the Instrument of Surrender made the authority of the Emperor and the Japanese government subject to the Supreme Commander for the Allied Powers in Japan (SCAP), General Douglas MacArthur of the United States, who took the initiative in procedures relating to the war crimes prosecutions as well as the whole occupation policy.[2] The occupation of Japan started when MacArthur arrived in Japan on 30 August 1945.

The occupation forces started to arrest war crimes suspects as early as September 1945.[3] The first round of arrest warrants included General Tōjō Hideki, Prime Minister at the time of the attack on Pearl Harbor. By the end of the year, more than 100 people were being held in custody as suspected 'Class-A war criminals', or major war criminals, having perpetrated 'crimes against peace'.[4] The Tokyo Tribunal was established based on the Charter of the International Military Tribunal for the Far East, issued on 19 January 1946. The Charter was modelled on the Nuremberg Charter and included 'crimes against peace', conventional war crimes and 'crimes against humanity' as its jurisdiction. The tribunal was composed of 11 judges from the nine signatories of the Instrument of Surrender – Australia, Canada, China, France, Great Britain, the Netherlands, New Zealand, the Soviet Union and the United States – plus India and the Philippines, each one of which also offered a member for the prosecution section. The selection of the accused started from March 1946, and indictments were issued for 28 defendants on 29 April 1946. Among those indicted were Tōjō, and 17 other military officers. Four of the defendants were former prime ministers, and most others were members of wartime cabinets.[5]

The Tokyo Trial opened on 3 May 1946. The prosecution case lasted until 24 January 1947. During this period, prosecutors developed the case that

> the accused participated in the formulation or execution of a common plan or conspiracy to wage declared or undeclared war or wars of aggression and war or wars in violation of international law, treaties, agreements and assurances against any country which might oppose them – against any country or countries which might oppose them – with the object of securing military, naval, political and economic domination of East Asia and of the Pacific and Indian Oceans, and all countries bordering thereon and islands therein and ultimately the domination of the world.[6]

The case was developed under 14 phases plus the one developed against individual defendants.[7] Prosecutors also raised issues concerning 'war crimes' and 'crimes against humanity'.

During the prosecution case, the defence, unlike the Nuremberg Trial, was given an opportunity to put forward a motion to challenge the jurisdiction of the tribunal. The defence lawyers claimed that the Tokyo Trial was *ex post facto* legislation because the Potsdam Declaration referred only to the trial of war crimes but not to 'crimes against peace' and 'crimes against humanity'. The defence also argued that the declaration limited the jurisdiction of the tribunal to the Pacific War and thus charges on the incidents that are unrelated to the war or had already been settled in the past should be excluded. In addition to those points, defence motions included the following claims: the trial comprised of the representative of the nations that defeated Japan 'can neither be fair, legal nor impartial'; 'war is not a crime'; 'individuals may not be charged with responsibility for wars'; 'killing in war is not murder follows from the fact that war is legal'; and violations of the laws and customs of war are punishable by a trial by a military commission but not by an international military tribunal as such.[8] The prosecution replied by emphasizing the significance of already existing international law and the unconditional aspect of Japan's surrender. At this stage, defence motions were dismissed by the president of the tribunal 'for reasons to be given later'.[9]

The defence took its turn from 24 February 1947 until 12 January 1948. The defence started its case with a joint presentation, which was broken down into five sections: general problems, relations with Manchuria and Manchukuo, with China, with the Soviet Union and the Pacific War. The presentation aimed at two things: the minor one was to deny 'the existence of the conspiracy and joint action by the defendants in committing crimes against peace'; and the major one was to claim that 'all of the acts committed by the defendants and the government of Japan were acts of self-defense against provocative acts of other nations threatening and interfering with Japan's recognized and legitimate rights in Asia and her right of national existence'.[10] The joint presentation was followed by individual defences.[11] The case for the defence was followed by rebuttal, surrebuttal, prosecution summation, defence summation and prosecution reply.

The trial closed its cases on 16 April 1948. There were 417 court days in total, during which 419 witnesses testified in court and 4,336 documents were accepted as 'Exhibit in Evidence'. The transcript of the proceedings covered 48,412 pages.[12] The number of sessions and witnesses and the duration of the proceedings of the Tokyo Trial were double that of Nuremberg.

The 11 judges spent seven months writing the judgment, which took eight days to read out, starting on 4 November 1948. On 12 November 1948, the judgment was rendered to 25 defendants, excluding two defendants who had died during the trial and one who had been discharged because of a mental disorder. All of the 25 defendants were found guilty. Seven including Tōjō were sentenced to death, 16 to life imprisonment, one to 20 years' imprisonment and one to seven years' imprisonment.[13] Responding to defence motions, the Tokyo judgment rejected challenges that aggressive war was not a crime, that there was no individual responsibility for war and that the Tokyo Charter was *ex post facto* legislation, reasoning mostly based on the Nuremberg judgment of October 1946: 'The Charter is not an arbitrary exercise of power on the part of the victorious nations but is the expression of international law existing at the time of its creation'.[14] The judgment also rejected the defence claim that a tribunal comprised of the governments of the victorious nations could not conduct a fair and impartial trial.

The Tokyo judgment was not unanimous. The majority decision was signed by nine judges out of 11. Five judges wrote separate opinions, including two dissenting opinions by the French justice Henri Bernard and Justice Radhabinod Pal of India.[15] Delfin Jaranilla, a judge from the Philippines, stated that sentencing was too generous to expect a deterrent effect;[16] the Dutch justice B.V.A. Röling claimed that Hirota Kōki, former Prime Minister and the only civilian sentenced to death, was not guilty of any charge; and William Webb, the president of the tribunal, expressed a reservation about applying death sentences, questioning its deterrent effect and also questioning the immunity given to the Emperor. The most powerful was the 1,235 pages of dissenting opinion of Justice Pal.[17] Arguing that the Tokyo Trial was *ex post facto* legislation and that there was no evidence for the existence of a conspiracy in Japanese foreign policy during 1930s and 1940s, and accepting the defendants' claim that the wars fought by Japan were self-defensive, Pal concluded that every defendant was not guilty of any charges and thus should be acquitted of all charges. An opportunity was not given for these separate opinions to be read out at the tribunal.

On 24 November 1948, with his power under the Tokyo Charter, MacArthur gave a final confirmation of the judgment of the tribunal. However, sentences were not executed immediately, as the defence counsel appealed on 29 November 1948 to the US Supreme Court for habeas corpus. The Supreme Court dismissed it on 20 December citing absence of jurisdiction in the case. The execution of the seven defendants sentenced to death was finally conducted on 23 December 1948. The judgment of the Tokyo Tribunal was officially accepted by the Japanese government through the San Francisco Peace Treaty of September 1951, the enforcement of which in 1952 ended the American occupation.

The strategic purposes

In an opening statement on 4 June 1946, Joseph Keenan, chief of prosecution, read out the purposes of the Tokyo Trial:

> Our purpose is one of prevention or deterrence. It has nothing whatsoever to do with the small meaner purpose of vengeance or retaliation. But we do hope in these proceedings that it is neither impossible nor improbable that the branding of individuals who visit these scourges upon mankind as common felons, and punishing them accordingly, may have a deterring effect upon aggressive warlike activities of their prototypes of the future, should they arise.[18]

By confirming that individuals of a nation who planned and conducted aggressive war would receive punishment, the prosecutor expected that the international tribunal, by establishing aggression as an international crime, would contribute to the maintenance of post-war international peace and security; 'the prevention of the scourge of aggressive war' was embedded in this grand strategy.[19] Indeed, the Tokyo Trial, just like Nuremberg, set itself out clearly as 'the trial to end all wars': 'we are waging a part of the determined battle of *civilization* to preserve the entire world from destruction', Keenan declared in his statement.[20]

At the same time, the Tokyo Trial was strongly connected to US policy towards post-war Japan. For the United States, the principal organizer of the Tokyo Trial, the issue of war crimes and punishment had been conceived within the framework of policies on the occupation of Japan. The American military occupation aimed to achieve the 'ultimate objectives' laid out in SWNCC 150/4/A (21 September 1945):

a To insure that Japan will not again become a menace to the United States or to the peace and security of the world.
b To bring about the eventual establishment of a peaceful and responsible government which will respect the rights of other states and will support the objectives of the United States as reflected in the ideals and principles of the Charter of the United Nations.[21]

The 'ultimate objectives', in other words, were the transformation of Japan. The 'political tasks' of the military occupation to achieve those objectives were threefold: disarmament and demilitarization as the primary tasks, following the prosecution of war criminals, and the encouragement of democratization.[22] In sum, the establishment of the International Military Tribunal constituted a major part of the political task of occupation, which aimed to transform Japanese society, through demilitarization and democratization, into a nation that would never again threaten the United States, and international peace and security.[23]

US policy regarding the issue of Japanese war criminals was specifically discussed at the State–War–Navy Coordinating Committee on 12 September 1945. The committee confirmed that 'the procedures and policies contemplated or already being applied in Europe relating to the trial and punishment of war criminals will be generally applicable in the Far East'.[24] The crimes to be punished and the authority of the SCAP over the coming trial were also defined by the committee. This 'American policy' on Japanese war criminals formally became the 'Allied policy' later, through the admission of the Far Eastern Commission, an organization empowered to formulate the basic policy to govern the terms of surrender.[25]

Devices of the trial

Just like Nuremberg, the international prosecution of Japanese war crimes was expected to endorse demilitarization and democratization. To achieve these ends, the punishment of war criminals was not enough; the criminality of those prosecuted had to be accepted by the Japanese people. The United States saw little problem in achieving these political ends by applying the devices and strategy of the war crimes trial conceived for Nuremberg.[26] In this context, the impact of the pursuit of individual responsibility and the creation of a record of the war and associated war crimes was well recognized.

The pursuit of individual responsibility

The Allies' policy on war crimes prosecution clearly embraced the idea of avoiding blame and responsibility being placed on the Japanese nation as a whole. Article 10 of the Potsdam Declaration clarified that the Allies' war crimes prosecution was not targeting the Japanese as a whole but specific individuals: 'We do not intend that the Japanese shall be enslaved as a race or destroyed as a nation, but stern justice shall be meted out to all war criminals, including those who have visited cruelties upon our prisoners'.

The de-collectivization of responsibility was regarded as an important tool for the demilitarization and democratization of Japan. Article 10 continued from above: 'The Japanese Government *shall remove all obstacles* to the revival and strengthening of democratic tendencies among the Japanese people. Freedom of speech, of religion, and of thought, as well as respect for the fundamental human rights shall be established' (emphasis added). Article 6 of the declaration clearly stated that 'obstacles' that the Allies viewed as being necessary to eliminate comprised a handful of individuals responsible for the war, who were clearly differentiated from the Japanese people in general:

> There must be eliminated for all time the authority and influence of those who have deceived and misled the people of Japan into embarking on world conquest, for we insist that a new order of peace, security and justice will be impossible until irresponsible militarism is driven from the world.

By prosecuting the wartime leaders, the Tokyo Trial sought to eliminate those figures from the post-war Japanese government, which was expected to transform itself into a democratic entity. This signified the *physical* demilitarization.

On examining US policy to demilitarize Japan, Meirion and Susie Harries regarded the Tokyo Trial as 'an integral part of the campaign for *psychological demilitarisation*'.[27] Indeed, the tribunal intended to demarcate wartime leaders and other Japanese people not only physically but also psychologically. For this purpose, the Tokyo Trial attempted not only to show that the defendants were war criminals but also to indicate that the people in Japan were their victims. The prosecution's opening statement said:

> We must reach the conclusion that the Japanese people themselves were utterly within the power and forces of these accused, and to such extent were its victims. With the permission of the tribunal, we would point out that the forces of occupation, who have the full power under the terms of surrender to implement its terms in such manner as they should see fit, have given full opportunity to the Japanese people and to the world to observe the fair manner in which the same is being conducted.[28]

Prosecuting individual war criminals was also a way to respond to the victim's cry for justice. Just as the voices demanding the prosecution of Nazi war crimes suspects were initially raised by representatives of the nine governments-in-exile in Europe, it was China, the biggest victim of wartime Japan, who first raised a clear voice in support of the international prosecution of Japanese war crimes suspects.[29]

Keenan expressed strong concern about the situation in which people were required to enforce the law by themselves against their leaders. Indeed, people in Japan had been under constant oppression and censorship before and during the war, which had prevented them from expressing their objections to national policy. Many anti-war movements were regulated and those engaged in peace movements were arrested and severely punished. Keenan insisted that the importance of 'Stern punishment imposed by orderly international tribunals', arguing that the trials at Tokyo 'are neither blood purges nor judicial lynchings, but if they are not held, the people in impatience and disgust, will have their own lynchings and blood purgings'.[30]

For the United States, punishing individuals responsible for the war and the alleged war crimes was regarded as being necessary for constructing a new relationship with Japan. Indeed, the United States, for its part, had a need to be reconciled with its former enemy over the attack on Pearl Harbor. According to an opinion poll in August 1945, 67 per cent of Americans wanted to treat the Japanese in general, and war criminals in particular, in a harsh manner. Accordingly, as Meirion and Susie Harries pointed out, 'a show trial of "Tojo and his gang" would seem to have been the obvious answer'.[31] General MacArthur himself had a strong feeling that 'Pearl Harbor should be avenged'. However, whether he expected the Tokyo Trial to achieve this end is doubtful. According to one judge at the Tokyo Tribunal, MacArthur would in fact have preferred a swift trial examining only the attack on Pearl Harbor, and in this sense he was against the Tokyo Trial, which indicted responsibility for the war itself.[32] In any case, as an American who worked in a prison accommodating major war criminals pointed out, war crimes trials provided 'the psychological moment of restoration' for the victors.[33] Such restoration was vital to enable the United States to construct a new relationship with Japan, against whom it had fought the war, characterized by mutual demonization and dehumanization.[34]

The Japanese people and the soldiers of the Allies were not the only victims of the Japanese military, however. What was missing from the Tokyo Trial was civilians in other Asian countries who had suffered most from Japan's war and colonial rule. The Tokyo Trial did not examine in detail their sufferings for political reasons that are addressed below. In this sense, the trial did not offer a forum for 'victim's justice' and reconciliation between Japan and people in her neighbouring countries.

The creation of an historical record

The goal of the Tokyo Trial was broader than mere punishment. This is even more apparent from the tribunal's enthusiasm for establishing an authoritative historical record that would be accepted by the Japanese. The Tokyo Trial's history lesson was expected to have educational effects for demilitarization and democratization.

To start with, the Japanese people had little information about the war they were fighting. Therefore, to reveal the facts through documentary evidence alone was expected to have a great impact on post-war Japan. However, this was not enough. The historical account of the Tokyo Trial had to be accepted by the Japanese: 'The purpose of the trial was to *convince* the Japanese people that their leaders misled them into war', Owen Cunningham, a member of the defence counsel stated.[35] Establishing the history in the minds of the Japanese was an important part of the 'psychological campaign for demilitarisation', and the Tokyo Trial was expected to play a certain role in it. This is clear from the fact that in December 1945, before the establishment of the Tokyo Trial, the major newspapers started to serialize the history of the Pacific War, based on the sources offered by General Headquarters, SCAP, the so-called GHQ.[36] This historical account took a similar line to the indictment and judgment of the Tokyo Trial and emphasized that the militarists in the government had been hiding the truth from the nation, depicting how they had terrorized the country, how Japan, despite propaganda to the contrary, had been fighting against heavy odds from an early stage in the war, and how brutally the Japanese military had fought in China and the Philippines, perpetrating war crimes against the Allies soldiers and locals. Considering the fact that this history was serialized in major newspapers all at the same time, that GHQ was the source of this account and that the Japanese media at the time was subject to GHQ censorship, it can be concluded that GHQ had been preparing the ground for the Japanese to accept the trial and its account of the war.[37]

The history lesson was not only for the Japanese. B. V. A. Röling, a Dutch judge at the Tokyo Tribunal, stated that 'a trial was also desired to show the American people and the whole world the criminal treachery of the attack on Hawaii'.[38] For the American leaders, the trial also meant to appeal to their own people and ease the anger over Pearl Harbor and other wartime sacrifices. It was also expected to show the world the righteousness of the war they had fought, even including dropping two atomic bombs.

Resorting to legal procedure rather than summary execution was expected by itself to have an educational effect as an ethical example of democracy, showing that law and justice can be applied even to enemies through a fair trial.[39] The United States was well aware of the importance of the justice as well as the authority of the tribunal being made clear to the Japanese people. SWNCC 57/3 of 12 September 1945 emphasized: 'the international character of the court and of the authority by which it is appointed should be properly recognized and emphasized, particularly in dealings with the Japanese people'.[40] This interestingly shows US awareness of the importance of the Japanese perception as well as the recognition of 'justice' and 'authority' in terms of the 'international' character of the trial.

Tokyo and Nuremberg compared

As seen above, the Tokyo Tribunal was modelled on the Nuremberg Tribunal, and it was expected to function and impact in more or less the same way as Nuremberg. However, the two tribunals are not as identical as is often assumed.

The two are different in critical ways, reflecting differences in the background and context of the defeat of the two countries.

The level of fairness and politicization

In general, the Tokyo Trial is more often said to be unfair and politicized than Nuremberg. Defects in the Tokyo Trials were pointed out even by American officials involved in the prosecution of Japanese war criminals. For example, US Brigadier General Elliott Thorpe, who had participated heavily in the process of selecting high-ranking war crimes suspects, reflected years after the end of the trial that he still did not believe the Tokyo Trial was the right thing to do: 'I still believe that it was an ex post facto law'.[41] The ambivalent and complex nature of the Tokyo Trial is symbolized also in the fact that judges of the tribunal could not speak with one voice at the final judgment.

On the fairness of the trials, many argue that the procedural flaws at the Tokyo Trial were greater than those at Nuremberg. In the words of John Appleman, compared with Nuremberg, 'the proceedings before the International Military Tribunal for the Far East seem strangely disorganized'.[42] Justice Henri Bernard of France dissented from the majority opinion on procedural grounds: 'A verdict reached by a tribunal after a defective procedure cannot be a valid one'.[43] Justice Pal also raised, as a reason for his dissent, that rules of evidence had been slanted in favour of the prosecutor. This point was put forward strongly to MacArthur, shortly after the close of the Tokyo Trial, by defence lawyer Ben Blakeney, representing the whole group of the defence counsel:

> The tribunal accepted from the prosecution 'evidence' in the form of newspaper reports, second and third-hand rumours and hearsay, opinions of self-styled 'experts', and made its findings and verdict on the basis of such 'evidence'; it ignored all defence evidence in its verdict, saying that the evidence of Japanese witnesses (although not those who testified for the prosecution) was unsatisfactory and unreliable.[44]

In addition, the prosecution was allowed greater resources than the defence, including translators; the prosecution having 102 at its disposal at the beginning of the trial compared to three for the defence.[45] Even though the Japanese defendants were permitted to have American lawyers in addition to Japanese lawyers, there is no doubt that they were involved in a trial based on an unfamiliar Anglo-American legal system, in a language in which they were not perfectly proficient.

The poor quality of the staff at the Tokyo Tribunal is also pointed out. William Webb, president of the tribunal, is described as 'coarse, ill-tempered and highly opinionated'.[46] In addition, his career in Australia from 1943 as a commissioner under National Security Regulations to investigate Japanese war crimes is raised to question his impartiality as president of the tribunal; Webb's prejudice towards Japan and its military is often pointed out.[47] Some others point to the inadequacy of Joseph Keenan as the chief prosecutor both in terms of his ability and his character, described as he was by his colleagues as 'a disgrace'.[48] Röling commented: 'Certainly, he was not up to his job. That is of course of great importance, because he was the chief prosecutor'.[49] With regard to judges, the Soviet and French judges were said to be not able to command English sufficiently well to do their job.

Whether the verdict and sentences of Tokyo were more severe than Nuremberg is not a simple question.[50] Some see Tokyo as harsher, pointing out that none were acquitted, while three were acquitted at Nuremberg.[51] Regarding the death sentence as the criterion of severity, Nuremberg was harsher than Tokyo, sentencing 12 out of 22 defendants to death, compared to seven out of 25 sentenced to death in Tokyo. Richard Minear compares the number of those who were sentenced to death *and* life imprisonment and argues that the Tokyo judgment, by sentencing 23 out of 25 defendants as such, was more draconian than Nuremberg, where only 15 out of 22 were sentenced either to death or life imprisonment.[52] What is more, the Tokyo judgment was signed by judges, some of whom expressed the view that the sentences were harsher, either regarding their content or regarding certain individuals, than they should have been.

As for the level of politicization, the Tokyo Trial, especially its aftermath, was far more susceptible to the politics of the Cold War than Nuremberg, which closed in October 1946. Already in the summer of 1947, the United States and Great Britain had lost enthusiasm for the originally planned second round of the Tokyo Trial. Entering 1948, it became clear that no further international trial of Class A war criminals was conceived.[53] In July of that year, Joseph Keenan wrote to the Secretary General of the Far Eastern Commission, regarding the release of some Class A war crimes suspects, stating that 'There is no further trial contemplated for any of the suspects on charges of planning, negotiating and waging aggressive warfare in violation of treaties, assurances, or international law'. He attributed this to 'the greatly prolonged proceedings before the present International Military Tribunal for the Far East' and stated that under such a situation 'no reasonable estimate of the time involved in such subsequent proceedings could be safely made'.[54] Indeed, the slow process of the Tokyo Trial, due to the number of countries involved and language problems, was clearly one of the reasons for the passive attitude of the Allies towards further international war crimes prosecution.[55]

This reluctance, however, had significantly more to do with the rapid changes in international relations. Relations between the United States and the Soviet Union were worse than they had been at the time of the Nuremberg Trial. In addition, there was also the rise of the communist threat in East Asia. As the original purposes, demilitarization and democratization, were regarded as already being on track as early as 1947, it was not thought to be a good idea to continue a punitive policy against Japan; the United States started to seek a conciliatory policy to transform Japan into a bulwark against communism in Asia. This shift in American policy on Japan was clearly outlined in NSC 13/2, 7 October 1948, which illustrated a policy that was less punitive and more focused on economic recovery. NSC 13/2 commented on the war crimes trial as follows:

> The trial of Class A suspects is completed and decision of the court is awaited. We should continue and push to an early conclusion the screening of all 'B' and 'C' suspects with a view to releasing those whose cases we do not intend to prosecute. Trials of the others should be instituted and concluded at the earliest possible date.[56]

The development of the Cold War strongly influenced the aftermath of the Tokyo Trial. On the day following the execution of Tōjō and others in December 1948, 19 Class A war crimes suspects waiting for the second round of the Tokyo Trial were released. The policy of 'no more trials on major war criminals in Japan' was officially announced by MacArthur in February 1949. The Japanese government, for its part, had been working behind the scenes for the release of the war criminals, a reduction in their sentences or pardons. It speeded up its effort after the occupation formally ended. In autumn 1952, Japan asked several states for the release of its war criminals, on the understanding that with the formalization of the peace, the war criminals issue should be solved politically. By the end of 1958, all the prisoners under sentence, including Class B and C war criminals held by the Allies, excluding the Soviet Union and the People's Republic of China, were released.[57]

US initiative in the Tokyo Trial

In addition to the general points on fairness and politicization noted above, there are several specific differences in appearance, procedures and background between Tokyo and Nuremberg. These can be attributed to the difference in the degree of American involvement at each tribunal.

Unlike Nuremberg, Tokyo was more of an 'American' tribunal than an international tribunal, as it was named. The Charter of the International Military Tribunal at Nuremberg was issued by the London Agreement in the form of a joint declaration of the Four Powers – the United States, France, the Soviet Union and the United Kingdom – and endorsed by 19 other countries later on. However, the issuance of the Charter of the Tokyo Tribunal took the form of an executive decree of General MacArthur. What is more, the Charter, though it was modelled on the Nuremberg Charter, was drafted by the International Prosecution Section, which at the time of drafting was staffed only with American prosecutors.[58] According to the Tokyo Charter, MacArthur had the authority to appoint the justices as well as the president of the tribunal,[59] while in Nuremberg the four signatories had appointed judges, who in turn appointed their president. Furthermore, MacArthur was given the authority to review their judgments.[60] It was clear to the participants that it was the United States who was taking the initiative in respect of the tribunal and its procedure. Röling reflected: 'In fact the Americans were in control of most aspects of the trial. The trial was very much an American performance'.[61] The structure of the tribunal also reflected the central role of the United States. Unlike Nuremberg, where there were four chief prosecutors, one each from the Four Powers, in Tokyo the prosecution consisted of one chief prosecutor from the United States and ten associate prosecutors from other countries.[62]

A significant effect of American domination of the Tokyo Trial procedure can be seen in the selection of people and issues judged by the trial, which was susceptible to US political considerations, that is, the US occupation policy and its Cold War strategy in the Far East. Accordingly, several important issues were absent from the trial's legal investigation. First was the research and human-body experiments of biological weapons conducted by the so-called Unit 731 based in Manchuria.[63] The conduct of Unit 731 led by Lieutenant General Ishii Shirō was a serious type of 'crimes against humanity'. However, it, together with Japan's alleged use of biological weapons in the war in China, was given immunity and not even examined during the trial, in exchange for the research results achieved by the unit. The United States wanted to monopolize the information the unit obtained, hiding it especially from the Soviet Union: 'Apparently the American military were eager to profit from the crimes committed by the Japanese, to enhance their knowledge of biological warfare', states Röling.[64] He sees with hindsight that one defendant was directly responsible for the establishment of a biological laboratory: 'I am ... convinced that one of our accused, who got life imprisonment, escaped a well-deserved death penalty because our Court was not informed about what he had done'.[65]

Significant immunity was also given to the Emperor, under whose name Japan fought the war, MacArthur being a strong opponent of the indictment of the Emperor.[66] The former enemy having immediately become a vital strategic ally with the start of the Cold War, the United States wanted to avoid a 'convulsion' among the Japanese people and anger towards the United States for disgracing their sacred figure.[67] What is more, it was seen that the confused war-torn society would be easily reunited under the name of the Emperor. Accordingly, the Emperor was not indicted or even summoned to the tribunal. The decision not to indict the Emperor was supported also by China and the Soviet Union in accordance with their own political interests at the beginning of the new phase of international relations.[68]

The third element that was put beyond the remit of the Tokyo Trial was 'Asia'. The degree of Asian element could be seen in the composition of judges at the tribunal: out of 11 there were only three judges from Asia – China, India and the Philippines – in spite of the fact that it was people in Asian countries that suffered most from harm caused by the Japanese army. During the trial, Japan's conduct of war crimes in China, especially the 'Nanjing massacre', was examined to some extent. However, Japan's acts in Taiwan and Korea, countries under Japan's colonial rule, were not investigated; the forced migration and labour of Koreans were all left untouched. Some argue that these acts can be defined as 'crimes against humanity'. It is also argued that given the fact that people under Japanese colonial rule had been Japanese subjects, non-humanitarian acts against these people could have been punished under the charge of 'crimes against humanity', just like the Nazis' acts against the German Jews.[69] However, alleged crimes relating to Japan's colonial rule and policy were not dealt with by the tribunal. The exclusion of these crimes reflected the primary interest of the United States: the war fought in the Pacific. At the same time, the tribunal was operated by many countries that were themselves colonial powers. The voice of the victims of colonialism was blocked. 'The plight of the Koreans was, in its way, emblematic of the larger anomaly of victor's justice as practiced in Tokyo', John Dower argues:

> The tribunal essentially resolved the contradiction between the world of colonialism and imperialism and the righteous ideals of crimes against peace and humanity by ignoring it. Japan's aggression was presented as a criminal act without provocation, without parallel, and almost entirely without context.[70]

This may be relevant to the fact that there was less focus on 'crimes against humanity' in the Tokyo Trial, where they played a minor role compared to Nuremberg.

Prosecutorial strategy regarding alleged crimes

While Nuremberg had only four counts for indictment – conspiracy, 'crimes against peace', war crimes and 'crimes against humanity' – there were 55 counts in Tokyo, which were separated into three groups under headings of 'crimes against peace' (Group I: counts 1 to 36); murder (Group II: counts 37 to 52); and conventional war crimes and crimes against humanity (Group III: counts 53 to 55).[71] Interestingly, 'crimes against humanity' was not dealt with independently but combined with conventional war crimes under Group III. Some argue that in the Tokyo Trial, 'crimes against humanity' were actually not examined because the three counts of Group III were in practice the charge with conventional war crimes.[72] This is related to the fact that Japan's war crimes, no matter how horrendous and evil they were, were different from the Nazi war crimes in nature, falling short of being 'crimes against humanity', which originally had Nazi crimes in mind. This was recognized by members of the Tokyo Tribunal. Webb stated in his separate opinion that 'The crimes of the German accused were far more heinous, varied and extensive than those of the Japanese accused'.[73]

In comparison to the little focus on 'crimes against humanity', the focus on 'crimes against peace' was far higher in the Tokyo Trial than at Nuremberg. A comparison of the charters of the two tribunals illustrates this point. Article 6 of the Nuremberg Charter gives the tribunal the power to try and punish persons who 'committed any of the following crimes': 'crimes against peace', war crimes and 'crimes against humanity'. On the other hand, Article 5 of the Tokyo Charter restricts war criminals tried and punished by the tribunal to be those who 'are charged with offenses which include Crimes against Peace'. In other words, no defendant was prosecuted without a charge of committing crimes against peace.[74] In addition, out of 55 counts, 36 represented crimes against peace.[75]

The Tokyo Trial's focus on crimes against peace needs to be examined also from the standpoint of the actual judgment and sentences. Out of 55 counts, the tribunal actually examined only 17 counts; most of the others were dismissed from the judgment because they were repetitious and were in effect charging the same type of offences.[76] Out of 17 counts, judgment was made on ten counts: count 1 (conspiracy), 27, 29, 31–33, 35–36 (crimes against peace), 54 and 55 (war crimes and crimes against humanity).[77] Interestingly, as is the case with Nuremberg, no one was hanged for conspiracy and crimes against peace alone.[78] However, at Tokyo, 22 defendants out of 25 were found guilty of at least one count in the category of crimes against peace, while in Nuremberg, 16 out of 22 defendants were charged for crimes against peace and 12 were found guilty. As for crimes against humanity, Nuremberg found 16 out of 18 defendants guilty, while in Tokyo only ten out of 24 defendants were found guilty of either count 54 or count 55, or both. Judging from the sentences alone, it may not be too simplistic to conclude that the Tokyo Trial was focusing on crimes against peace much more than had been the case at Nuremberg.

The impact of specific features of the Tokyo Trial

As seen above, the Tokyo Tribunal was not a clone of the Nuremberg Tribunal; on applying the Nuremberg model to the case of Japan, several 'adjustments' were made to suit the situation in Japan, or US policy on Japan. However, these adjustments, in the longer term, hurt the general perception of the Tokyo Trial and sowed various seeds for future problems of a kind that did not necessarily emerge in the case of post-war Germany.

First, Tokyo's heavy focus on 'crimes against peace' meant that the trial was examining less *the way* Japan had conducted the war but more *the reasons* why Japan had conducted it. Crimes against peace, or aggressive war, was a much more disputed concept than conventional war crimes and crimes against humanity, because it dealt directly with the nature and cause of war, which is recognized differently by different participants, and differently at different times. In the case of the war in Europe, there is little argument that it was aggression started by Hitler to dominate the continent.[79] However, the nature of the war in Asia is still under debate: whether Japan's war was purely aggressive in nature or had some element of self-defence, or whether it was a colonial war that had been also waged by the Allies. Accordingly, there was a question over whether Japan alone had to take responsibility for 'starting' the war. The point is still raised by right-wing critics in Japan and is brought to the centre of the debate of the Tokyo Trial among the Japanese.[80]

Several researchers on the Tokyo Trial see the fact that 'crimes against peace' was the central charge of the trial as the reason why it is more controversial than Nuremberg. Philip Piccigallo reflected: 'had the Tokyo defendants been tried on conventional war crimes charges only – as lesser Japanese suspects were – most likely no substantial controversy or criticism of the IMTFE would have arisen'.[81] 'I am fully in favor of conventional war crimes trials', Minear stated: 'But when the issue is not conventional war crimes but aggression ... then I must demur'.[82] The difficulty of the concept 'crimes against peace' is reflected in the failure of the post-Second World War international community to codify and criminalize aggression; it was not at all easy to reach a definition that differentiates the crime from a war of self-defence.[83] Since the Tokyo Trial, 'crimes against peace' has not been included in the jurisdiction of any ad hoc international war crimes tribunal.

Second, issues that had been given immunity or were not examined under the Tokyo Tribunal became, several decades later, issues of dispute, which came to be talked about even more fiercely than before. The absence of the Emperor at the Tokyo Trial is often raised as evidence that the Tokyo Trial was a political trial: 'The political objective of the American occupation policy conspicuously distorted the trial', Ōnuma Yasuaki claims.[84] In addition, unresolved responsibility, Japan's war responsibility towards its Asian neighbours, has left a deep scar on both the victims and victimizers. Issues and people eliminated from the legal procedures at the Tokyo Tribunal were not necessarily acquitted of their responsibility in any sense; they were buried and left untouched for such a long time that they became too complex and controversial to be handled. For these reasons, some of the left-wing critics in Japan are reluctant to accept the Tokyo Trial positively.[85]

Conclusion

'Regardless of the important differences between the European and Pacific wars', Minear argues, 'Tokyo was to be the Nuremberg of the Pacific'.[86] As this chapter has examined, the overall structure and proceedings of the Tokyo Tribunal were modelled on the Nuremberg Tribunal. What is more, the expected impact of the Tokyo Trial on society, especially the effect of the individual criminal punishment of wartime leaders and an historical account of the war through legal procedures, were more or less identical to those in the Nuremberg Trial on post-war Germany, which were examined in the previous chapter. However, post-war Germany and Japan seem to have reacted differently to the International Military Tribunals they experienced: while the former actively discussed it and acknowledged the outcome, the latter was relatively silent over the tribunal and the issues with which it dealt.

The difference in attitude of the people in the two countries can be attributed to several critical differences between the two tribunals, as well as their contexts, examined above. The specific character of the Tokyo Trial raised several problems of kinds that were absent in the case of Nuremberg and thus created an impact of a different kind on the people and society of post-war Japan. In this sense, such an impact is unique to the Tokyo Trial, and it may be concluded, accordingly, that the Tokyo Trial worked differently, or did not work at all, on post-war society because of its unique features. The following analysis of the Tokyo Trial's impact on post-war Japan cannot ignore this point.

However, what this research focuses on in the following chapters is whether and to what extent the impact and effect of the trial can be attributed to the two devices of the international tribunal: the individualization of responsibility and the creation of an historical record of the war, which were considered also for Nuremberg and are considered for ongoing international war crimes tribunals. Before examining each of these devices and their impact, the next chapter overviews the general reaction and perception of the Japanese people regarding the Tokyo Trial from 1946 to 2006.

4 The Japanese perception of the Tokyo Trial, 1946–2006

This chapter illustrates chronologically the attitude of the Japanese towards the Tokyo Trial from 1946 to 2006. The general view held by the Japanese now, and then, is that the Tokyo Trial was 'victor's justice'. It was, and is, perceived as 'a display of power' rather than of morality or justice. B. V. A. Röling, the Dutch judge at the tribunal, reflected his experience in Japan during the trial:

> I sometimes had contacts with Japanese students. The first thing they always asked was: 'Are you morally entitled to sit in judgement over the leaders of Japan when the Allies have burned down all of its cities with sometimes, as in Tokyo, in one night, 100,000 deaths and which culminated in the destruction of Hiroshima and Nagasaki? Those were war crimes'.[1]

The Tokyo Trial is regarded as 'victor's justice' because of legal shortcomings in its foundation and procedures and political elements that influenced the creation and operation of the tribunal. As is the case with Nuremberg, Tokyo too has been criticized as a trial based on an *ex post facto* law because it is disputable whether 'crimes against peace' and 'crimes against humanity' were 'crimes' at the time they were committed. It is also questioned whether prosecuting individuals under international trials for committing conventional war crimes was already regarded as an international custom.[2] The Tokyo Trial is also criticized as a unilateral trial, having prosecuted Japan's conduct only. 'Crimes against peace' raised questions not only regarding whether Japan only was guilty of starting the war, but also whether the Soviet declaration of war against Japan on 8 August 1945 was not an act of aggression, a breach of the 1941 non-aggression pact with Japan. 'Crimes against humanity' raised the American use of atomic bombs against Hiroshima and Nagasaki, which was not examined under the Tokyo Trial.[3] 'Punishment should be meted out', a sense that was shared by the Allies in the aftermath of the war, was 'noble sentiments, to be sure', says Richard Minear, the author of *Victors' Justice: The Tokyo War Crimes Trial*: 'Yet they do not alter the uncomfortable facts. Gross injustice was committed at Tokyo. The leaders of the defeated nation, and they alone, were offered as a sacrifice to a better world'.[4]

In spite of a widely held understanding of 'victor's justice', the general reaction of the Japanese people towards the Tokyo Trial has been a passive acceptance, or apathy. This chapter illustrates this attitude, by putting it in the context of the time, and analyses how perceptions of the Tokyo Trial developed, changed or remained unchanged over time. The chapter also considers whether there is any difference in perception and attitude between the intellectuals and the general public, by analysing the publications on the Tokyo Trial, media reports, events related to the trial and public discourse surrounding them.[5]

American occupation and the Tokyo Trial: 1946–51

The opening of the Tokyo Trial in May 1946 received almost totally supportive coverage from the Japanese media.[6] This remained as such all through the trial's procedures. On the day of the judgment, the editorial of *Asahi Shimbun*, a daily newspaper with one of the biggest circulations in Japan, representatively stated:

> The judgment of the Tokyo Trial has a special significance in the history of Japan and the world because it is a global expression of the determination for peace, which can be commonly held both by the victors and the vanquished, and is an oath of its practice among related countries.[7]

The media paid little attention to Justice Pal's dissenting opinion that all the defendants were not guilty, but reported more the tribunal's president William Webb's opinion that the Emperor also had some responsibility for the war. The media also reported that many of the people on the street regarded the trial as generally fair.[8]

The reporting of the Japanese media cannot be interpreted without considering the fact that GHQ conducted strict censorship covering newspapers and radio, as well as theatres and films, which lasted until the end of the occupation in 1952. The targets of deletions and suppression included 'Criticism of military tribunal' and 'Justification or defense of war criminals', together with 29 other items.[9] As a result, the information that the Japanese people received on the Tokyo Trial was not complete.[10] The impact of censorship cannot be underestimated in influencing the atmosphere of the society.[11] The coverage of the media, however, was not insensitive to the general feelings of the society at the time. The Japanese for their part had reasons for accepting the trial, albeit passively.

The general reaction

The Tokyo Trial was accepted by the Japanese as a consequence of defeat in the war. The Japanese embraced their old saying *'Kateba Kangun, Makereba Zokugun'* (Win and you are the official army, lose and you are the rebels), equivalent to the Western saying, 'might is right', with which they swallowed frustration: why should only Japan face a trial? What is more, facing the overwhelming American military presence, the Japanese felt that there was no other choice for the vanquished; 'victor's justice' was regarded as a 'physical necessity'.[12] Japanese acceptance of the Tokyo Trial was connected to their initial acceptance of the American occupation. The absence of systematic looting, violence or rape by American soldiers that had been fully expected by the Japanese, together with the 'spontaneous generosity' of the Americans, gave a favourable impression of the American occupier.[13]

At the same time, there existed among the Japanese nation anger towards their wartime leaders. Sudden defeat in the war profoundly shocked people who had been informed very little of the war they were fighting. A man born in 1935 reflected:

> We had always been told that we would win the war. So when I found out that Japan has lost the war, I could not stop crying and was totally stunned for a while. I was just ten-years old but I can imagine how bad it was for the grown-ups at the time. Total change had occurred so suddenly.[14]

Many people possessed a strong sense that they were betrayed and deceived by their own government.[15] This, together with post-war poverty, hunger and devastation, raised the rage towards the wartime cabinet and the military, especially Tōjō Hideki, Prime Minister at the time of the outbreak of the Pacific War. Tōjō's popularity among the Japanese further declined when he, in September 1945, attempted to commit suicide and failed at the time of the arrest by GHQ.

The people needed someone to blame for their wartime and post-war misery; there existed within the Japanese a sense that they were the victims of a war recklessly conducted by a military clique.[16] People's strong disbelief in the wartime leaders detached them from the defendants at the tribunal. The trial, in other words, was accepted by the Japanese as punishing 'the bad fellow' on their behalf.[17] This may be one of the reasons why the Tokyo Trial, together with other minor war crimes trials, created very little resentment and anger from the Japanese people at the time. According to private letters among the Japanese, which were secretly censored by GHQ, 34 per cent of those who mentioned the Tokyo Trial praised it, and 39 per cent were critical, sympathizing with the defendants for their heavy sentences – but not necessarily protesting against the trial per se. Another 27 per cent, GHQ analysed, showed no clear opinion.[18] The only exception was the tribunal's death sentence on Hirota Kōki, a civilian political leader, which disturbed many Japanese and led to a movement for petition. Hirota, since the trial, has been seen as a tragic hero of the Tokyo Trial, having tried to avoid the war as Prime Minister and Minister of Foreign Affairs but becoming the only civilian sentenced to death together with the military clique.[19]

In addition to a consequence of defeat and anger towards their leaders, the easy acceptance of the Tokyo Trial was due to general disinterest. War crimes prosecution was an issue of little importance compared with serious post-war poverty and hunger. Disinterest was cultivated also by the slow progress of the Tokyo Trial together with its dry legal procedures, which deprived it of its maximum impact. 'It was only at the beginning that each news agency mobilized all of its journalists and reported the trial in detail', a journalist from *Kyōdō Tsūshin* reflected:

> However, when it came to technical arguments between the prosecutor and the defence counsel, they lost interest.... Within a month, the press box was filled only with a few sleepy-looking journalists staying there for appearance's sake. Others were relaxing in a waiting room.[20]

As the trial had extended over a long period, even sympathy towards the defendants increased. With the closing of the tribunal, the media stopped not only reporting on the Tokyo Trial but even mentioning it.[21]

Issues in which the people took specific interest were Tōjō's defence and the judgment of the tribunal. Unlike many other defendants, during his defence from 26 December 1947 to 7 January 1948, Tōjō did not deny his political and administrative responsibility as former Prime Minster. At the same time, he powerfully justified the policy of Japan and denied the aggressive nature of the war Japan fought, which appealed to those Japanese who were frustrated with 'victor's justice'.[22] With his 'very long and very impressive speech', According to Röling, Tōjō 'restored his dignity in the eyes of the Japanese people'.[23] However, in general, the degree of public interest in the Tokyo Trial was low, which was a matter of concern even for academics and commentators at the time.[24]

The reaction of academics

Unlike the general public, academics and scholars were not uninterested in the Tokyo Trial. With the close of the Tokyo Trial, various academic journals issued special editions on the trial,[25] some of which sought to identify the political and historical significance of the Tokyo Trial, focusing on the meaning of judgment for the denial of wartime militarism. Some articles argued that the Tokyo Trial on its own was not enough, pointing out that the Emperor and *zaibatsu* (conglomerate) were not tried.[26]

The interests of academics during this period were mostly focused on the legal aspects of the trial: the concept of war crimes, the development of international law and the jurisdiction of the tribunal.[27] Legal scholars at Waseda University conducted research on the background, structure, indictment and procedures of the Tokyo Trial.[28] In 1948, after the judgment of the Tokyo Trial, Takayanagi Kenzo's *The Tokio Trials and International Law* was published.[29] Takayanagi was a member of the defence counsel at the Tokyo Tribunal and the publication was based on his statement for defence summation at the trial, pointing out legal defects of the trial. He raised a concern about the negative impact of such a trial on the Japanese. In contrast to Takayanagi, Yokota Kisaburō was a vocal supporter of the Tokyo Trial and its political significance. Yokota, an international legal scholar, while recognizing problems in the form of law at the tribunal, emphasized the importance of the essence of the trial, that is, the substantive reasons for the punishments given, which, according to him, should not be dismissed by legal and technical arguments.[30] Yokota argued that the true objective of the trial and punishments was to pay a price for aggressive wars and violence that Japan had conducted in the past and 'draw a line in the sand', opening the way to Japan's rehabilitation towards the future.[31] His comments were published in major newspapers on the day of the judgment, as a 'scholar's view of the Tokyo Trial'.

Overall, the view expressed by academics and commentators of the Tokyo Trial was positive, in spite of their awareness that there were several defects in the trial.[32] It seems that academics and intellectuals held a sense of mission to cultivate positive significance of the trial for the sake of post-war Japan. Scholars of Waseda University stated that the Tokyo Trial was an attempt at a new world order for perpetual peace and that its record was vital reading for people in post-war Japan. At the same time, they wrote in the preface of their volumes of research: 'We are aiming to faithfully report the facts and opinions presented at the tribunal, but not to criticize. Each article should adhere to strict academic standards and refrain from any exaggeration or prejudice in making comments on the trial'.[33] The fact that they had to state this in a strong tone implies that they were having some difficulty or dilemma in examining the trial 'frankly' and analysing it 'critically', be it due to their own views or to social atmosphere. This comment is intriguing because it already indicated the difficulty that Japanese academics and intellectuals were going to face hereafter in researching the Tokyo Trial.

After the occupation: 1952–60

With the San Francisco Peace Treaty of September 1951 coming into effect in April 1952, Japan regained its sovereignty, and the American military occupation that lasted for six years and eight months formally ended. At the same time, with the acceptance of the Peace Treaty, the Japanese government officially accepted the judgment of the Tokyo Trial, and issues of war crimes prosecution were solved in terms of international law.[34]

Critical view emerges

The end of the occupation meant an end to censorship conducted by GHQ, and criticism of the Tokyo Trial became more visible, some of it as a reaction to the censorship. Takigawa Masajirō, a member of the defence counsel at the Tokyo Tribunal, published in 1952 a book titled *Judging the Tokyo Trial*, in which he argued that the judgment was prepared beforehand and that there was no scope for the defendants to justify the war they fought. He strongly claimed that the Tokyo Trial was a retaliatory punishment:

> Being based on the illusion that a World Government could be created by the victor alone, the Tokyo Trial judged the vanquished arbitrarily in the name of 'civilization' with the primitive idea of retaliation, but without any self-examination on their part. It was not even an unjust trial but was a vice

> that does not deserve to be called a trial. The Tokyo Trial did not contribute to the progress of international law but rather made it relapse for several centuries.[35]

On the other hand, even after the end of censorship, there was a reluctance to criticize the Tokyo Trial. The research group of *Asahi Shimbun*, while pointing out the problem of 'victor's justice', expressed concern that criticism of the trial would lead to the justification of Japan's militarist past: 'If the Japanese come to see the lofty idea of the trial negatively as a reaction to GHQ's censorship, we may repeat the tragedy of turning back the clock'.[36] Against this backdrop, Takigawa expressed frustration:

> During the occupation, self-examination through the Tokyo Trial was said to be the starting point for re-establishing the country.... To regret guilty past actions and apologize to the world was said to be the only way for Japan to re-enter international society. But that was the occupation policy of the United States to weaken the mentality of post-war Japan.[37]

Takigawa wrote in 1978 that in the 1950s his book was bitterly criticized as a 'bad book' by journalists and critics.[38] Sugawara Yutaka, another member of the defence counsel of the Tokyo Trial, lamented: 'Although the Government formally regained sovereignty a year and half ago, no effort has been made to tell the nation about the truth [of the war and occupation]'.[39] He pointed out the defects of the Tokyo Trial and criticized it as 'savage revenge', having tried to destroy Japanese tradition. Sugawara's essay written in 1953 was actually published in 1961 because, according to him, he had been given advice that the time was not yet ripe for his book. Kobori Keiichirō, an academic specializing in comparative culture, who has been strongly criticizing the Tokyo Trial, argued that the journalism during this period conducted 'self-censorship and self-regulation' on behalf of the occupation army.[40]

It was in 1952, four years after the end of the trial, that Justice Radhabinod Pal's dissenting opinion was published in Japan.[41] In his 'dissentient judgment', Pal concluded that all the defendants were innocent, arguing that the Tokyo Trial was an *ex post facto* legislation:

> It has been said that A VICTOR CAN DISPENSE TO THE VANQUISHED EVERYTHING FROM MERCY TO VINDICTIVENESS; BUT THE ONE THING THE VICTOR CANNOT GIVE TO THE VANQUISHED IS JUSTICE [*sic*]. At least, if a tribunal be rooted in politics as opposed to law, no matter what its form and pretenses, the apprehension thus expressed would be real, unless 'JUSTICE IS REALLY NOTHING ELSE THAN THE INTEREST OF THE STRONGER' [*sic*].[42]

In the 1960s, two books on Pal's judgment were published, both of which support the judgment. Interestingly, while one book was entitled *Justice Pal's*

Argument of Japan's Innocence,[43] the other suggested that the claim of 'innocence' was misleading; the latter argued that Pal had not stated that Japan was morally innocent and that his argument should not be taken as a total acquittal of modern Japan.[44] In any case, with his judgment, Judge Pal became one of the most known and important figures in Japan regarding the Tokyo Trial.[45] Especially for those who strongly criticized the tribunal, his above-quoted words became a mantra.

Besides the legality and justice of the Tokyo Trial, the account of the war presented at the tribunal's judgment came to be openly discussed. The research group of *Asahi Shimbun*, who supported the Tokyo Trial in general, nonetheless expressed some reservations at the way the tribunal created the record of the war. Pointing out the dubious selection of the defendants and the tribunal's failure to examine the rise of Communism in Asia, the group stated that 'the trial was influenced by international politics and thus distanced itself from *the historical truth*'.[46] The historical account was criticized also from different standpoints. Tsurumi Shunsuke emphasized the importance of examining Japan's war against China, which was not the centre of focus of the Tokyo Trial. Rather than using the term 'Pacific War', which focuses on Japan's war against the United States, Tsurumi used in 1956 the term 'Fifteen-years War', and by doing so regarded three different armed conflicts – the Manchurian Incident of 1931–35, the Sino-Japanese Conflict of 1937–45 and the Pacific War of 1941–45 – as a chain of Japanese aggressive wars.[47] On the other hand, Takigawa, as part of his criticism of the Tokyo Trial, rejected the idea that Japan had conducted an aggressive war; he claimed that it was a war of self-defence.

The general perception

On the part of the Japanese people, once the occupation had ended, general apathy towards the Tokyo Trial further increased. In May 1952, a month after Japan's recovery of sovereignty, *Asahi Shimbun* conducted an opinion poll on the occupation policy, in which 47 per cent answered that some positive things had been done during the occupation (14 per cent finding nothing positive) and 28 per cent answered that some negative things had been done (26 per cent finding nothing negative). Being asked what, in concrete terms, was positive or negative, the Tokyo Trial or war crimes prosecutions were deemed to fall into neither category.[48] Considering the supposed impact and significance of the Tokyo Trial, this is rather odd; it seems as if the Tokyo Trial had completely disappeared from the Japanese memory. At the same time, 39 per cent responded 'do not know' to the question whether there was anything positive in the occupation, and 46 per cent for anything negative. This may imply the passive attitude as well as ambivalent feelings of the Japanese towards the occupation, which may not be unrelated to their perception of the Tokyo Trial.

The nation's interest was now focused on the rapid growth of the country's economy. Regarding the economic situation, the government declared in its economic white paper in 1956 that 'the post war is over [*mohaya sengo deha nai*]'. In 1964, Tokyo hosted the Olympic Games. The interest of the nation was immediately shifted from the country's recovery from the war to its further development; in such an atmosphere, reference to the Tokyo Trial was not actively made.[49]

Instead of the Tokyo Trial, in which major war criminals, having perpetrated 'crimes against peace', were judged and punished, people after the occupation came to take more interest in the trials of minor war criminals, having conducted conventional war crimes and crimes against humanity, the so-called 'Class B and C' war crimes trials. They were conducted by the United States, Britain, Australia, France, Holland, Philippines, China and the Soviet Union, in their own occupied territory in Asia, based on their own laws and jurisdiction. More than 55,000 individuals were taken into custody and 5,700 faced trial as Class B and C war criminals. A total of 984 were sentenced to death, 475 to life imprisonment and 2,944 to limited prison sentences.[50] These figures exclude war crimes trials conducted by the Soviet Union, details of which are still unknown.

Many Class B and C war crimes trials were said to have had many defects: the absence of interpreters, wrongful arrests, and unfair procedures and judgments caused by various problems in the law as it was applied. In addition, many Japanese prisoners suffered serious torture and ill-treatment conducted by vengeful locals; yet those acts did not receive any punishment.[51] However, these facts had not been known to the Japanese people at home during the occupation. Instead, with the despair of the defeat and poverty together with the Allies' propaganda, people soon after the war showed anger at war criminals as well as the families of those criminals.

It was not until the end of occupation that the details of those trials became known to the public through the words of the ex-servicemen and the publication of memoirs and farewell notes of the indicted.[52] Accordingly, sympathy and interest regarding minor war criminals increased.[53] The tragedy of those minor war criminals became better known through the story of a man who was prosecuted and executed for killing American POWs, which he had conducted unwillingly following orders. The story, *Watashi ha Kai ni Naritai*,[54] was made into a TV drama and a film in 1959 and elicited national compassion. Those soldiers had obediently followed orders, as was the custom of the Japanese military based on the Imperial Rescript of 1882; nonetheless, they were punished after the war for committing war crimes. In many of these trial cases, following orders was not regarded as a mitigating circumstance. 'The discrepancy between the legal concept held by countries running trials and the customs of the Japanese military', which had the same effect as actual law, 'made the fate of soldiers so tragic', the *Asahi* emphasized.[55] The tragedy and suffering of Class B and C war criminals were easily shared by the people, because they, unlike the major war criminals at the Tokyo Tribunal, were ordinary citizens who participated in the war as foot soldiers. At the same time, minor war crimes trials were seen 'to be connected in an unbroken chain' with the Tokyo Trial.[56] In that sense, the Japanese view of the Tokyo Trial has been influenced, to some extent, by their view of the trials of minor war criminals, which gave overall war crimes prosecutions a negative image.

Instead of taking over the investigation of war crimes from the hand of the Allies, post-occupation Japan welcomed back former war criminals into society. While all remaining Class A war crimes suspects had been released soon after the execution of Tōjō and others in December 1948, the Japanese nation came to regard those who remained in prisons as 'the victim of international policy'. With the end of the occupation, the responsibility for the management and control of the Sugamo Prison in Tokyo, which interned Class A as well as B and C war criminals, was passed over to the Japanese government. Accordingly, the treatment of prisoners improved immensely.[57] Regarding war criminals not as ex-convicts under domestic law, the government started to prepare financial support system for such prisoners as well as their families.[58] As Utsumi Aiko examines, it was certainly 'not an atmosphere in which Japan's post-war soul-searching as a 'peaceful nation' could incorporate the defendants' experience in the trials and in their imprisonment' and what they had thought about the problem of war responsibility.[59] Japan after the occupation also welcomed former Class A war crimes suspects back onto the political stage. Kishi Nobusuke, who was one of the released Class A war crimes suspects that were waiting for the future trial at the time of the Tokyo Trial, became the Prime Minister in 1957 and served two consecutive terms until 1960. Shigemitsu Mamoru, sentenced by the Tokyo judgment to seven years in prison, became the Foreign Minister in 1954.[60]

The 1960s and 1970s

A revival in the interest among academics towards the Tokyo Trial took place in the mid-1960s.[61] One of the reasons for this was the Vietnam War and the reported atrocities there, which recalled 'crimes against peace', war crimes and 'crimes against humanity'. These crimes were examined at the International Military Tribunals and, thus, raised interest in the Tokyo Trial. The normalization of Sino-Japanese diplomatic relations in 1972 also raised Japanese interest in China, together with the issue of Japan's war crimes against the Chinese. However, raised interest brought to the fore different standpoints from which the Tokyo Trial was examined: the awareness of responsibility for the past war, and frustration and cynicism towards the trial.

Sumitani Takeshi argues that the Vietnam War together with a series of radical social movements in Japan during this period prompted the Japanese to see themselves as aggressors in relation to other Asian countries.[62] Kinoshita Junji stated: 'The reason why I came up with an idea to write a play on the Tokyo Trial was because I thought that one of the origins of this strangely distorted post-war Japan might be found in the trial'.[63] His play was first staged in 1970. *Kami to Hito tono Aida* (Between God and Man) consists of two parts: the first half is a recreation of the Tokyo Trial and the second deals with a minor war crimes trial of a private.[64] The play pointed out that the Tokyo Trial had not offered an opportunity for the Japanese to achieve self-examination because it had 'dealt with the matter in terms of expediency'.[65] By involving the audience in the recreation of the Tokyo Trial and by showing the agony of a private in a minor war crimes trial, Kinoshita pushed the audience to think about each person's own guilt and responsibility: the play dealt with 'the act and art of self-judgment, the first half by obvious silence, the second by active demonstration'.[66]

At the same time, the realpolitik of international relations during this period raised cynicism over the Tokyo Trial. The fact that war crimes, 'crimes against humanity' and 'crimes against peace' of the post-Second World War wars were generally left unpunished strengthened the view among the Japanese that the Tokyo Trial was after all the victor's justice and that war crimes prosecutions would and could only be done by the victor against the vanquished. 'The Tokyo Trial is an exact reflection of various contradictions in current international society', *Asahi Shimbun* press corps wrote in 1962: 'the weakness of international law is revealed by the fact that the vanquished of the unconditional surrender can easily be brought to court but the great power's "dirty hand" cannot be judged'.[67]

In addition to the international neglect of the legacy of the International Military Tribunals,[68] cynicism among the Japanese towards that legacy was due to the threat of nuclear war caused by the two members of the former Allies. Tanaka Masaaki, a vocal opponent of the Tokyo Trial, claimed that the International Military Tribunals, embracing the motto of 'peace and humanity', had ended in total fiasco: 'We are now threatened not only by a possible Third World War but also by brutal mass slaughter comparable to no past events'.[69] Frustration derived from 'victor's justice' was a driving force for anti-Tokyo Trial polemicists, who saw the Tokyo Trial as utterly unfair and vengeful and had gone against the development of international law, all of which endorsed the anarchy of the post-Second World War world. Peace now was threatened by those who punished the aggressors of the Second World War in the name of civilization. This was a strong setback for the Tokyo Trial, which was claimed by the prosecutor, and accepted by the Japanese people, as a great trial whose 'proceedings could have a far reaching effect on the peace and security of the world'.[70] Kiyose Ichirō, associate chief of the Japanese defence section, argued that perpetual peace could not be attained with a mere 'revenge tragedy', like the Tokyo Trial.[71]

The Tokyo Trial and the debate on the nature of the war

In the 1960s, the term *Daitōa Senso* (the Greater East Asia War) came to be used in public again to refer to Japan's war during the 1930s up until 1945.[72] The usage of the term was prohibited by GHQ during the occupation because of its connection with wartime ultra-militarism.[73] In the contemporary context, the term connotes the justification, sometimes glorification, of Japan's war history. During the 1960s, most of the terms currently used to describe the war surfaced: 'the Second World War', 'the Pacific War', the 'Fifteen-years War', the 'Greater East Asia War'; each of these terms is strongly related to how one sees the nature of the war, which is not free of political and ideological colour.[74]

The Tokyo Trial came to be related to the debate on the nature of the past war because the trial itself had offered a specific account of the war, that Japan prepared and waged wars of aggression from the late 1920s until 1945. For this reason, the Tokyo Trial became the principal target to attack for those who regard the war as self-defensive in nature or as an attempt to liberate Asian countries from Western imperialism and create the Greater East Asian new order.[75] Awaya Kentarō analyses the debate over the trial during this period as follows:

> The already present confrontation between the different views of the Tokyo Trial became even more controversial with the added political and ideological flavours of the 1970s. What is more, through the pros and cons of the trial, the confrontation between the different views on the history and present status of Japan became radicalized.[76]

Because of such political and ideological flavours, the Tokyo Trial became difficult as well as delicate as an issue to be researched. It is worth noting that authors of those anti-Tokyo Trial publications during this period were often non-academics or academics not specialized in the field. Up until the late 1970s there was a lack of diversity in authors writing on the Tokyo Trial; books written by the same authors were republished or published under different titles, and they were mostly written from anti-Tokyo Trial and right-wing points of view. Academic works on the Tokyo Trial, except those conducted by legal scholars, or positive reviews of the trial were rarely published. Writing on the Tokyo Trial in 1971, Richard Minear pointed out that Japanese scholars were either staying away from the Tokyo Trial, perhaps for ideological or personal reasons, or 'tended to affirm the validity of the trial and its verdict' when they had to comment on it.[77] This kind of attitude frustrated people like Tanaka, who claimed that the 'servile' Japanese unconditionally accepted that 'Japan had conducted an aggressive war' and still did not understand, or even try to understand, the real intention of the Tokyo Trial, which he saw was a means of propaganda under the occupation.[78] The result, he claimed, was the obsequious national attitude of the Japanese, burdened with a sense of guilt. There was a clear contrast between those vocal rightist critics and leftist or 'liberal' intellectuals who remained silent.

The general reaction

During the 1960s and 1970s, several books providing overviews of the Tokyo Trial were published, many of which were written by people who had directly or indirectly participated in the trial.[79] However, a slight increase in the number of publications during this period compared to the 1950s did not necessarily mean an increase in general interest regarding the Tokyo Trial. Rather, most of the books were based on the authors' concerns about apathy among the Japanese people regarding the trial. Sumitani, who started to take an interest in the Tokyo Trial in the early 1970s, looks back at the period and states that he thought the issue had already faded away because he had rarely heard about the trial during this period.[80] The nature of the silence and indifference during this period may be different from that of the occupation period. With the passing of time, the memory of the war started to fade and the so-called post-war generation, without the experience of the war and the Tokyo Trial, increased. Many publications implicitly or explicitly targeted the younger generations who were enjoying post-war economic development and might not know much about pre-war and wartime history.[81] The general apathy, at the same time, may not be irrelevant to the cynicism created by the Cold War as noted above.[82]

Kojima Noboru, who critically reviewed the trial, is the author of perhaps the most widely read Japanese-written work on the Tokyo Trial. He claimed that constructive effects of the Tokyo Trial were nowhere to be seen. What may be worse, he argued, 'the Tokyo Trial might have led post-war Japan and international society in untoward directions'.[83] Kojima claimed, in 1971, that exactly because of such an impact, 'the Tokyo Trial, together with the Pacific war, should be the starting point to which people now should go back and rethink Japan and where it should go'.[84] For this purpose, he raised a fundamental question: 'What was the Tokyo Trial'? The question seems to be the central concern of most of the literature on the Tokyo Trial up to the present time, which focuses on how the tribunal was established; how its procedures were carried out; who was sentenced and for what reason, and so on. Whether to claim the wrongfulness of the trial or to emphasize its positive impact, each author is strongly aware that one has to start by depicting what actually happened. In other words, there was, and still is, a common understanding that the people in Japan know very little about the Tokyo Trial.[85] The people's long-time indifference kept arguments on the Tokyo Trial focused on the historical facts, rather than on its significance and lessons learnt.

The 1980s

Up until the late 1970s, most of the argument on the Tokyo Trial had been focused on either whether the trial was victor's justice or not – in other words, whether the trial itself was just or not, or whether the trial's historical account of the period between 1928 and 1945 was right or not – in other words, whether Japan's war was a criminal aggressive war or inevitable self-defence. Focusing on the former easily leads to cynicism, because the more research on the trial develops, the more the inherent defects of the trial come to light.[86] Cynicism ends the discussion and thus leads to indifference to the whole issue. Focusing on the latter often ends up in less constructive debate, as it is often accompanied by emotional and ideological zeal. In sum, the Tokyo Trial had been either ignored in general or debated emotionally among a rather limited circle in an extreme form. Given such a situation, very little interest was shown in the Tokyo Trial's 'universal' significance or the lessons that could be learned from it. During the 1980s, however, attempts to reinvestigate the Tokyo Trial from this perspective started to emerge.

Beyond dualisms

Andō Nisuke, an international legal scholar, pointed out that the question 'What is the Tokyo Trial'? has various faces: 'what it was for the judge', 'for the judged' or 'for the third parties'. Or, it can be seen as a question of the past: 'what it was' or 'what it should have been', providing lessons for the future. Andō saw it in terms of what the Tokyo Trial should be to the Japanese now.[87] After more than 30 years, the memory of the Tokyo Trial had already faded. Nonetheless, the significance of the Tokyo Trial, Andō emphasized, was too important for the contemporary Japanese to allow to fade with the passing of time.[88] He proposed that instead of the conventional 'all-or-nothing' style of analysis, the assessment of the Tokyo Trial required facing the facts with open-mindedness and having 'courage and practice to look for the truth within grey areas'.[89]

The point that had been absent in previous debates on the Tokyo Trial was how the people in Japan themselves see the trial and how they learn lessons from it for the future. Another international legal scholar, Ōnuma Yasuaki, emphasized the importance of re-examining the way the Japanese had reacted to the Tokyo Trial, and tried to examine the trial within the context of 'post-war responsibility [*Sengo Sekinin*]' of the Japanese people, especially responsibility towards the Asian victims. He pointed out that what had been symbolically absent from the Tokyo Trial was 'Asia' and the Japanese people themselves.[90] By regarding the war as the Pacific War fought against the United States and referring to Hiroshima and Nagasaki, the Japanese strengthened their feeling of being victimized by the war, which allowed them to dismiss, to some extent, Japan's war crimes. Ōnuma claimed that this perception should not be used to offset Japan's conduct against the Asian people.[91]

It is also during this period that empirical research based on primary sources started to be conducted, representatively by Awaya Kentarō.[92]

Symposium, film and general reactions

With Andō and Ōnuma, together with Hosoya Chihiro, an international political theorist, playing a central part, the International Symposium on the Tokyo War Crimes Trial was held in Tokyo in May 1983. It was the first opportunity to examine the trial in public on such a scale within an international and interdisciplinary context. The two-day symposium focused on historical, legal, international and contemporary aspects of the Tokyo Trial and the panellists of the symposium were academics and journalists from both Japan and abroad.[93] The symposium achieved great success, with about 1,000 participants. While there was broad agreement among panellists that the Tokyo Trial had serious defects, the symposium emphasized that it was more important to recognize the positive aspects of the trial for international peace and security. The symposium thus set forth a new direction for research of the Tokyo Trial, adding issues and perspectives that had been absent in past discussion of the trial. Examining the emergence in the late 1970s of a small group of scholars and journalists working on the Tokyo Trial, a chairman of the symposium stated:

> thirty years after the end of the war, and of the trial itself, we were liberated from emotional bias and were able to evaluate the Tokyo Trial from a position of relative calm. This is one of the reasons the time is ripe for a re-examination of the Tokyo Trial.[94]

The symposium, however, also revealed that it was difficult, even after 35 years, to talk about the Tokyo Trial calmly. One of chairmen had to remind the participants at one point: 'the purpose of our gathering here is not to take nationalistic positions against one another. Please bear this in mind in making statements'.[95] Debates at the symposium became heated especially on the historical aspects of the tribunal and its historical record of the war. Questions regarding the veracity of the tribunal's historical record were constantly raised even during the session focusing on legal, international or contemporary aspects of the trial. The record of the symposium shows that the chairmen interrupted a number of members of the audience, pointing out that the issue raised should have been discussed in the session on 'The trial in historical perspective'.[96]

The symposium was held as the pre-release event of a feature-length documentary film of the Tokyo Trial. *Tōkyō Saiban* [The Tokyo Trial] released in 1983 was based on films that were shot and had been kept by the US Department of Defense. Director Kobayashi Masaki's intention was to 'illustrate the Tokyo Trial, the historical truth, as objectively as possible', and 'to examine, within a historical context, the significance of the trial for the Japanese ... in order to think about war and peace'.[97] The film achieved great success. However, to his surprise, Kobayashi received comments from the audience which he had not expected, such as: 'Those 28 defendants were praiseworthy', 'That trial was a political trial' or 'The trial was coloured with racism'.[98] Several film critics and journalists had warned that the film might highlight problems with the trial and lead people to justify Japan's past.[99]

Ōnuma observes that the public responded more acutely to Hiroshima and Nagasaki than Nanjing, both of which were depicted in the film.[100] He points out the popularity of the story of the tragic life of Hirota Kōki, the only civilian sentenced to death in the trial, in spite of the fact he, according to general understanding, had tried to avoid the war: 'The Japanese people's feeling towards the Tokyo Trial is reflected in the fact that the whole significance of the trial is condensed into the injustice of Hirota's death sentence'.[101] People were embracing the feeling that 'something is wrong with the Tokyo Trial', and the reaction to the film, Ōnuma saw, was easily understood as the eruption of 35 years of pent-up feelings: 'Through the tragic hero, Hirota, the Japanese in 1983 reacted to the film acutely, most feeling negatively towards the trial'.[102] Rather than to educate the people, the film stimulated emotions that had long laid dormant among the Japanese: a sense of 'victor's justice'.

Frustration against the Tokyo Trial was associated with national pride. Having attained huge economic development and been reputed 'Japan as Number One',[103] Japan in the 1980s regained self-confidence, which at the same time lessened its long-time inferiority complex towards the United States.[104] In the process, the emphasis on Japanese pride grew stronger, and along with this the Tokyo Trial came to be targeted. In the summer of 1985, Prime Minister Nakasone Yasuhiro set out his 'General Reckoning with the post-war [*Sengo Seiji no Sōkessan*]', in which he emphasized the importance of cultivating Japanese national identity that could stand tall in the world. Although he acknowledged that some of Japan's war conduct deserved harsh judgment, Nakasone questioned the way in which the Tokyo Trial had been conducted and expressed concern that the trial had created a masochistic tendency among the Japanese to regard everything as wrong with Japan.[105] In the same year, Nakasone became the first Prime Minister to conduct an 'official visit' to the controversial Yasukuni shrine, which holds the souls of about 2.5 million Japanese war dead since the Meiji Restoration in 1868, including 12 convicted Class A war criminals and two defendants who died during the Tokyo Trial, who were enshrined in 1978. The visit was strongly objected to by China, South Korea and other countries in South-East Asia as an expression of glorifying the past war. Having received these protests, Nakasone gave up the visit the following year.

In the 1980s, several 'hawkish' members of the cabinet publicly expressed their frustrations with the Tokyo Trial as well as the 'Tokyo Trial view of history'. In 1986, the Minister of Education commented that the Tokyo Trial was a 'black trial [*ankoku saiban*]'.[106] He was dismissed for having also stated that 'Korea on her part had her own responsibility for Japan's annexation of the country'.[107] These people, however, were a minority among Japanese politicians. In fact, most politicians rarely referred to the Tokyo Trial. This is in stark contrast to their German counterparts, who do not hesitate to speak positively of Nuremberg.[108] The words and deeds of Japanese politicians, together with the 'textbook row' in 1982, which was caused by a media report that the Japanese Ministry of Education had ordered some textbook authors to change the account of the war, damaged Japan's relations with China.

The film *Tōkyō Saiban* in 1983 clearly was the catalyst for an increase in interest in the Tokyo Trial among the Japanese. This was well reflected in the sudden rise in the number of publications on the Tokyo Trial that year.[109] Although public interest declined at the end of the film's distribution,[110] the release of the film had stimulated academics and intellectuals. Various journals, of both right and left ideological persuasion, issued editions specifically focused on the Tokyo Trial,[111] and articles and books written by academics have appeared constantly ever since. Several signs of productive academic research of the Tokyo Trial also emerged, as the symposium indicated.

In spite of the expectations held by some academics, however, the passage of time did not curb the emotional and ideological reaction to the Tokyo Trial. The trial was still caught in irreconcilable dualisms, which were further strengthened during the 1980s through increasing interest in the trial and the domestic and international environment. In addition, the Tokyo Trial came to be caught in a third type of dualism: between an attitude that was inclined to face Japanese responsibility towards the suffering of Asian victims and an attitude that denied the existence of such sufferings and Japan's responsibility for them. Confrontation between the two attitudes became ever starker entering into the 1990s, when the victims of the Japanese Imperial Army broke silence and pressured the Japanese government for official acknowledgement and compensation.

The 1990s onwards

Academic approaches on the Tokyo Trial developed in the 1980s were passed on to the 1990s. In 1996 there was another symposium on the Tokyo Trial, 'Thinking about the Tokyo Trial: How the War was Judged', which attempted to examine academically and empirically the trial's historical and international political background, its approach to the military, diplomats, the Imperial Court, the Emperor and its overall significance.[112] Historian Higurashi Yoshinobu conducted a full-scale research on the Tokyo Trial based on fact-finding via primary sources, examining its significance as a foreign policy. Considering that the true facts of the Tokyo Trial were being distorted by the ideological confrontation between those who affirmed the trial and those who opposed it, Higurashi attempted to analyse the policy of the trial through the relations of 'norm' (or 'civilization's justice') and 'power' (or 'victor's justice') in international politics.[113]

The end of the Cold War gave access to Soviet documents that illustrate the Soviet policy on the Tokyo Trial. With these documents, Awaya Kentarō, together with NHK (Japan Broadcasting Corporation), conducted research on the origins of the Tokyo Trial, focusing especially on a decision process regarding the immunity given to the Emperor. The result of the research was made into a documentary programme and shown on NHK in August 1992.[114] Awaya, with other researchers, compiled and published the Numerical Case File, the International Prosecution Section's official records of interrogation stored in the National Archives.[115] A substantial number of the defendants' documents that had been rejected, not submitted, or withdrawn, were also compiled.[116]

The legacy of war crimes and war responsibility

In the 1990s, half a century after the war, several issues regarding the past war and war crimes were brought to the fore, which not only caused debates domestically over Japanese responsibility, but also harmed Japan's relationships with neighbouring countries. In 1991, several Korean women publicly testified about their experiences as military sexual slaves. The issue of the so-called 'comfort women', had been not heard in public until the victims themselves came to the fore, and thus their story shocked the Japanese. With archival documents coming to light in 1992 that backed up the claim that the military authorities of the day were directly involved in establishing and managing 'comfort stations',[117] the Japanese government, in August 1993, publicly acknowledged the issue, offered an apology and decided to sponsor an NGO, the Asia Women Fund, to provide 'sympathy money' to the victims. The fund did not constitute direct compensation by the Japanese government, who stated that it had no legal responsibility to pay compensation to individual victims because the issue of reparation had been solved with post-war state-to-state treaties. Some victims have been bringing suits against the Japanese government to receive official post-war compensation.

On the one hand, issues of comfort women as well as the year 1995, the fiftieth anniversary of the end of the Second World War, raised sensitivity over 'post-war responsibility', which, according to Takahashi Tetsuya, connotes the Japanese people's *political* responsibility to respond to the victims' claims and to make the government fulfil its responsibility.[118] The media and academics started to tackle the theme enthusiastically and, as part of that process, some referred to the Tokyo Trial.[119] On the other hand, issues of war crimes and the reaction of the Japanese and the government to them angered and frustrated right-wingers and conservatives. Frustration led to the so-called neo-nationalist movement, which criticized people's historical perception that accepted victims' claims. It is within this context that the Tokyo Trial and its account of the war were pinpointed and attacked severely as the cause of Japan's apologetic attitude. The movement also attacked post-war Japanese education and school textbooks that depicted war crimes committed by the Japanese Imperial Army. The textbook row has been a source of diplomatic tension between Japan and its neighbouring countries.[120]

In addition, Japanese ministers' regular visits to the Yasukuni shrine became a new source of tension during this period. The Yasukuni row became bigger under Prime Minister Koizumi Junichirō, who conducted a visit to the shrine every year since he took office in 2001 until he left in autumn 2006. Although Koizumi insisted that his visits were to pray for the dead and make a vow for peace, his deed immensely harmed diplomatic relations with China and South Korea, precluding any top-level meeting between Japan and China for five years and between Japan and South Korea for about a year, until Koizumi's successor took office in October 2006. On Koizumi's visit to the shrine in April 2002, the Chinese Foreign Ministry expressed 'strong dissatisfaction' with the action, saying that China 'resolutely opposes' all such visits. The South Korean Ministry of Foreign Affairs and Trade also commented: 'We are very concerned that the visit is made to remember convicted war criminals who made neighbouring nations undergo deep pain and suffer the ravages of war'.[121]

These issues and rows were widely covered in the media; however the Tokyo Trial itself was not yet very visible in Japanese public discourse up until 2005, despite the fact that the origins of issues of past war crimes, the textbook row, and the Yasukuni issue especially, can be traced back to the trial: who and what were prosecuted and how the war was depicted in it.[122] At the same time, far more books on the Tokyo Trial were published in 1995 alone, the symbolic year to look back on the past, than any other single year in the past.[123] These points indicate that the Tokyo Trial surely remained in the Japanese psyche, probably as a scar and ache, when contemporary Japan reflected on its past and its responsibility for that past. The Tokyo Trial finally became visible in the society in 2005, and even more so in 2006, the year that marked the sixtieth anniversary of thc start of the Tokyo Trial.

2005–06

The row of the Yasukuni shrine started in 2001 gained momentum in 2005 because of the sixtieth anniversary of the end of the war, when the Japanese had more occasions to look back on the past and re-examine the legacy of the war. In this context, the relations between the Yasukuni row and the Tokyo Trial finally came to be highlighted. As the row intensified into its highest level in 2006, politicians became more frank than in the past about commenting on the Tokyo Trial, in most cases openly criticizing the trial and questioning its righteousness.

The media, academics and intellectuals also began to tackle the Tokyo Trial more directly.[124] *Asahi Shimbun* and *Yomiuri Shimbun* picked up the Tokyo Trial in their editorial on 2 May 2006, the eve of the sixtieth anniversary of the start of the trial; they had never dealt with the topic on its own in their editorial since the close of the trial. In the field of art, Kinoshita's play in 1970 was performed again in 2006. During 2001 and 2006, Inoue Hisashi wrote a series of plays dealing with the Tokyo Trial, focusing on the historical significance of the trial and Japan's war responsibility.

In spite of its much greater exposure in the media, the fact and significance of the Tokyo Trial are still not very well known to the Japanese. According to opinion polls of *Yomiuri Shimbun* and *Asahi Shimbun* in 2005 and 2006, in which they, for the first time, directly asked about the Tokyo Trial, 60 per cent (*Yomiuri*), or even 70 per cent (*Asahi*), answered that they did not know the content of the trial.[125] During this period of time, traditional anti-Tokyo Trial criticism attacking the righteousness and justice of the trial and its historical account became even stronger, stimulated by the Yasukuni row and the history textbook row. However, at the same time, the Tokyo Trial, after 60 years, started to be debated in public within a wider context: contemporary Japan and the legacy of the war, war crimes and responsibility, slowly going beyond irreconcilable dualisms.[126] It is still not known, at the time of writing, whether this emerging trend is merely short lived or becomes a turning point for the Japanese understanding of the Tokyo Trial.

Conclusion

Having examined the Japanese attitude towards the Tokyo Trial since 1946 up to 2006, the following points can be made. First, right from the beginning, apathy can be observed as a general attitude of the Japanese towards the Tokyo Trial. Apathy towards the trial seems relevant to the Japanese long-term indifference to its past war and war responsibility. Second, the Tokyo Trial has been widely understood as 'victor's justice', which is accompanied by certain kind of frustration: why was only Japan's conduct prosecuted? This sentiment has been the driving force for the nationalist criticism of the Tokyo Trial. These two points lead to the third one: the Tokyo Trial is a topic that has been ignored by the majority of the population, on the one hand, and has been debated emotionally and ideologically within a limited circle on the other. Within that circle, focus is often on whether the trial was just or not, or whether Japan conducted aggressive wars and committed war crimes or not. These issues often cause irreconcilable debate and prevent general lessons from being learned from the Tokyo Trial for the contemporary Japan and the world. And fourth, in spite of the general apathy and invisibility of the Tokyo Trial in society, the trial in fact has been intricately connected to how Japanese people understand the nature of the past war and Japan's responsibility for that war.

These four points are important Japanese reactions towards the Tokyo Trial, which imply the trial's impact on post-war Japan. The rest of the book examines the content and mechanisms of these reactions – apathy, frustration, a sense of war responsibility and an historical perception – in more detail, with the two devices of the trial as pillars of analysis: the individualization of responsibility and the tribunal's record of the war. Rather than illustrating the Japanese perception as it is, the remainder of the book attempts to analyse and explain the Japanese attitude in relation to these two devices that are recurrent themes in the discourse of the 'Nuremberg legacy' within the context of current international war crimes prosecution and transitional justice. The aim is to examine whether these devices had any impact on post-war Japan, if so what kind, and analyse what can be learned from the experience of the Tokyo Trial for the pursuit of justice in post-conflict society.

5 The Tokyo Trial and the historical record of the war

Through its legal procedure and judgment, the Tokyo Tribunal provided an historical record of the war and war crimes conducted by Japan. Of its 1,218 pages of judgment, the tribunal devoted 1,050 pages to a detailed explanation of Japanese policy during the period between 1928 and 1945. This chapter examines what kind of impact, if any, the Tokyo Trial's historical record has had on post-war Japan.

Analysis is conducted from two perspectives: whether and in what way the tribunal's historical record helped demilitarization and democratization of Japan, the strategic purpose of the American occupation policy; and whether and in what way it had any impact on the cultivation of people's historical perception and collective memory, and reconciliation, which are raised by promoters of the 'Nuremberg legacy' as a key utility of the trial's historical record. It is not the aim of this chapter to explain post-war Japan's demilitarization and democratization process as the outcome of the historical record of the Tokyo Trial, which was merely one part of bigger American occupation policy.[1] What the following attempts instead is to examine the impact of the tribunal's historical record from the perspective of demilitarization and democratization. In the same vein, the chapter does not try to analyse Japanese historical perception, collective memory and reconciliation per se. These are topics of increasing popularity but very complex ones that consist of multiple elements, which cannot be explained only by the Tokyo Trial. Rather, the following attempts to examine whether the Tokyo Trial can be placed within a bigger framework of collective memory and reconciliation and see if there is any role that the trial's historical record played or plays in it. The aim of this chapter is to test, through the Tokyo Trial, one of the two pillars of the Nuremberg legacy: the positive impact of the trial's historical record on post-war societies.

The historical account of the Tokyo Tribunal

During the procedures at the Tokyo Tribunal, both the prosecutor and the defence counsel spent much of their time characterizing the wars Japan had fought between 1928 and 1945. The defence claimed that the wars Japan had fought were justifiable acts of self-defence to preserve the welfare and prosperity of the Japanese nation threatened by the Allies' measures to restrict the economy of Japan. Against this claim, the judgment of the tribunal, accepting the case for the prosecution, concluded that there was, in Japanese policy, a criminal conspiracy to wage wars of aggression: Japan had launched a war of aggression against China, had planned and prepared for a war of aggression against Britain, France, the Netherlands, the United States and the Soviet Union, and had launched a war of aggression against the United States and the British Commonwealth. The judgment defined the conspirators as the military and their supporters and found that they had succeeded in 'obtaining control of the organs of government of Japan and preparing and regimenting the nation's mind and material resources for wars of aggression designed to achieve the object of the conspiracy'.[2] They, according to the judgment, 'carried out in succession the attacks necessary to effect their ultimate object that Japan should dominate the Far East'.[3]

The tribunal also found that the Japanese military had perpetrated serious war crimes against the Allies' POWs and against civilians while waging war in China, including the notorious Nanjing massacre: 'from the opening of the war in China until the surrender of Japan in August 1945 torture, murder, rape and other cruelties of the most inhumane and barbarous character were freely practiced by the Japanese Army and Navy'. According to the evidence and testimony, the tribunal declared that only one conclusion was possible: 'the atrocities were either secretly ordered or wilfully permitted by the Japanese Government or individual members thereof and by the leaders of the armed forces'.[4]

Defects in the tribunal's account

Whether broadly in agreement with the verdict of the Tokyo Trial or not, it is now widely agreed among academics that it is risky to accept unconditionally the account of the war and Japanese wartime policy provided in the judgment of the Tokyo Tribunal. There are several defects in the tribunal's historical account of the war, of which this study focuses on the following three points, which directly influenced, or are said to have influenced, the perception and discourse of the Japanese people regarding the war and war crimes.

One of the fundamental defects was the tribunal's application of the concept of conspiracy to account for the wars fought by Japan. The term 'conspiracy' was originally conceived to apply to the case of Nazi Germany. The question raised here is whether it can also be applied to the Japanese case. First, the prosecution at the Tokyo Tribunal insisted: 'it is apparent from the evidence that there did exist a really carefully planned conspiracy or common plan for commission of the crimes set forth in the Indictment'.[5] However, as historian Iokibe Makoto states, in the case of Japan, the whole war was 'not the matter of the existence of cool-headed and evil "conspiracy" but the matter of its *non-existence*'.[6] The complexity and incoherence of wartime Japanese policy can be seen from the simple fact that the Japanese cabinet changed 17 times during the period between 1928 and 1945. What is more, the lack of conspiracy is well reflected in the stark confrontation during the trial between two defendants, Tōgō Shigenori, a career diplomat, and Admiral Shimada Shigetarō, over the attack on Pearl Harbor.

Second, the Tokyo judgment concluded:

> These far-reaching plans for waging wars of aggression and the prolonged and intricate preparation for and waging of these wars of aggression were not the work of one man. They were the work of *many leaders* acting in pursuance of a common plan for the achievement of a common object. That common object, that they should secure Japan's domination by preparing and waging wars of aggression, was a criminal object.[7]

Who, however, were those 'many leaders'? In practice, prosecutors of the Tokyo Tribunal had found it difficult to identify conspirators. Arthur Comyns Carr, British associate prosecutor, who took a central part in drafting the indictment, stated:

> the whole Japanese situation is infinitely more complicated than the German for the purposes of a prosecution, as all the politicians, soldiers and sailors were all squabbling and double-crossing one another all the time and it is by no means easy to pick the right defendants.[8]

A staff member in the attorney general's office also stated:

> the difficulties of drafting and agreeing the defendants have been much greater than over the Nuremberg indictment in that Japan never had any consistent party like the Nazis, and out of a plethora of possible defendants responsible since 1931, only a few can be picked from a very competitive bunch.[9]

These facts raise the question as to whether the count of 'conspiracy' can be applied to the Japanese case.

The structure of Japanese wartime decision making that lacked centrally given criminal order is a reason why the Tokyo Trial focused on another difficult criminal concept: 'negative criminality', or legal culpability for having failed to prevent the commission of war crimes.[10] The prosecution and punishment for the omission to stop crimes yielded doubtful judgments against several defendants.[11]

'Japan was not Germany; Tojo was not Hitler; the Pacific war was not identical with the European war', Richard Minear argues: 'Yet in spite of these crucial differences the legal trappings set up to punish the Nazis were applied in precisely the same manner to the Japanese leaders'.[12] Conspiracy is a convenient concept that enables wholesale prosecution of military leaders; however, it is too simplistic a concept on which to base historical narration. 'Declaring that documentary materials introduced revealed an eighteen-year-long "common plan" to wage aggressive war', John Dower notes, 'was much closer to propaganda than to serious historical analysis'.[13]

The second shortcoming of the Tokyo Trial's account of the war is its heavy focus on the role of the military clique. The judgment spent a great many pages under the heading of 'The Military Domination of Japan and Preparation for War' to describe how the military, through propaganda, persuasion or assassination, came to dominate Japan, created a 'reign of terror', and prepared for aggressive wars. The military, according to the judgment, gradually rose:

> to such a predominance in the government of Japan that no other organ of government, neither the elected representatives of the people, nor the civilian ministers in the Cabinet, nor the civilian advisers of the Emperor in the Privy Council and in his entourage, latterly imposed any effective check on the ambitions of the military.[14]

Blaming the military for Japan's wars of aggression may be inevitable, considering the fact that the Tokyo Trial was part of American policy to demilitarize Japan.[15] However, to explain 18 years of Japanese history only by a conspiracy of the military clique is too simplistic. Iokibe points out that the procedures of the Tribunal lacked two important civilian figures that played a significant role in expanding the war: Matsuoka Yōsuke, a former Minister of Foreign Affairs, who concluded the Axis Alliance, and Konoe Fumimaro, a former Prime Minister who contributed to the expansion of the Sino-Japanese war.[16]

Arai Shinichi, historian, claims that examining the developments to the war within the framework of extreme militarist versus moderate political leaders is the 'elitists' view of history', which lacks 'structural analysis of social and historical elements that have enabled Japan to conduct aggression'.[17] This was pointed out by the research group of *Asahi Shimbun* soon after the occupation:

> If the aim was to reveal the truth and avoid the tragedy of the war being repeated, wasn't it most important to investigate the reason why Japan had come to pursue aggression? For that purpose, as to national issues, it was first of all necessary to examine Japan's social structure, with the Emperor at the top, half-feudal farming villages at the basis and monopolistic financiers in the middle.... However, the prosecutor started off their argument with the fact that a chain of bad guys had planned the aggression and mobilized the whole structure of Japan. In this way, it avoided issues of the Emperor and *Zaibatsu* and ended up in targeting a few military men with 'star value', along with a very limited number of bureaucrats.[18]

As examined in Chapter 3, the Tokyo Trial exempted several important issues and people from prosecution as a result of political calculations by the United States. The significance of an historical record with important pieces missing is rather dubious.

The third shortcoming is that the Tokyo Trial, as well as its account of the war, focused heavily on the Pacific War. Awaya Kentarō, historian, points out that the Second World War in the Asian-Pacific sphere had three aspects: war among imperial powers; war between fascist and anti-fascist powers; and liberation war against colonialism. Rather than examining the complex nature of the war, the tribunal created a simple account based on the Allies' view of the war, i.e. war between fascist Axis vs anti-fascist Allies. This is because of the strong influence in conducting the Tokyo Trial of the United States, whose interest was in the Pacific War. Accordingly, 'the aspect of the war among the imperial powers was overlooked and the aspect of liberation against colonialism was dealt with subordinately'.[19]

The colonialist aspect of the war in the Asian sphere and Japanese colonial rule over its Asian neighbours were ignored at the tribunal in spite of the fact various war crimes had been allegedly conducted against civilians there. Kainō Michitaka, a member of the defence counsel at the tribunal, saw it as a problem to put Tōjō Hideki, Prime Minister at the time of the outbreak of the Pacific War, at the centre of the Tokyo Trial:

> The Tokyo Trial should have focused more on Japan's war against China. As a war, the Pacific War was bigger in scale and impact, causing greater harm to the world. However, on the point of immorality and aggressiveness, it is doubtful whether Japan's war in the Pacific should be focused on. Something is wrong with regarding the war crimes trial as being a mere Tōjō trial.[20]

Japan's war responsibility against civilians in Asian neighbours had been left half solved and rarely mentioned within the debate on the Tokyo Trial, until the late 1970s.[21]

The Tokyo Trial was conducted with a specific view of the war, and the pre-existence of such a view can be seen from the fact that the tribunal had set its jurisdiction between 1 January 1928 and 2 September 1945, implying that this was *the* period of Japan's war. On this temporal jurisdiction, Arnold Brackman examines that rather than present 'the link between the accused and the reign of barbarism they had conducted as state policy from 1931 to 1945, the prosecutors plunged into murky Japanese domestic politics of the 1920s and 1930s',[22] that is, the rise of the military clique. What is more, by setting the temporal jurisdiction, the tribunal could and did determine 'who will play the villain, who the victim'.[23] In any event, many Japanese academics believe that 'In a real sense … the Tokyo Trial sat in *judgment on the history* of the Pacific region up to the end of World War II'.[24] In other words, the trial had defined the nature of the war. John Pritchard states: 'There is, perhaps, a philosophical divide between those who call it the "Tokyo War Crimes Trial" and those who call it the "Tokyo War Trial". I prefer the latter'.[25]

In the Tokyo Tribunal's historical record, some find a problem of resorting to legal procedure for the account of the events. Minear's conclusion follows:

> Historical process does not yield to adjudication; and the attempt to make history justiciable is doomed from the start. The mistakes of Tokyo were attributable in part to bias and to restrictions on admissible evidence. But the larger share of the blame must fall on the basic misconception that the events at issue could be adjudicated.[26]

The documents and materials of the Tokyo Trial were collected and examined for the purpose of judicial procedures; that is to prove the guilt of the defendants, not for the pursuit of factual truth per se. In addition, the Tokyo Trial as well as the Nuremberg Trial, was a *military* trial. Donald Watt claims: 'the historian who reads the proceedings of the trial for the arguments of the prosecution and defense counsel is only too speedily made aware of the inefficiency of the adversary system of legal investigation, at least as practiced by Anglo-Saxon lawyers as a means of uncovering historical "truth"'.[27] Even some high officials in the US government expressed some doubts at the time on the appropriateness of the Tokyo Tribunal as a means of establishing a historical record: 'the validity of the trial itself doubtless will be long debated, as will the wisdom of using a court process to reveal this military past to the Japanese', wrote William Joseph Sebald.[28]

Impact on the people at the time

Although the experts seriously question the 'authoritativeness' of the Tokyo Tribunal's historical record, they commonly accept that without the structure of an international trial and the strong authority of GHQ controlling the country, it was not possible to assimilate the enormous amount of documents and records of wartime Japan. Indeed, the Japanese government and military organizations had tried to burn many of their secret documents before the start of the American occupation. Many important issues would never have come to light without the Tokyo Tribunal. Many Japanese academics accept this as a positive, or the most positive, aspect of the Tokyo Trial.[29] What is more, it was the procedures of the Tokyo Trial through which the Japanese people came to know in detail what had actually happened during the war and what kind of atrocities had been conducted by their soldiers.

The Tokyo Trial's account of the war had a significant impact on the Japanese people at the time.[30] The trial offered people facts about the war – who had planned and conducted the war in what way – which were for a long time concealed from the public. The significance of the Tokyo Trial's account rests not only on it revealing the hidden aspects of the war and wartime government but also on it 'interpreting and providing an overview of the period'.[31] Importantly, the information of the war and the way the war was portrayed by the judgment were accepted by the majority of the population.

Acceptance of the trial's historical account was natural, considering the fact that the Tokyo Trial itself was accepted albeit passively by the nation.[32] What is more, GHQ's campaign before the Tokyo Trial, such as a series of articles in major newspapers on 'The History of the Pacific War', may have had a substantial effect.[33] The trial's account, more importantly, was accepted because it was, in several aspects, 'comfortable' for the people at the time. First, by revealing the wartime politico-military structure, the Tokyo Trial pointed the finger at who should be blamed for the war and misery and poverty that accompanied it: the military. As is examined more in detail in Chapter 6, the story offered by the Tokyo Trial matched the national anger that existed at the time towards the wartime government and the military, as well as people's disassociation from them.[34] At the same time, the detail of atrocities committed by the Japanese army, such as the Nanjing massacre, revealed through the trial, shocked the Japanese. New information convinced the nation that they had been deceived by the military clique, a sense that had been already shared by the nation. 'During the war we were forced to suffer a poor life; but we lost the war that Tōjō had said that we would definitely win', an executive of a company said during the trial: 'Now I came to learn through the Tokyo Trial and others that it was a reckless, aggressive war pursuing the interests of the privileged class and capitalists, and realized that we had been completely deceived'.[35] The trial's account of the war further strengthened people's detachment from their wartime leaders.

Second, the tribunal's account of the war excluded the role of the Emperor, who was supported by the majority of the nation even after the war.[36] Here, an interesting US–Japan collaboration in the Tokyo Trial's historical record can be pointed out. The historical record without the Emperor could not have been created without cooperation from the Japanese side, including the defendants.[37] An often-noted episode is the testimony of Tōjō, who, during his defence on 31 December 1947, stated that 'there is no Japanese subject who would go against the will of His Majesty; more particularly, among high officials of the Japanese government or of Japan'.[38] This statement upset the US chief prosecutor Joseph Keenan because it implied war responsibility on the part of the Emperor. Keenan urged Tōjō via Kido Kōichi, the Emperor's close adviser, to retract his statement. On 6 January 1948, Tōjō claimed that his statement on the Emperor had been based on his 'feeling towards the Emperor as a subject, and that is quite a different matter from the problem of responsibility, that is, the responsibility of the Emperor'. He emphasized that war had been decided by his cabinet: 'It may not have been according to his will, but it is a fact that because of my advice and because of the advice given by the High Command the Emperor consented, though reluctantly, to the war'.[39]

The Tokyo Trial attempted to facilitate the demilitarization and democratization of Japan and demarcate wartime and post-war Japan. The Japanese, on their part, accepted the trial's judgment and its account because they themselves felt resentment against the military and were willing to leave the war behind and move forward. Thus, the Japanese albeit passive acceptance of the Tokyo Trial's account of the war was not a one-way story.[40]

The 'Tokyo Trial view of history' and revisionism

The account of the war for which so many people fought and died is never without controversy. For some people, the view that 'Japan has waged wars of aggression and committed terrible war crimes along the way' is hardly acceptable. Such a view is more unacceptable when it is seen as having been given, or imposed, through an international trial, and even more so when the trial is regarded as 'victor's justice'. The Tokyo Tribunal's historical record, together with the trial itself, has been bitterly criticized by the right-winger, the nationalist and the revisionist, who justify, even glorify, pre-war and wartime Japan.

The 'Tokyo Trial view of history' and its critics

The historical record of the Tokyo Tribunal has been targeted by right-wing polemicists under the banner of the 'war crimes trial view of history', or the 'Tokyo Trial view of history' (*Tōkyō saiban shikan*). What exactly the term 'Tokyo Trial view of history' means is not necessarily clear, and the term in fact has been used in various ways. However, it is rarely used academically and most of the time denotes the negation of the judgment of the Tokyo Trial. Fuji Nobuo, a user of the term, sees the 'Tokyo Trial view of history' as:

> an historical view which regards the account of the Tokyo judgment as totally true and considers that the wars conducted by Japan were 'wars of aggression' against international law and treaties and that Japan's past actions were all criminal and 'bad'.[41]

The biggest attack on the 'Tokyo Trial view of history' is made on the tribunal's conclusion that the wars Japan fought from the late 1920s until 1945 were aggressive in nature. While academics in the field, examined above, see it as a problem that the tribunal applied a concept of conspiracy to account for Japan's aggressive war, such an account itself is the problem for the anti-'Tokyo Trial view of history' critics. For them, the historical account of the Tokyo Trial is simply not true: they emphasize, echoing the assertion of defendants at the tribunal, the self-defensive aspect of Japan's wars or the aspect of the wars to liberate Asia from Western imperialism. 'The view that Japan had conducted aggression was *created* and *proliferated* based mostly on the judgment of the Tokyo Tribunal', argued Satō Kazuo, international legal scholar.[42]

The 'Tokyo Trial view of history' becomes even more unacceptable as it is seen as the creation of 'victor's justice': the war fought by the vanquished was judged as criminal aggression by the victor unilaterally and retroactively.[43] Takigawa Masajirō, a member of the defence counsel at the tribunal, stated: 'Whether the war Japan conducted was an aggressive war or a war of self-defence should be left to future historians. It is not an issue left to the judgment of the victor'.[44] Fujioka Nobukatsu, a strong opponent of the 'Tokyo Trial view of history', states: 'The history was written according to the prepared conclusion that Japan was the villain and the Allies were good. It was based on information that corresponded with such a conclusion'.[45] Kobori Keiichirō, an academic specializing in comparative culture, claims that the trial's view is not a substantiated historical fact. He argues that the 'Tokyo Trial view of history' was based on the argument of the prosecutor coloured with bias: 'This was an historical *interpretation* of the "victor" of the trial'.[46]

In the place of the 'Tokyo Trial view of history', those critics are willing to promote an affirmative, or glorifying, account of pre-war and wartime Japan. This is why anti-'Tokyo Trial view of history' critics show stronger resentment of the tribunal's account of Japan's war crimes than of its silence over American alleged war crimes: Hiroshima and Nagasaki. The Nanjing massacre first came to be known widely to the Japanese public through the Tokyo Trial, which recorded that the Japanese Imperial Army had killed, raped and tortured more than 200,000 people in the city. The massacre has been one of the prime targets of the right-wing critics as it harms their account of wartime Japan. For those who refuse to accept the fact of the massacre, the Tokyo Trial is detestable as the origin of the 'fictionalization' of the crime. The title of Fuji's book, *The 'Nanjing Massacre' was Invented in This Way: The Deception of the Tokyo Trial* [*'Nankin Daigyakusatsu' ha Kōshite Tsukurareta: Tōkyō Saiban no Giman*], is symbolic in this sense. Tanaka Masaaki, a strong opponent of the Tokyo Trial, also wrote a book entitled: *The Fiction of the Nanjing Massacre* [*Nankin Gyakusatsu no Kyokō*]. Satō claims that the 'Nanjing incident' was 'extravagantly publicized' by the Tokyo Trial, based on insufficient evidence in order to make Japan unreasonably into a criminal state equivalent to Nazi Germany.[47]

This kind of claim, however, had been relatively muted, until the 1990s when the nationalists and conservatives found an atmosphere developing within Japanese society where their assertion could be heard.

The revisionist and neo-nationalist movement in the 1990s

The death of the wartime Emperor in 1989 signified the end of an era that began in 1926, and the Japanese started re-examining the bright and dark sides of this tumultuous period. At the same time, entering the 1990s, individuals in Japan's neighbouring countries started to raise their voices, asking for an apology and compensation for the suffering inflicted on them by Japan half a century ago. The nature of Japan's responsibility for the past war and war crimes was talked about both inside and outside Japan. Facing increasing claims from the victims of the 'comfort women', the Japanese government publicly acknowledged the issue in 1993 and sponsored the establishment of an NGO to provide 'sympathy money' to the victims.[48]

The end of the domination of Japanese politics by the Liberal Democratic Party (LDP) enabled the Japanese government to face Japan's past more frankly. In 1993, Hosokawa Morihiro, the first Prime Minister outside the conservative LDP since 1955, expressed 'profound remorse and apologies for the fact that Japan's actions, including acts of aggression and colonial rule, caused unbearable suffering and sorrow for so many people'.[49] The year 1995 marked the fiftieth anniversary of the end of the Second World War, a milestone that encouraged Japan to look back on the past. The so-called 'war apology' resolution was passed in that year by the National Diet under Prime Minister

Murayama Tomiichi of the Social Democratic Party of Japan. It aimed to put to rest criticisms from its neighbours for not having apologized properly for its past war and war crimes.[50] Murayama himself expressed a more unequivocal apology to Japan's neighbours, with a clear statement that Japan, 'through its colonial rule and aggression, caused tremendous damage and suffering to the people of many countries, particularly to those of Asian nations'.[51]

While the Japanese government's actions during the first half of the 1990s were criticized as insufficient from one side,[52] they angered and frustrated some others as too 'apologetic'. What angered the latter was the government's as well as the nation's uncritical acceptance that 'Japan had conducted wars of aggression and committed war crimes' and their 'ignorance' and apathy towards the past. These frustrations led to a series of 'revisionist' movements, which directly challenged the general Japanese historical perception of the war. The movements especially attacked journalism, the 'progressive intellectuals' and the school teachers' union, which, since the end of the war, has been strongly influenced by the leftist, or Marxist, approach to modern history, for having been proliferating and sustaining the 'enemy propaganda' ever since the occupation and undermining the morale of the Japanese, especially the young.

In 1996, Fujioka Nobukatsu, Professor of Education, established the Association for Advancement of Liberalist View of History (*Jiyūshugi Shikan Kenkyūkai*). Fujioka's 'liberalist' view claimed that it attempted to go beyond the dichotomized historical arguments between the left that totally rejects the element of self-defence in the war and the right that rejects the aggressive aspect of the war. However, his arguments have very much in common with the traditional right-wing view of history.[53] Fujioka argues that the seven years of the US occupation, especially the censorship conducted by GHQ, was focused on the 'thought-reform' of the Japanese nation, brainwashing the people with the story that only Japan was evil and making them embrace a sense of guilt.[54] Fujioka also regarded the comfort women as 'an unfounded scandal created in the 1990s for the political purpose of bashing Japan'.[55] The association claimed that the Japanese attitude towards the war and alleged war crimes were caused by a 'masochist view of history [*Jigyaku-shikan*]', which had been imposed by the victor of the Second World War through the war crimes trial.

The revisionist movement gained momentum in 1996 when the Ministry of Education approved junior high school history textbooks that started to depict the issue of comfort women.[56] Fujioka being one of its promoters among other academics and public figures, the Japanese Society for History Textbook Reform (*Atarashii Kyōkasho wo Tsukuru Kai*) was established in 1997. The society, so-called 'Tsukurukai', claimed:

> Especially in modern history, Japan is dealt with as a criminal that is destined to apologize down the ages. In the post-Cold War era, this masochist tendency has been strengthened and current history textbooks have even come to treat an account of the propaganda of the former enemy as fact. There is no country in the world that conducts such history education.[57]

Alternatively, Tsukurukai prepared a new textbook, which put forward the view that the colonization of Manchuria and the 'Greater East Asia War' were part of a series of Asia's liberation wars against the Western powers. According to them, 'The textbook the Society writes illustrates a self-portrait of Japan and the Japanese, with dignity and balance, with a global historical view'.[58] Having gone through several corrections, Tsukurukai's textbook for junior high schools was finally given the government's certification and was published in 2001. Although only a very small number of schools actually decided to use the textbook, its depictions of Japan's war in Asia caused strong criticism from China and South Korea, and raised heated debates both domestically and internationally.

Revisionist and the so-called neo-nationalist arguments in the 1990s have been widely publicized and supported by a number of public figures. In 1994, the Minister of Justice was made to resign for his statement: 'The Nanjing massacre was a fabrication' and 'the war was not an aggressive war'.[59] The slogan of the neo-nationalism was most powerfully conveyed by Kobayashi Yoshinori, a cartoonist, who made himself, with his medium of expression, a cartoon, an effective spokesman of the movement. He, in his comics, glorified the Japanese Imperial Army and dismissed the Nanjing massacre and comfort women as fiction. Kobayashi claimed:

> Only Japan refuses to recognize its own justness. Is this because its people have turned into mice with electrodes stuck into their head? Remove the electrodes, Japan! There was justice in Japan's war! We must protect our grand father's legacy![60]

His *On War* has sold nearly one million copies and has become a social phenomenon.[61]

It is in this series of revisionist and neo-nationalist movements that the Tokyo Trial, especially its verdict and historical record of wartime Japan, came to be attacked as the source of Japanese masochistic attitude. The title of Kobori Keiichirō's book, *Re-examining the Tokyo Trial: The Starting Point that Ruined Japan*, illustrates the nature of frustration those people had felt towards the Tokyo Trial.[62] Unlike the previous time, in the 1990s these frustrations and attacks on the Tokyo Trial and its account of the war were raised more loudly, and echoed by many more people. The fact that several heads of large corporations joined the criticism may not be irrelevant to a sudden decline of Japanese economic activity and a recession during this period, a period that challenged the Japanese national identity and pride that had been built on economic development and transformation since the end of the war.

Maeno Tōru, a businessman born in 1926, saw that many Japanese people were losing the pride and identity as the 'Japanese race [*Nihon minzoku*]'. He found reasons for this in the 'Tokyo Trial view of history':

> The guilty verdict at the Tokyo Trial that concluded that Japan was the aggressor totally denied Japanese tradition and culture, which had been

> established up to then. Japanese history was distorted and the truth of the Greater East Asia War was concealed. Since then, the Japanese have been overcome with a sense of guilt, and many Japanese have come to regard Japanese history and traditional culture negatively based on the Tokyo Trial view of history.[63]

Maeno's book is recommended by the Governor of Tokyo, Ishihara Shintarō, a popular outspoken conservative politician who did not hesitate to deny bluntly the Nanjing massacre.

Nakajō Takanori, another businessman of the wartime generation, was concerned about the young generation's ignorance about the unfair trial and their being 'brainwashed' with the idea that 'Japan's past was totally wrong'. He wrote in his best-selling book, *Granddad, Tell Me about the War*, that he wanted the historical facts to be known to the young generation, who did not know that Japan had been convicted by an unreasonable trial.[64] He claimed that Japan's war against Western countries led to the liberation of Asian countries: 'To conclude that everything was wrong because we lost the war is to distort history'.[65] Arguments of people like Maeno and Nakajō are not based on thorough academic analysis; but because they are based on the perceptions of individuals who have lived through wartime and post-war Japan, and because of their casual and straightforward style of writing, these publications have been accessible and have appealed to the public.

In 1998, a film on the Tokyo Trial was released. Unlike the one in 1983,[66] *Puraido: Unmei no Toki* [*Pride: The Fateful Moment*] focused on the 'heroic agony' of Tōjō Hideki at the Tokyo Tribunal, paralleled with the struggle of the Indian judge Pal and India's movement for independence from Great Britain. Itō Shunya, the director of the film, stated:

> Tōjō was the one who saw the real nature of the trial and fought against it ... that the trial was a continuation of the war by the Allies, especially the United States, within the context of its post-war strategy. It was a trial to drag Japan into a subordinate relationship to the United States in order to stop it from once again becoming a military threat. In addition to demilitarization, the trial stepped even into the Japanese mentality and labelled the war an inexcusable act of aggression.[67]

The film created a controversy. In Japan, several groups held meetings criticizing the film for trying to acquit Japan of the responsibility for aggression and wrongdoing. Some of them even campaigned for the suspension of the screening. The film, at the same time, did evoke some sympathy from Japanese viewers. Tsugawa Masahiko, who had played the role of Tōjō, claimed: 'A comment, "I am glad that I was born in Japan", made to me by a member of an audience pleased me the most'.[68] Tsugawa's comment implies the core logic of neo-nationalism and revisionism: the Japanese have been ashamed of themselves because of the sense of being an 'ex-convict nation' imprinted by the

Tokyo Trial; such a sense can be eradicated and replaced with pride through 'enlightenment', by telling the 'truth' through things like the film *Puraido*.

One group indicated the reason why they criticized the Tokyo Trial as follows:

> With the criticism of the Tokyo Trial that concluded that the Greater East Asia War was an aggressive war, we want to wipe out the Tokyo Trial view of history enveloping our nation and to redeem the honour of a thousand of our countrymen who suffered disgrace, having been regarded as war criminals.[69]

Indeed, neo-nationalist criticism of the Tokyo Tribunal appealed to not a few war-bereaved who resist the idea that the war was an aggression, because to accept that would be to disgrace the soul of their family members and to admit that they died in vain. Examination of Japanese reaction regarding the Tokyo Trial, reaction especially of wartime generations, cannot ignore the fact that many people at the time supported the war and, up to a point, its causes.[70]

A generation gap in perception of the war exists to some extent. According to an opinion poll conducted in October 1993 by *Yomiuri Shimbun*, 53.1 per cent agreed with the statement that 'Japan was an "aggressor" in World War II'; 24.8 per cent disagreed and 22.1 per cent did not answer. The percentage of those who agreed to the statement was highest among those in their twenties (61.7 per cent), and lowest among those over 70 (41.1 per cent). At the same time, what should be pointed out is that in every generation from those in their twenties to those over 70, those who agreed with the statement exceeded those who disagreed.[71] This importantly shows that the neo-nationalist voices were not necessarily shared by the majority of the population. In fact, voices having been raised against the Tokyo Trial and the 'Tokyo Trial view of history' were a reaction to the current Japanese people's acceptance of criminality in the country's war history.

Collective memory, apathy and the Tokyo Trial

In spite of the above events and movements and the media coverage, both in Japan and overseas, on Japanese nationalist posture since the 1990s, the negation of the past Japanese war and militarism and the preference for pacifism are still strong among the nation.[72] In the opinion poll conducted by *Mainichi Shimbun* in August 2005, asking about the nature of Japan's wars against the US and China, 43 per cent responded that they were 'wrong wars', while 29 per cent said they were 'inevitable wars'.[73] Another opinion poll conducted by *Asahi Shimbun* in August 1994 showed 72 per cent thought that 'Japan has not done enough compensation to people under the Japanese colonial rule and occupation'.[74] Focus groups and intensive interviews conducted by the author in the autumn and winter of 2003 also confirmed that people more or less hold the view that Japan conducted an aggressive war led by the military clique and committed war crimes that cannot be excused; the view that corresponds to the central line of the Tokyo Trial's verdict.[75] In interviews, most people distanced themselves from the revisionist view, some showing disgust and immediate refusal to accept the view, and some expressing that they felt 'something is wrong' with such an account of the war and the Tokyo Trial.

Interestingly, while revisionists criticize the widely held view of the war by attributing it to the Tokyo Tribunal, those who see criminality in Japan's war do not relate their historical view to the Tokyo Trial. In fact, most interviewees, while recognizing the revisionist movement and argument, did not know the term 'Tokyo Trial view of history' and the criticisms made against it. Just as illustrated in the previous chapter, the general attitude towards the Tokyo Trial examined through focus groups and intensive interviews was apathy. However, close examination based on interviews revealed that the apathy consists of multiple elements: 'indifference', 'cynicism' and a sense of 'taboo'. These are three different states of mind, but all lead to easy, or passive, acceptance of the Tokyo Trial. The following examines the deeper significance of the Japanese apathy regarding the Tokyo Trial and analyses the impact of the Tokyo Trial's historical record on the Japanese view of the war.

Indifference: ignorance and demarcation

Apathy can be attributed to indifference, that is lack of interest, and the current Japanese indifference to the Tokyo Trial is caused primarily by ignorance: the simple lack of knowledge. According to an opinion poll of *Asahi Shimbun* in May 2006, 70 per cent answered that they did not know well about the content of the Tokyo Trial.[76] Details of this ignorance were observed by the author's interviews, each of which began with a question whether s/he knows anything about the Tokyo Trial. Most of the interviewees, except for those the age of 60 and beyond, answered that they had heard about it or recognized the event had taken place, but that they did not know about it in detail. Some of those born in the 1980s did not even know it as an event that took place in history.[77]

Interestingly, while many of the current generation regard Japan's previous war as 'bad' and 'punishment-worthy', they only have a very vague idea exactly who was prosecuted under the Tokyo Trial and for what reason. An immediate response of the interviewees tended to be 'war crimes' or as vague as 'wrongdoing'. Having been asked in more detail about exactly what crimes they thought the war criminals had been tried for, several interesting points were raised. First, as for the war crimes judged by the Tokyo Trial, many mentioned Japan's wartime conduct against China and other Asian countries, be it the war itself, aggression or war crimes against civilians. Having been asked about Pearl Harbor, a woman in her fifties clearly stated: 'That does not occur to me as the first thing about the Tokyo Trial. What occurs to me first is what Japan has done to its neighbouring countries'.[78] Some younger people stated that the trial could not have been for Japan's conduct against the United States, pointing out the American use of atomic bombs.[79] These responses may be the effect of wide media coverage since the early 1990s of the comfort women and other alleged war crimes against Asian civilians, which made a strong impression as being representative of Japan's past war crimes.

This relates to the second point: some, especially the young, claimed that the Tokyo Trial could not have been conducted in relation to the starting and waging of war per se, because, if so, every country, including the victor, was responsible. An interviewee in her thirties stated: 'If it was for a crime to start the war, other countries should have also taken some responsibility. But the fact that Japan was tried in such a manner may mean that it was about aggression towards Asian countries'.[80] The comment reflects the differentiation between the 'war' against the Allies and the 'aggression' towards their Asian neighbours, which can be observed quite often in Japanese perception.[81] And third, it is pointed out, especially by the over-forties generation, that wartime leaders were responsible for the crimes against their own nation for having led Japan in the wrong direction.[82]

These are 'images' held by many interviewees, which do not necessarily correspond with the facts: there is a gap between people's image of the Tokyo Trial and what the trial actually was. First, the Tokyo Trial provided a platform for examining Japan's war against the Allies, not for Japan's war crimes against Asian civilians. Second, the trial examined every aspect of the war from the perspective of a conspiracy, focusing more on Japan's war against the Allies. Third, not necessarily all the 'wrongdoing' and all those 'responsible' were examined by the Tokyo Trial because of political calculation on the part of the Allies.[83] It tends to be regarded, from the contemporary perspective, that what was punished was 'crimes against humanity' or aggressive war against Asian neighbours that accompanied the atrocities against civilians. However, this was not the case. This is exactly why Arnold Brackman expressed concern that his attempt to write on the Tokyo Trial might 'unnecessarily offend today's pro-Western Japanese'.[84] I shared this concern over conducting interviews. A question arose as to whether people's perception of the Tokyo Trial would become more hostile if they knew the detail of the Tokyo Trial. And, this is exactly what right-wingers and revisionists have been trying to do, by stressing the defects and political aspects of the trial.

In addition to ignorance, general indifference arises also from the passage of time. 'Why care about the Tokyo Trial now?' was an immediate reaction shared by most interviewees. More interestingly, there is a strange kind of 'temporal demarcation'. As some academics analyse, there is 'a radical break in 1945' in the Japanese psyche, that is a clear demarcation between pre-war and post-war Japan.[85] The Tokyo Trial was conducted at the juncture of war and peace, as 'the last act of the war and first act of the peace'.[86] However, to the Japanese, it was more 'the last act of the war'. 'The US army of occupation and the Tokyo Trial do not exist in parallel in my image', a man in his late thirties stated.[87] Although the two were issues of the same period of time, the former is the image associated with the beginning of peace. A man born in 1959 stated: 'For me, even though the Tokyo Trial took place not that long before when I was born, it seems like a thing from the distant past'.[88] These comments imply that the Tokyo Trial for the Japanese is an event that is related to pre-war and wartime Japan and, thus, is detached from the current Japan and pushed to the bottom of their collective memory together with the war itself.

Cynicism: 'victor's justice'

In addition to indifference based on ignorance and demarcation, apathy among the Japanese derives also from cynicism, which is strongly based on a widely shared understanding that the Tokyo Trial was 'victor's justice'. Irrespective of the amount of knowledge acquired and of age, almost all the interviewees expressed their belief or supposition that the Tokyo Trial was an unfair trial *because* it had been conducted by the victor of the war against the vanquished. In talking about the trial, most of the interviewees repeatedly used terms such as 'victor', 'vanquished', 'winning' the war or 'defeat' in the war.

Unlike the revisionists, the 'Tokyo Trial view of history' as such was rarely mentioned by the interviewees; however, a number of them believed that the trial had succeeded in stigmatizing Japan as an evil villain. 'The Allies wanted to create the impression that Japan was wrong', commented a businessman in his forties.[89] 'It was needed as a symbol of whom to blame', stated a student, 'Otherwise, why was such a thing needed? Everybody was wrong, weren't they? I wondered when I first heard about the Tokyo Trial whether defeat equals wrong doing'.[90] The view is shared by various other interviewees who echoed that the Tokyo Trial had been conducted by the victor in order to justify the war *ex post facto*.[91] Some sensed that the trial was a punishment given for disciplinary purposes. A student in a focus group commented as follows:

> It was a show trial, perhaps for people in China and Korea. After the war, you need a 'bad guy', you need to clarify who was bad. The Tokyo Trial was a way of clarifying that. That is my image. Image of a scapegoat.[92]

The victor's mentality of 'establishing the history' by a trial to prove they had had a just cause in fighting against the evil enemies was also pointed out by various Japanese academics.[93]

In general, however, 'victor's justice' has not necessarily caused an emotional reaction, except in the case of some nationalists and revisionists. Instead, it has created cynicism: 'The Tokyo Trial was a result of the defeat, nothing more'. This is based on the logic of 'might is right'.[94] Cynicism deprives the trial of the positive educational impact it expected to convey to the Japanese. This attitude was already of concern to some academics and commentators at the time of the Tokyo Trial. Gushima Kanesaburō lamented soon after the Tokyo judgment that many people recognized the trial with 'might is right' logic and that their understanding of the trial's legal basis and jurisdiction and of its significance were insufficient.[95] Ōhara Yasuo, an academic, saw the Tokyo Trial as mere 'victor's justice' and doubted if there were any lessons to be learned from it: 'The only way to make use of the Tokyo Trial is to examine the fact that the trial did not contribute to post-Second World War international peace at all'.[96]

'Victor's justice' also lessens the educational impact by confusing people about exactly what the Tokyo Trial judged. The dialogue between two interviewees in their thirties and forties on 'what was judged' is indicative:

I: Aggressive war, the responsibility for the war, I think. It was to do with starting the war.
J: But if you talk about responsibility for starting the war, regardless of winning or losing, how about Bush and the Iraq War?
I: Well, if we talk about starting the war, I think it was the responsibility more of the Emperor rather than Tōjō.
J: That's true.
I: Then, the Tokyo Trial may not have been to do with starting the war.... Then was it to do with the treatment of POWs?
J: But it was the victor's trial against the vanquished, right?
I: The Allies judged Japanese war criminals ...
J: Does that mean Japan was tried because it lost the war? If it had won, it wouldn't have been judged?
I: Yes, yes.
J: That's funny.[97]

Interviews also showed that there were some, though a minority, who expressed strong antipathy against 'victor's justice', through which the nature of the influence of neo-nationalism and revisionism could be observed. In each of three focus groups with university students, consisting of three to eight people, there was one person who vocally criticized the Tokyo Trial.[98] They were the ones who showed the most interest in and knowledge of the Tokyo Trial. Focus groups embodied what is illustrated in Chapter 4: those who enthusiastically talk about the Tokyo Trial tend to be strongly critical of it. These small minorities all stated that they had gained knowledge of the Tokyo Trial through their readings of well-known right-wing authors, and the logic of their arguments exactly echoed those of the neo-nationalists and revisionists: that the Tokyo Trial was imposed by the victor to destroy the Japanese mentality, that it disgraced Japanese-ness and pride and that many Japanese hold the 'masochist view of history'. 'With hindsight, I think I was very much brainwashed by my education', said an undergraduate student in a focus group: 'At the time, I strongly held the view that the war was wrong and the Tokyo Trial was right'.[99] A postgraduate student in another focus group supported the anti-'Tokyo Trial view of history' movement:

> After having read books like Kobayashi's, I thought Japan has been too obedient to the United States. We have also leaned too far to the left. We should push ourselves a bit more towards the right. And as a start, I welcome the movement that is re-examining the Tokyo Trial. Through

> reading right-wing literature, I have found that there are so many things that the United States is hiding. I think it is wrong to accept a given history.[100]

A businessman said he was currently interested in the Tokyo Trial after having read Nakajō's book. He stated: 'The history class at school was boring. I now know that this was because it portrayed a masochist view of history'.[101]

Overall, 'victor's justice' deprives people of the will to reflect on the Tokyo Trial and learn the lessons from it. People fail to understand not only for what reasons their past leaders were prosecuted and punished but also what such prosecution meant to Japan. At worst, it provides justification to nullify the significance of the war crimes prosecution as a whole. Awaya is concerned that there has been 'a social illusion that one can avoid facing Japan's war crimes and war responsibility by pointing out the defects of the Allies' war crimes tribunals'.[102]

Education and long-term educative impact of the Tokyo Trial

As mentioned earlier, although there are those who sympathize with neo-nationalism and revisionism, most of the interviewees distanced themselves from the revisionist view that affirms Japan's past war. Interestingly, comments made by interviewees suggest that people do not agree with the revisionist claims not merely because of the content of those claims but also because of the political and ideological agenda they sense behind those claims. According to an interviewee in her thirties, 'After all, what those revisionists are saying is a self-justification of aggression. I cannot sympathize with that'.[103] A student stated:

> I wonder if those who claim that the Tokyo Trial has had a negative impact on current Japanese society are raising their voices because they are ashamed of the defeat of the past. I feel some concern about their stirring up nationalism in such a way.[104]

An interviewee born in 1949 commented:

> I do understand what those people are trying to say, because you can interpret history totally differently depending on your standpoint. But I think we should not mix up what one wanted to have happened and what has actually happened. It does not change the fact. … It is a distortion of history to deny a certain view of history by saying that it would harm the pride of Japanese youth. I do understand them wanting to think that Japan has not done such a thing, but it is not the fact.[105]

These comments, however, are not necessarily backed up by solid knowledge and understanding of history. The above interviewee in her thirties, for example, based her view on a number of claims made by Asian victims. She could not deny the revisionist's claim that she as well as the Japanese as a whole were 'brainwashed'. Nonetheless, she said:

> I don't want to say that Japan's war was *not* aggressive. I don't want to justify past militarism in such a way. As a Japanese person, I don't want people in other countries to equate Japan present-day with militarism or a country that invaded Asian nations. That may be why I admit the aggression, detaching myself and present-day Japan from its past militarism.[106]

Several interviewees saw points in the neo-nationalist and revisionist assertion that the Japanese have been brainwashed. Interestingly, however, this did not lead to accepting their argument. A man in his late thirties stated:

> For them, my view is the 'Tokyo Trial's view', right? If they say I am brainwashed, yes, I may be. If you examine the history in detail, it is true that it was not only Japan who was wrong and you can say that there was no need to try Japan in such a harsh way. But I think at that time there was no other option but the 'Tokyo Trial's view'. It may be possible from now on to redeem history by relativizing the 'Tokyo Trial's view', and defending Japan's conduct as a necessary evil within international relations as they were then.... But, can wrongdoing be justified if you did it for the sake of your country? Things done were wrong because they were conducted by sacrificing people in other countries.[107]

Some students saw a positive meaning in being 'masochistic'. A student in a focus group commented:

> I don't know about the authenticity of each historical view. But without some elements of a 'masochistic view', the war will keep on being justified, while self-examination diminishes. The war might have been just and such a claim may be right, and in that sense, we may not need to be totally masochistic. But we should not forget self-examination; otherwise, we can go to extremes.[108]

Another student in the group agreed: 'I've read Tsukurukai's textbook but it was romanticizing Japan too much. Why can't we have a middle ground? We need to have both views'.[109] A student in the same focus group who expressed strong criticism towards the Tokyo Trial's view of history also agreed with these comments. Without direct experience of the war and being detached from the past, the younger generations are more 'pragmatic' and future-oriented, seeking what is needed for present-day Japan. An interviewee born in 1974 stated: 'For our generation, it is more constructive to admit what has happened in the past. It is not being obsequious'.[110]

However, these comments also indicate people's reluctance to examine and understand the country's past and to verify the view they hold. It seems that the Japanese people are feeling 'comfortable' or 'safe' in admitting criminality in their country's past, whether it is true or not; in other words, stick to the 'Tokyo Trial's view of history', rather than dig-up and face the painful past.

This attitude, while accepting the country's past wrongdoing, does not mean, in a real sense, that 'Japan is facing its history'. And, it is here that the neo-nationalist and revisionist has a point in criticizing the Japanese people's easy acceptance of the 'given history'.

At the same time, regarding such a general attitude, another, albeit more subtle, aspect of the Tokyo Trial's 'educational impact' can be observed. Asada Sadao, scholar of diplomatic history, pointed out: 'Not knowing about the Tokyo Trial per se, people are well-aware of its legacy: anti-war and anti-military consciousness and pacifism. In many ways, they may be indebted to the educational impact of the Tokyo Trial'.[111] Asada's point was echoed especially by the post-war generation. 'The Tokyo Trial says that you become a villain if you wage war, becoming war criminals and tried', an interviewee born in 1959 concluded.[112] An undergraduate student at a focus group regarded the Tokyo Trial as good because it had changed the Japanese perception of the war.[113]

It is here that the Tokyo Trial's historical record and its educational impact are ambivalent. On the one hand, the Trial had encouraged the spirit of anti-militarism and pacifism, which since have been very strong in the Japanese. On the other hand, the trial did not provide a 'history lesson' as such, as some promoters of the tribunal had intended. Instead, in the long run, the Tokyo Trial's historical record prevented the enhancement of the Japanese people's understanding of the war and war crimes, by giving them an excuse for not examining detail of the war and making judgment on it by themselves. Ara Takashi argues that the limitations of the Tokyo Trial lie in the fact that it pursued responsibility mostly of the 'aggressiveness' of the wartime national power and authorized the American view of history along the way; what was required was 'a historical perception from the view of the Japanese people and the pursuit of war responsibility based on it'.[114] Kojima Noboru argues that the 'Tokyo Trial view of history' has put 'a brake on dispassionate research on the history of the period'.[115] He expresses a concern that the strong influence of the 'Tokyo Trial view of history' 'shrouds the most important aspects of history and leads us to forfeit opportunities for reflection and research'.[116]

In spite of some educational impact and legacy, the Tokyo Trial and its historical record has not been visible in Japanese society. The Japanese are well aware of their ignorance of the Tokyo Trial. Most of the interviewees excused themselves more than once for their lack of knowledge of the trial. Interestingly, most of them attributed this to their having not learned about it at school; almost all the interviewees of the post-war generation said that they had no memory of having learned about the Tokyo Trial. A high school history teacher admitted that very little is taught about the Tokyo Trial at school.[117] She immediately attributed this to the Japanese education system based on the needs of the university entrance examinations, in which pre-Second World War history only is questioned in detail. However, she also stated that history after the end of the Second World War has not yet been clearly established, even after more than half a century: 'On the part of teachers, there is not yet agreement regarding from which standpoint and in what way the history of the period can be taught, or what is right and wrong'. She pointed out that some teach August 1945 as 'the end of the war', and some as 'the defeat in the war'. The Tokyo Trial is embedded in this delicate period, which is not yet settled in the eyes of the Japanese. The teacher concluded: 'History education in Japan does not deal with raw incidents of modern history; it only deals with issues about which no one disagrees'.[118] This is sensed by former students. A woman in her mid-fifties reflected on the education she had received in the 1960s: 'We were not taught about the Tokyo Trial at school *not* because of a lack of space within the timetable, but because of the topic itself. People don't want to touch it. I sense that in our society'.[119]

Taboo and silence over the Tokyo Trial

Several interviewees admitted that issues of 'this kind' – the war and war crimes of the past – are what the Japanese have been reluctant to talk about in public.[120] The very problem surrounding the Tokyo Trial and the Japanese people is that it is either talked about emotionally and ideologically within a limited circle, or simply ignored by the majority of the population in spite of its importance in Japanese modern history.[121] In addition to indifference and cynicism on the part of the Japanese, this attitude is strongly related to the general perception that the Tokyo Trial is a national taboo. Intensive interviews revealed this perception as well as the complex features of this perceived taboo, which consists of multiple elements.

The first element of the taboo is the Japanese people's reluctance to face the issues that were examined by the tribunal. Asada states that it has been difficult to talk about the Tokyo Trial in Japan because an examination of it makes people face the tribunal defendants:

> I think there is a kind of guilty consciousness among the Japanese, a consciousness that there were many others who could have been tried but were not tried. People may be reluctant to re-examine only the victims of the Tokyo Trial.[122]

Many interviewees of the post-war generation pointed out that their parents and grandparents often talked about the national sufferings of the war but rarely about war responsibility and the Tokyo Trial. They sensed significance in the older generation's silence over the trial. An interviewee stated:

> For the wartime generation, talking about the Tokyo Trial would mean talking about their own guilt. They supported the war but only their leaders were tried. The desire to evade one's own responsibility, the desire to put the blame on someone else, has prevented people from talking about the Tokyo Trial. They don't want to touch the war anymore. The issue of the Tokyo Trial, I think, is a taboo for them.[123]

Asada also points out that the things and events that were revealed in the trial were not at all comfortable for the Japanese to look at closely, especially after more than half a century. 'I think the Tokyo Trial is a national taboo', states Asada, who himself did not give a lecture on the Tokyo Trial during his seminar on the history of US–Japan relations. 'I think I had been avoiding the topic unconsciously. It is not a topic that can be dealt with from a neutral standpoint'.[124] 'I don't think there is a country that makes a point of emphasizing its own stain and disgrace', a man in his forties stated.[125] His view is echoed by another.[126] It is not only issues examined at the tribunal but also the war crimes trial itself that are uncomfortable for the Japanese to face. This may be related to the point examined earlier: although it was conducted after the war under the US occupation, the Tokyo Trial, unlike other occupation policies, is associated not with post-war but with wartime Japan and, thus, people have preferred to banish it from their memory. The Tokyo Trial simply does not fit in well with Japan's post-war identity.

Second, the taboo comes also from the issues that were *not* examined by the tribunal: the Emperor, human-body experiments and war crimes under colonial rule.[127] For the Japanese, the re-examination of the Tokyo Trial means opening Pandora's Box. How does the nation face the responsibility of the Emperor and Unit 731, both of which were left untouched even by the tribunal? On the issue of the Emperor's war responsibility, for example, it is not until his death in 1989 that it gradually came to be actively discussed in public. However, even after the death of the Emperor, the issue remained a taboo, or at least a difficult issue to discuss in Japan. In 1990, the mayor of Nagasaki was shot by an ultra-nationalist because of his comment that the Emperor had responsibility for the war. Indeed, the issue of the Emperor is one of the focal points of strong disagreement between the rightist and leftist view of the war. At the same time, some of the wartime generation felt relieved that the Emperor's war responsibility was 'settled by outsiders'.[128] In other words, the Tokyo Trial has given a good excuse for the Japanese to close the debate on the Emperor's wartime responsibility, which is too delicate for them to face by themselves.[129]

The third and most significant aspect of the taboo is the fact that the Tokyo Trial is strongly related to another sensitive issue: how to see the nature of the war, which has been debated politically and ideologically. In fact, in Japan, there is even now no consensus on how to refer to the war that ended in 1945: 'the Second World War', 'the (Asian-)Pacific War', 'Fifteen-Years War' or 'the Greater East Asia War', each of which is strongly associated with different views on the nature of the war.[130] Many of the government's and the Emperor's statements still call the war 'the *previous* war' (*saki no sensō*). This illustrates well the delicacy of the issue.

The Tokyo Trial is related to this unsettled issue because the trial itself has offered a specific account of the war. And, it is the Trial's account of the war, rather than its general significance and lessons, that has been the focus of debates on the Tokyo Trial. This can be seen from the fact that even in interdisciplinary symposiums on the Tokyo Trial in 1983 and 1996, there were heated debates especially on the tribunal's historical account and the issue of the trial's historical significance.[131] Igarashi Takeshi, one of the organizers of the 1996 symposium, expresses his particular interest in the reason why the symposium was so successful. At the same time, he expresses some anxiety about the fact that the symposium heated up in ways different from what the organizers had expected. The symposium, according to Igarashi, was different from ordinary ones: the participants actively expressed agreement and disagreement with presentations and some even stood up and shouted at panel members. Igarashi, as an historian, states: 'our understanding about how much the Tokyo Trial had left a deep scar on the Japanese people's perception of history was not enough'.[132]

Because of its account of the war, the Tokyo Trial became surrounded by political and ideological arguments, and these various 'isms' have become obstacles to a frank examination of the Trial. Andō Nisuke, an international legal scholar, pointed out that under the 'absolute pacifism' proliferating in post-war Japan, 'criticizing the Tokyo Trial itself was a taboo'.[133] Being critical of the Tokyo Trial does not necessarily mean denying the tribunal's judgment that Japan conducted aggressive war and war crimes, and valuing the trial is not equal to the acceptance of the whole judgment. However, they are inseparable in the Japanese mentality. The connection between the Tokyo Trial and its account of the war is so strong that it is not possible to repudiate the former without being seen to challenge the latter,[134] and doing so, as Andō pointed out, has been a taboo in post-war Japan with its new image of a peace-loving nation. Indeed, soon after the occupation, there was some hesitation among the media to criticize the trial, because of a fear that the criticism would have led to a justification of Japan's militarist past.[135]

On the other hand, valuing the trial is easily targeted by nationalists as a masochistic attitude towards history, lacking national pride, confidence and patriotism. It is here that the revisionists and neo-nationalists are trapped by the strong link between the trial and its historical account: it is not always clear whether a 'masochist attitude' refers to the acceptance of the fact that Japan conducted aggressive war and war crimes, or to the acceptance of the historical account that was imposed by the victor through an international trial. In other words, those who attack the 'Tokyo Trial view of history' seem to base their claim on the inaccuracy of the view as much as on the inappropriateness of the way the view was proposed by the trial. These are two different issues that need to be examined separately; just as an inaccurate historical account can be given through appropriate procedures, a correct historical account can be given through inappropriate methods. It is unfortunate that the two are put together as part of the same emotional argument that aims at the total negation of the Tokyo Trial. At the same time, it should be noted that although those who denounce the trial and its judgment tend to adopt the nationalist and revisionist posture, to regard their denunciation simply as a newly emerged, ultra-nationalist tendency misses the significance of those criticisms that point out problems related to the trial that need to be re-examined.

The fact that the Tokyo Trial has not been a popular topic for academics in the field is relevant to the above point. Some point out that in Japan modern history is regarded as 'too fluid, too political, too controversial' for an academic topic and thus as 'something best left to journalists'.[136] Emotional and ideological debates conducted by journalists, polemicists or academics not specialized in the field, in turn, might have 'scared away' serious academics from conducting research on the Tokyo Trial. In the eyes of a non-Japanese Tokyo Trial researcher, Japanese scholars have been avoiding the Tokyo Trial. Minear wrote in the 1970s: 'Where some coverage was unavoidable, they have tended to affirm the validity of the trial and its verdict. Apparently, they fear that denigration of the trial will lead to a positive reevaluation of Japan's wartime policies and leadership'.[137]

The pitfall in criticizing the Tokyo Trial is acknowledged by Minear himself. In the preface for the Japanese version of his *Victors' Justice*, he stated that he hoped that Japanese readers would learn that the Tokyo Trial was a large-scale, staged event based on a dubious US presumption. At the same time, he did not forget to emphasize: 'I also hope that the Japanese reader will understand that this book does not immunize or defend Japanese policy during the 1930s and 1940s. The problem of historical responsibility remains irrelevant to innocence in legal terms'.[138] Despite Minear's concern, it was his book that impressed Fujioka very much: 'The scales fell from my eyes', he commented having read Minear's book.[139] The difficulty of criticizing the Tokyo Trial constructively can also be seen from the fact that Judge Pal, who wrote a dissenting opinion challenging the jurisdiction of the Tokyo Tribunal and acquitting every defendant, has been a favourite figure for the nationalists and revisionists, who regard him as the person Japan should be grateful to, and his opinion as the bible. His comment, 'The name of Justice should not be allowed to be invoked only for the prolongation of the pursuit of vindictive retaliation', is often quoted in those anti-Tokyo Trial publications.[140] When he died in 1967, an association of the relatives of convicted war criminals held a memorial service in Tokyo.[141]

The difficulty sensed by academics and intellectuals in examining the Tokyo Trial is also shared by the general public. Almost all the interviewees, who at first had shown very little interest in the Tokyo Trial, expressed at the end of the interview that they had enjoyed talking about it and had realized its significance to contemporary Japan. Many said that they wanted to know more about the Tokyo Trial as well as Japan's war history. However, they also expressed their reluctance and discomfort to talk about it in public, for fear of being involved in ideological disputes. 'I hear about the Tokyo Trial from debates on the pros and cons of the trial', stated an interviewee in her late twenties: 'The debate seems to be conducted among people with very biased ideas, and I don't want to be involved in it'.[142] Participants of one focus group said that they enjoyed having talked about the Tokyo Trial, having exchanged various opinions with other participants. However, one commented at the very end: 'We usually cannot talk about this kind of issue on the street or in a casual manner. People would think we are "wacky"'. Another also agreed and stated that was why she usually did not talk about the Tokyo Trial.[143]

'I don't mind talking about the Tokyo Trial to you', said a man in his mid-sixties: 'But I don't want to talk about this kind of issue to strangers. I don't want to be misunderstood'.[144] He regarded the fact that comments on war and responsibility are very easily taken either as a right- or left-wing stance to be a serious problem. After having strongly criticized the Tokyo Trial, a businessman in his forties excused himself: 'Don't take me as being on the far-right. I am not one of those Emperor worshipers'.[145] A woman in her mid-fifties showed discomfort during the interview in case her comments were taken as those of a leftist.[146] This kind of hesitation was not seen among undergraduate students born in the 1980s. This is an interesting difference between the generations. For these students, it was not right/left political ideology but a lack of knowledge that made talking about the Tokyo Trial difficult.[147] They were not only ignorant of the Tokyo Trial but were seemingly unaware of political debates and taboos that surround the issue. A focus group with third-year undergraduate students gave an impression that substantive discussion of the Tokyo Trial is difficult to conduct with people in their early twenties and below. It is worth examining what kind of perception the young generation, with little knowledge of Japan's past, is going to hold from now on.[148]

Andō states that in the Tokyo Trial there are several points that the Japanese can positively adopt: 'The Tokyo Trial can be a good textbook for seeing things from a wider perspective, instead of doing so from the right and left in their extreme forms'.[149] It is ironic that the Tokyo Trial and its historical record have become the fuel for such an ideological debate. The Tokyo Trial's account in fact satisfies neither the right nor left. They are both unhappy about the trial's account, as well as the Japanese people's indifference to the past war and war crimes. The rightists cannot accept the Tokyo Trial for having conveyed the view that has made the Japanese obsequious and masochistic, and the leftist criticizes the Tokyo Trial for not having done enough to reveal Japan's war crimes against Asian civilians. Caught in the middle, the majority prefers to remain silent.

The trial's historical record and post-war Japan's reconciliation and transformation

This last section conducts some analysis on how the Japanese historical perception in relation with the Tokyo Trial affects Japan's reconciliation with neighbouring countries as well as its own past. Regarding the relation between Japan and other Asian countries, Funabashi Yōichi, the chief diplomatic correspondent for *Asahi Shimbun*, claims that it is a deepened historical consciousness more than an apology that is necessary for reconciliation: 'We have apologized at various times. But that would make the current young generation resistant and obstinate. What is important is not an apology but the historical consciousness of why we have to apologize'.[150] Facing and addressing the past war and cultivating historical understanding are the important first steps for reconciliation not only with victims but also with one's own past, which is necessary for social transformation, in a real sense, of post-war society. According to the 'Nuremberg legacy', the historical record of the event created through an international war crimes tribunal endorses and contributes to these processes. A question here is whether this is the case with the Tokyo Trial and post-war Japan. Examination of this chapter so far suggests a rather negative picture.

The 'history problem', even after more than 60 years, is a major, sensitive political issue between Japan and China and South Korea.[151] Japanese historical consciousness of and atonement for the past have been questioned by its neighbouring countries whenever high-ranking politicians make 'careless' comments about the war and responsibility for it.[152] Since the late 1990s, the problem has become even more serious over the revisionist textbook rows and Prime Minister Koizumi Junichirō's visits to the Yasukuni shrine. On Yasukuni, Koizumi was criticized by China and South Korea for having visited as Prime Minister the place that enshrines the spirit of Class A war criminals.[153] On the Prime Minister's visit to the shrine in August 2004, the Chinese Foreign Ministry released a strong statement: 'The Chinese side hopes the Japanese side will honour its word by *facing up to history*'.[154] In 2005, when the latest version of Tsukurukai's revisionist textbook passed the government's check and certificate process, the nations of China and South Korea reacted so fiercely as to have caused critical diplomatic tension between Japan and the two countries, especially China. Reactionary uprisings in China, which put Japanese people and property there in danger, in turn, caused national resentment on the part of Japan. The Tokyo Trial itself is not the direct focus of these rows. However, the facts that Class A war criminals are the core problem of the Yasukuni row and that the revisionists have been working hard to proliferate an alternative to the 'Tokyo Trial view of history' indicate that the Tokyo Trial plays a role, though possibly an indirect and subtle one, in history problems that have been preventing reconciliation in East Asia.

As examined above, the neo-nationalist movement does not embody the general historical perception held by the Japanese. The majority of the population regard the aggressive nature of the past war, and unlike the assertion made by China and South Korea, Japanese children, especially since the 1980s, do learn at school about Japan's war crimes.[155] Nonetheless, compared to post-war Germany, Japanese society has been relatively 'permissive' to nationalist and revisionist words and deeds. This permissiveness is partly based on the idea that people are free to hold whatever view they like, which was expressed by several interviewees who distanced themselves from the revisionist view of the past war.[156]

However, it is also based on the Japanese people's passive attitude and ignorance of their past. Having been asked about the victims' demands for compensation and apology as well as the revisionists' claim to oppose those requests, several interviewees confessed that they did not have enough knowledge to accept or deny those views. A student at one focus group stated that the revisionist claim 'confused' her, so that she did not know what to believe.[157] This is echoed by some others. 'We don't even know much about the whole picture of the war. So we cannot say anything even when we talk about it with other Asian people', an interviewee commented: 'That must be irritating for them'.[158] Indeed, such a Japanese attitude is often criticized as 'collective historical amnesia' and may be an obstacle, together with loud but minority voices that deny Japan's past war crimes, for Japan's reconciliation with its neighbours.

With this ambivalent historical perception, some interviewees stated that they felt better admitting to the past war crimes and apologizing in order to create friendly relations with their Asian neighbours; some others were frustrated about the fact that they were forced to respond to the issue of war crimes that they were not sure actually happened.[159] The former prefers not to challenge the criminality of the past war and 'received view of history'; to the latter, the claims of the neo-nationalist that provide a release from the burdens of the past appeal immensely. In either case, they are not helpful not only for reconciliation but also for cultivating historical understanding and healthy national identity.

The Japanese passive attitude towards the past or its oft-cited collective historical amnesia is in some part the legacy of the Tokyo Trial's historical record. The Japanese did not have to face the war directly because they were given a judgment on and explanation of their war by an international tribunal in the name of international justice. In the long run, this deprived the Japanese of the will and opportunity to face and judge their past and build up their own historical view. This is why some students majoring in history saw the neo-nationalist and revisionist claims as in a sense a 'healthy' and 'natural' reaction, compared to the national hesitation to discuss and challenge the taboo of the war and war crimes.[160] At the same time, debates on the nature of the war in general and the Tokyo Trial's account of the war in specific, are often conducted ideologically and emotionally; accordingly, the majority of the population find it difficult to examine the trial as well as war crimes frankly and keep quiet. The 'silence' examined in this chapter is different from 'amnesia' but the difference may not be clear in the eyes of the victims.

The logic of the 'Nuremberg legacy' goes: the 'authoritative' record of the event offered by an international tribunal not only discredits responsible leaders but also preserves and cultivates collective memory, which is necessary for restoring the national identity, and thus social transformation of war-torn society.[161] However, Japan is still struggling to come to terms with the war and cultivate post-war national identity exactly because of an absence of reconciliation and an unsettled past. The Tokyo Trial not only failed to contribute to but also became an obstacle to the Japanese becoming reconciled to the past. It is questionable whether the trial's record of history was the catalyst for cultivating the sound national historical consciousness or hindrance to it.

Conclusion

The Tokyo Trial attempted to promote the demilitarization and democratization of post-war Japan through presenting an 'authoritative' historical record of the war. In one aspect, the trial contributed to these strategic purposes by revealing the facts and criminality of the war, which had been hidden from the nation. Although the trial's account of the war had several factual defects, Japanese people accepted the account with shock and a distrust of their wartime leaders;

and the majority of the nation still perceive the aggressive nature of their past war and war crimes committed there. However, it is not clear whether this perception can be attributed to the Tokyo Trial's historical record, as the neo-nationalists and revisionists claim. Collective memory of the war is not so simple as to be created and cultivated only by war crimes trials; the American occupation policy consisted of various elements and the Tokyo Trial was merely one of its tactics. The fact that the Tokyo Trial itself is not visible in Japanese collective memory may suggest that the trial in fact did not play a direct or major role here.

However, at least it can be concluded that the Tokyo Trial's historical record *did not* contribute to finalizing the history of a traumatic experience and a controversial period of the Japan's past. The Japanese still, after more than 60 years, hold an ambiguous and unsettled view of the war, and have not successfully come to terms with their past. This can be seen from the simple fact that even in the twenty-first century, major newspapers conducted opinion polls asking the nation questions like 'whether Japan's war was aggressive or not' and that the result showed a number of people responded 'do not know'. This reflects the nation's ambivalent attitude towards their past. In the midst of the confusion and despair after the defeat, the Japanese were given a judgment on their war by an international tribunal, which they were prepared to accept, albeit, unenthusiastically, instead of re-examining the painful event by themselves, at the time or later on. In this sense, the International Military Tribunal deprived the Japanese of the will and opportunity to judge their own past. This promoted a general indifference to the war and war crimes.

At the same time, the Tokyo Trial has left fertile ground for emotional debates over the interpretation of the war. This can be seen from the fact that the historical account of the past is debated by some by referring to the Tokyo Trial. The 'authoritativeness' of the trial's account of the war has been severely attacked by revisionists and nationalists, not only on the content of the account but also on the fact that such an account was the creation of 'victor's justice'. What is more, as ongoing arguments over textbooks and the Yasukuni shrine show, the Tokyo Trial itself is embedded in the 'history problem' between Japan and its neighbouring countries. Instead of establishing a history in the eyes of the Japanese, the Tokyo Trial haunts the nation whenever it turns its face to the past.

The interpretation of the Tokyo Trial's verdict is strongly associated with how one views the past war and present-day Japan and recognizes one's own national identity, which makes the trial a highly political, ideological and emotional topic. As interviews and focus groups clearly showed, these ideological and emotional debates surrounding the Tokyo Trial deter the majority of Japanese people from thinking and talking about the trial and war crimes in a casual and frank manner. Above all, the issues that were judged, and not judged, by the Tokyo Trial as well as the trial itself are traumatic events for the Japanese. In sum, the Tokyo Trial itself came to be perceived as a national taboo. This is an important element, together with indifference and cynicism, that constitutes the national silence, or 'historical amnesia', as perceived from the outside.

The Tokyo Trial has stimulated nationalist and revisionist zeal on the one hand, and contributed, unintentionally, to the majority's 'apathy' on the other, both of which hinder Japan's reconciliation with its Asian neighbours. This unsettled past and lack of reconciliation are serious obstacles to Japan's social transformation in a real sense, which is frustratedly held back by the past even after 60 years. These points lead to a conclusion that the Tokyo Trial plays rather negatively to reconciliation and the social transformation of post-war Japan. This not only questions one aspect of the contemporary 'Nuremberg legacy' regarding the positive impact of the historical record of an international trial on post-conflict societies, but also shows an example of how such a record actually influences the difficult processes of transformation that post-war society has to go through.

This ambivalent Japanese historical view of the past directly relates to the ambivalence shown towards the issue of war responsibility. Utsumi Aiko argues that the fact that there is still no consensus among the Japanese on what to call the past war synchronizes with the Japanese omission to examine actively the war and its responsibility.[162] Indeed, reconciliation as well as 'coming to terms with the past' consists not only of how the nation perceives the past war; it needs to be accompanied by 'how people become aware of their war responsibility and how they fulfil that responsibility'.[163] The following chapter analyses in what way the Tokyo Trial influenced the Japanese sense of war guilt and responsibility, focusing on another device of the tribunal: the individualization of war responsibility.

6 The Tokyo Trial and the individualization of responsibility

According to current understanding of the 'Nuremberg legacy', individual criminal punishment in the aftermath of mass atrocities is necessary for the de-collectivization of responsibility, which contributes to the detachment of the leaders most responsible from the majority of the population, the de-collectivization of hatred felt by the victim, and the endorsement of social transformation of the nation by freeing them from the burden of guilt and the traumatic past.[1] The aim of this chapter is to examine whether this applies to the case of the Tokyo Trial, by focusing on the perception and understanding of the Japanese, both at the time and at present, regarding responsibility for the war. The chapter does not analyse the Japanese sense of war guilt and responsibility per se. With regard to the aim of this study, the chapter limits the examination of the people's sense of war responsibility to its relationship to the Tokyo Trial; that is, whether, and to what extent, people's sense of war responsibility is affected by their leaders having been prosecuted under the international war crimes trial.

The chapter first examines the way the Japanese understood through the Tokyo Trial the individual responsibility of their leaders, then moves on to examine how people perceived their own responsibility for the war. The chapter also examines, through intensive interviews and focus groups, how the current generation perceives 'collective guilt' for the war. People's sense of war responsibility and guilt is an important barometer for grasping the impact of individualized criminal punishment and its effect and limitations with regard to de-collectivizing responsibility and guilt. Finally, the chapter analyses how the current Japanese sense of war responsibility influences Japan's reconciliation with its victims as well as its own past.

Individual responsibility pursued: the effects of individual criminal punishment

The Tokyo Trial was embedded in the Allies' policy to demilitarize and democratize post-war Japan. By pursuing the individual responsibility of Japanese wartime leaders through a legal process, the trial aimed to detach the military from the majority of the nation both practically and psychologically.[2] This itself was not a very difficult task for the Allies, as in the aftermath of the war, the Japanese felt shock, frustration and anger towards their wartime leaders for wartime hardship and defeat in the war that the nation had been told they would win.[3] George Atcheson, Jr, the Acting Political Adviser in Japan, pointed out the general mood among the Japanese 'of fixing war responsibility on the major suspects' and the probability of changes in that mood in the coming months and noted in December 1945: 'it accordingly seems to me highly desirable to start the trials and get them over with as soon as possible during this period when the prosecution will, as regards the majority of those listed, receive popular support'.[4] While the United States had tried to take advantage of Japanese people's negative sentiment towards their military leaders in conducting war crimes prosecutions, it attempted to strengthen such sentiments through the Tokyo Trial.

Towards demilitarization and demarcation

By prosecuting and punishing individual wartime leaders, the Tokyo Trial clarified whom to blame for national suffering, pointing a finger at the military clique. At the same time, the trial labelled the Japanese as victims of their military leaders. Joseph Keenan, chief prosecutor of the tribunal, stated in his opening statement: 'We must reach the conclusion that the Japanese people themselves were utterly within the power and forces of these accused, and to such extent were its victims'.[5] The Tokyo Trial thus tried to appeal to people's 'victim consciousness'.[6] A sense of 'having been deceived' by wartime leaders, which was widely shared in the aftermath of the war, was also strengthened by the Tokyo Trial's account of the aggressive aspects of Japan's war and war crimes committed by the Japanese Imperial Army, of which the nation had not been informed.[7] A sense of 'having been deceived' and 'victim consciousness' were important elements that promoted the nation's detachment from their wartime leaders, especially the military.[8] The trial's direct impact on people's detachment from the military can be seen from the fact that many ex-servicemen, who had been sent off with great support, came back home after the war to find that they were regarded by society as 'war criminals'.[9]

Through individual criminal punishment, the Tokyo Trial also sent the message of demarcation from the past, the era of militarism. On the day of the judgment of the trial, the editorial of *Asahi Shimbun* emphasized:

> What we need to bear in mind is that this trial demands *the complete burial of the past Japan* coloured with the militarism which was cultivated by the defendants. The Trial also clearly prescribes that the country we, the nation, should construct in future is a peaceful nation.[10]

Mainichi Shimbun's editorial also echoed:

> The whole Japanese nation should support the zeal for peace and the spirit of democracy expressed in the judgment. Our focus on this point would be a

> big driving force in *moving Japan on from a past sealed 'aggression'* towards a new peaceful nation.[11]

These editorials show that Tokyo was regarded as a trial that eradicated the militarist past while providing Japan with a future based on new ideas: peace and democracy. The message of demarcation was firmly received by the Japanese who themselves were strongly hoping to start all over again.[12]

The Tokyo Trial had a symbolic effect: the Japanese were not only detached from their wartime leaders but also given a setting in which to bury the militarist past. The trial impressed upon the Japanese that they were the victims of the military clique who had deceived the nation and conducted aggression, and the people accepted the Tokyo Trial, albeit passively, as punishing 'the bad fellows' on their behalf. What is more, people recognized in the trial an opportunity to start from scratch as a peace-loving democratic nation, concentrating on the restoration of society without looking back on its militarist past. The Tokyo Trial's pursuit of individual responsibility succeeded in this sense. However, individual criminal punishment left an ambiguous 'legacy' in the Japanese understanding of war guilt and responsibility.

The side effects of the individualization of responsibility

The individualization of responsibility means the de-collectivization of responsibility. However, in cases of war, there are responsibilities that cannot be de-collectivized; the responsibility of leaders for having decided to wage war and the responsibility of the nation for having supported the leaders should be differentiated. This point was raised by the Japanese media at the time. The editorial of *Mainichi Shimbun* wrote after the judgment in Tokyo:

> What matters for all Japanese people is how they as a whole reflect on the end of the Tokyo Trial and its judgment. It is a big mistake to think that everything is completed and that the Japanese as a whole were purified by the punishment of several people in certain official positions having conducted certain actions. It is also a big mistake to assume that the matter is only relevant to the defendants. The defendants were punished for their own crimes and were not sacrificed for the crimes of the Japanese. Every Japanese person has to reflect deeply on 'crimes against peace'.[13]

Mainichi Shimbun also wrote on the day of execution of seven defendants:

> Nobody can assert that they are the only criminals and that all other Japanese people opposed the war … the responsibility of having caused the tragedy should be shared by the whole nation. Facing their executions, the Japanese should think over this point solemnly.[14]

On the part of the Japanese government, Prime Minister Higashikuni-nomiya Naruhiko announced, as early as late August 1945, the so-called 'collective repentance of the hundred million [*Ichioku Sōzange*]', claiming that the whole Japanese nation should be repentant to the Emperor for the defeat in the war. This claim indicated equal responsibility of the leaders and the nation and, in fact, meant that 'responsibility rested with nobody and [was] pursued by nobody'.[15]

The argument that the nation as a whole should embrace responsibility for the war, however, did not appeal to the Japanese at the time. This is not merely because of their anger towards wartime leaders but also because of the symbolic impact of the Tokyo Trial. The trial's punishment of the wartime leaders sent the majority of the nation messages, which caused four side effects: people's self-immunization from war responsibility, the limited understanding of war responsibility, the symbolic effect of the Emperor's immunity and the hasty closure of war crimes issues.

First, the de-collectivization of responsibility enabled the majority of Japanese people to protect themselves from personal responsibility for the war their country had fought. This was a result of 'victim consciousness' and a sense of 'having been deceived' by the leaders, which were, as seen above, reinforced by the way the Tokyo Trial was conducted. People's victim consciousness, that they were the 'victims' of the war recklessly fought by the military, prevented the Japanese from facing their role as the victimizers and thus facilitated self-immunization from war responsibility. While the Japanese people were shocked and appalled by the Tokyo Trial's account of the Nanjing massacre, such a reaction did not, at least during the occupation, encourage the people further to reflect on the suffering that their military had inflicted on other nations. Japan's war responsibility towards Asian countries was barely raised in public.[16] Some point out that the symbolic 'absence of Asia' in the trial enabled such Japanese attitude.[17] A sense of 'having been deceived' prevented the Japanese from taking war crimes examined under the trial as their own business. It also allowed people to rationalize their own wartime cooperation. This is well expressed in the following comment by a political cartoonist at the time: 'All of us people were deceived and used by them, and cooperated in the war without knowing the true facts. Looking back now, this was because of ignorance and being deceived'.[18] The result is self-justification and self-immunization of one's own responsibility for the war that the whole nation supported.[19]

With 'victim consciousness' and a sense of 'having been deceived', the Japanese at the time could and did, consciously or unconsciously, put the burden of all their war guilt and responsibility on the shoulders of the defendants at the trial. Accordingly, not only the defendants but also the crimes examined under the trial and its verdict were seen with a sense of detachment by the nation. In other words, the Japanese remained as 'bystanders' to the Tokyo Trial and did not take it actively and personally.[20] They could remain as such because the Tokyo Trial was not a stage on which the war responsibility of the Japanese nation was examined.

During the occupation, several Japanese scholars debated the Tokyo Trial from the perspective of war responsibility, including responsibility towards the Asian countries and the collective responsibility of the Japanese nation.[21] Some were even aware of responsibility for their having been deceived, and showed self-criticism on their having supported the government.[22] Although these arguments were elaborated in various forms, debates on the nation's war responsibility could not develop fully during this period. Arai Shinichi points out the Allies' strategic purpose in pursuing the leaders' responsibility, that is, the transformation of Japan, and argues that this is why 'it was very difficult at that point to talk about the nation's responsibility. It may have led to the total negation of the Tokyo Trial, the result of which might not have been positive at that time'.[23] There were strong warnings among academics and commentators that to bring up the issue of the collective war responsibility of the nation might nullify the Tokyo Trial that had pursued its leaders' individual responsibility. Accordingly, collective responsibility was pushed below individual responsibility pursued under the Tokyo Trial.[24]

Second, the pursuit of leaders' responsibility made people pay attention to 'responsibility for defeat' in the war, which could be taken only by high-ranking individuals. 'Responsibility for defeat' was easily perceived by the Japanese who had been suffering from the war and its aftermath and were conscious of being victims. A view of 'victor's justice' also reinforced the impression that what mattered in the trial was the defeat, not the waging of the war.[25] This 'limited' responsibility was expressed also by the defendants at the trial. In his affidavit read on 30 December 1947, Tōjō Hideki stated that there was a clear difference between the issue of whether the war was just or not and that of the responsibility for the defeat:

> I believe firmly and will contend to the last that it was a war of self-defense.... As to ... the responsibility for defeat, I feel that it devolves upon myself as Premier. The responsibility in that sense I am not only willing but sincerely desire to accept fully.[26]

The problem with the 'responsibility for defeat' was that it diminished the understanding of war responsibility, as it focused on the responsibility of leaders towards their nation, but not towards other nations.[27] In addition, 'responsibility for defeat' was a concept that related closely to the Japanese people's identification of themselves as victims of the war and the defeat. Nevertheless, the 'responsibility for defeat' might have had an extra positive effect from the Allied Powers' viewpoint. In the eyes of the Japanese public, the 'primary victimizer' for their suffering was no longer the enemy but their 'irresponsible leaders' who had been in charge of the war. Whether intended or not, this redirection of their hatred was vital for the United States to transform Japan into a friendly ally.

The third issue that had an important impact on the Japanese sense of war responsibility is the Tokyo Tribunal's treatment of the Emperor. The tribunal's individual criminal punishment was not applied to the Emperor, the Supreme Commander of the war. The extent to which the Emperor played an actual and vital role in planning and waging the wars of aggression has been fiercely debated. However, it is undeniable that the Japanese fought the war in the name of the Emperor, and all orders followed by soldiers during the war were given in his name. Many of those tried under Class B and C war crimes trials were soldiers from the battlefield who had followed orders from an immediate superior, which were taken as orders from the divine Emperor.[28]

On the part of the Japanese in the aftermath of the war, not a few voices longed for the Emperor to admit his war responsibility in some forms.[29] However, this was overtaken by the nation's acceptance of the new face of the Emperor as a 'human being' and a 'symbol of democracy'.[30] The Tokyo Trial's granting of immunity to the Emperor was welcomed by the Japanese people: 'The absence of the Emperor at the War Crimes Trial was a relief to most Japanese', Tsurumi Shunsuke reflects.[31] However, he continues: 'At the same time, it was considered a denial of the very logic of the trial for war crimes. This ambiguity is the most important aspect of the Japanese reaction'.[32] By means of the silence of the Tokyo Trial, the Emperor was seen to be innocent. By extension, the Emperor's innocence symbolized the innocence of the Japanese people who had waged the war in his name. In the words of Ian Buruma, 'like their emperor, they had been "deceived" by the military leaders'.[33]

The immunity of the Emperor given by the Tokyo Trial made the Japanese perception of war responsibility and war guilt ambiguous. John Dower frankly states what the Japanese themselves hesitate to say:

> If the man in whose name imperial Japan had conducted foreign and military policy for twenty years was not held accountable for the initiation or conduct of the war, why should anyone expect ordinary people to dwell on such matters, or to think seriously about their own personal responsibility?[34]

By immunizing the Emperor, the Tokyo Trial obscured Japanese war responsibility in a rather distorted way. 'The result is that responsibility for the Pacific War came to rest with "everybody and nobody"', Dower argues: 'the issue accordingly became terribly complex'.[35]

Japanese perceptions of the Tokyo Trial and the issue of war responsibility cannot be detached from the responsibility of the Emperor. This could be observed from intensive interviews and focus groups I conducted for this study. During interviews, not a few people referred to the fact that the Emperor was not prosecuted at the Tokyo Trial.[36] A man in his forties stated: 'Even if he were utilized by the military, something should have been done about the Emperor's responsibility, in order to promote reflection on Japan's war conduct'.[37] Indeed, examination of the Emperor's responsibility – not necessarily criminal, but political or moral – is a vital exercise for examining the Japanese nation's war responsibility. However, this itself has not been an easy topic to talk about, especially for the wartime generation. An opinion poll conducted by *Asahi Shimbun* soon after the death of the wartime Emperor in 1989 revealed this. Regarding the question as to 'whether the Emperor has some kind of war responsibility', among male respondents, while those who answered 'yes' exceeded those who answered 'no' among generations between their twenties and forties, the ratio reversed among those over 50.[38] 'In the end, it all comes down to the Emperor', said an interviewee in his mid-sixties: 'But I think, in an emotional sense, this should not be touched. Even in Britain, prosecuting the Royal Family may be a problem. Whether right or wrong, this is a different matter from prosecuting Milosevic'.[39] Overall, 25 per cent answered 'yes' to the war responsibility of the Emperor, 31 per cent 'no' and 38 per cent answered that 'it cannot be said either yes or no'.

The immunity of the Emperor surely added, in the eyes of the Japanese, an element of taboo to the Tokyo Trial that itself is already a very delicate issue.[40] Awaya Kentarō, a scholar of the Tokyo Trial, suggests: 'Granting of immunity to the Emperor is not only significant in itself but also became an obstacle for the Japanese to develop a sense of war responsibility actively, in other words, to "come to terms with the past"'.[41] This point was expressed by an interviewee in her fifties: 'There are many Japanese people who think about the Emperor's war responsibility, but they don't express it in public. This is problematic for us to reflect on where the responsibility for the war lies'.[42]

And fourth, there is the issue of 'rush to closure'. According to Ara Takashi, an historian, 'the Tokyo Trial was the pursuit of *legal* responsibility, of the leaders, for *objective* criminal acts under international law, and the subject of the pursuit was the Allies'.[43] He points out that what the Tokyo Trial did not, and could not, pursue was *political* responsibility, which requires the participation of the Japanese people, who were absent from the international trial. Given that the leaders were being prosecuted and punished under an International Military Tribunal, it may have been possible to prosecute others under domestic law, in which the Japanese themselves could be more actively involved in the process of examining the nation's war crimes. Political and moral responsibility can be pursued also by means other than criminal punishment.[44] In any form, what is required is a people's serious inner reflection on their and others' war responsibility.

However, the Tokyo Trial, whether intended or not, worked towards closure, in the eyes of the Japanese, of the entire issue of war crimes and responsibility. As examined below, GHQ's prevention of war crimes prosecutions by the Japanese government in 1946 deprived the nation of a chance, for the time being, to prosecute war crimes by themselves. This, however, was merely a practical matter. What is even more significant was the psychological closure. For the Japanese, the issue of war crimes was settled with the execution of seven defendants in December 1948, in spite of issues remaining regarding responsibility of other types and of other people, including that of the whole nation.[45] The Tokyo Trial, for its part, gave the impression that issues that were not examined in the tribunal were guilt free. In this way, individual criminal punishment not only freed the Japanese from war responsibility but also deprived them of the will to reflect further on their personal war guilt. At the international trial, not only were different concepts of guilt and responsibility – criminal, political, moral and ethical – blurred and obscured, but the opportunity to examine different types of responsibility in different ways was also lost.

The Japanese accepted the Tokyo Trial as part of the American occupation, the result of being defeated. Thus, it may be natural that people regarded the trial as something that had to be gone through in order for Japan to re-enter the international community, but not as something for deep inner reflection. Symbolic demarcation from the past as set out by the Tokyo Trial also enabled the people to evade a re-examination of the dark events of the past. Instead of sincere self-reflection on war crimes, Yoshida Yutaka, an historian, points out, there was a sense that the pursuit of democratization would cancel out responsibility for the war, 'even without reflectively facing the nation's war cooperation and responsibility'.[46] This intention to 'actively bury the past', Yoshimi Yoshiaki suggests, matched the mood of post-war Japan that embarked on rapid reconstruction and development. At the same time, he points out that the Japanese people's will to move forward as 'a peaceful and democratic nation' reflected their own sense of war responsibility. The problem, Yoshimi argues, was that 'it was pursued without facing the past sincerely'.[47]

It should be emphasized that the Tokyo Trial alone is not the cause of these 'side effects'. The trial did strengthen victim consciousness and sense of 'having being deceived', which had been held by the people at the time. The Japanese, for their part, consciously, or unconsciously, took advantage of the Tokyo Trial in order to blame their wartime leaders for their misery and to free themselves from the burden of war guilt. In other words, in the Tokyo Trial the Japanese could find an excuse for not taking seriously personal responsibility for the war that brought devastation to the country as well as its neighbours. In any event, all these 'side effects' prevented the Japanese from cultivating good understanding of the war responsibility. This would be relevant to public disinterest and silence regarding the trial, as well as war crimes and responsibility, which remained as such until the 1980s, when the issue came to be raised by the Asian victims of the Japanese Imperial Army.[48]

Collective responsibility perceived (I): the limitations of individualizing responsibility

If the Allies' intention to pursue individual responsibility under the Tokyo Trial was to free the Japanese from collective responsibility of war and war crimes, as well as from an epoch of militarism, the analysis above then illustrates that the goal was achieved, perhaps too well. However, war responsibility and a sense of collective guilt are not so simple as to be brushed away by individual criminal punishment. Instead of freeing the Japanese nation from the issue, the Allies' prosecution and punishment of a handful of wartime leaders twisted Japanese perceptions of war responsibility and sense of war guilt, and even made them perceive collective responsibility. The rest of this chapter examines this point: the limitations of de-collectivizing war guilt and responsibility through individual criminal punishment and the long-term significance of this. Analysis of de-collectivization is divided into two aspects: 'horizontal' de-collectivization and 'vertical' de-collectivization. The former denotes an attempt to avoid war responsibility from being borne by the whole Japanese people at the end of the war; the latter indicates an attempt to avoid collectivized war responsibility being passed on to future generations.

This section examines 'horizontal' de-collectivization and its limitations based on two points: whether, and to what extent, the limitation can be attributed to the idea and measure of individualization of war responsibility; and whether, and to what extent, the limitation can be attributed to the fact that the trial was conducted by the 'victor' of the war. Before moving on to an examination of 'vertical' de-collectivization, the section also examines whether domestic trials could have lessened the trial's side effects and better contributed to 'horizontal' de-collectivization.

The limitations of 'horizontal' de-collectivization

Pointing out the unpopular death sentence of the civilian leader, Hirota Kōki, Bernard V. A. Röling, Dutch Justice at the Tokyo Tribunal, stated that the effect of the Tokyo judgment 'might have been more positive if a clearer distinction had been made between those civilians who aimed at the greatness of Japan by peaceful means, and the military who were bent on direct military conquest'.[49] However, in the eyes of the Japanese, making a clear distinction and pursuing individual responsibility for the war by means of the trial were themselves dubious.

Practically, there is a question of whom to punish. In the Tokyo Trial, compared to Nuremberg, the selection of the defendants was not straightforward; individuals were selected, or eliminated, according to the political calculation of the Allied Powers, especially of the United States.[50] Dubious selection of defendants was, and is, clear in the eyes of the Japanese because some key figures were missing and some 'unexpected' names were included.[51] Many interviewees raised the question of which leaders' responsibility should be pursued at the trial, and whether the defendants at Tokyo were *those* leaders, or *all of them*. In addition to the Emperor, it was clear that certain individuals and groups were absent from the trial in spite of their active role in the war: industrialists (*zaibatsu*), leaders of the ultra nationalistic secret society and the military police. Unclear criteria for the selection of defendants gave the impression that 'the accused were selected as scapegoats' or were merely 'unlucky men', and thus even aroused sympathy towards the defendants.[52] What is more, it left an impression that the pursuit of war crimes was not done properly. The dubious selection of defendants, together with the immediate release, soon after the execution of Tōjō and other major war criminals, of remaining Class A war crimes suspects, made the Japanese reflect on the trial with the question: 'What was the Tokyo Trial after all?'[53]

The 'abrupt' selection of defendants made it unclear to the Japanese whom, and what, the Tokyo Tribunal was targeting and thus diluted the impact that the Allies expected through individual criminal punishment. In spite of the Allies' intention to avoid the collectivization of responsibility, this lack of clarity sent a contradictory message that the trial was prosecuting the Japanese collectively. 'Sometimes it seemed that the Tokyo Trial was punishing the state, and at other times individuals', wrote the research group of *Asahi Shimbun* in 1953.[54] Criticizing the Tokyo Trial soon after the occupation, Takigawa Masajirō, a member of the defence counsel at the Tokyo Tribunal, claimed: 'As long as the idea that "*we are* international criminals who have waged aggressive war" is indoctrinated in our minds, the Japanese nation will never prosper'.[55] The tone of his claim is totally different from those made by the media and leftist commentators on Japanese collective responsibility. Takigawa emphasized the collectivity to indicate the injustice of the Tokyo Trial. An emphasis on 'the collective responsibility pursued under the Tokyo Trial' is a common feature of the anti-Tokyo Trial criticism made by the conservatives and the nationalists thereafter.

In addition to the dubious selection criteria, there is strong scepticism over whether war responsibility and guilt can be targeted at individuals. The people, as a nation, supported the war that was accompanied by various war crimes committed by soldiers at the front. A man born in 1938 stated:

> The Nazis and non-Nazis can be differentiated. But in the case of Japan, were people in the military all guilty? It can be said that they did their best to protect our country, and in that sense, they become our fellow countrymen. So, clear demarcation is not possible.[56]

'In the case of Japan, things do not end by executing some leaders', an interviewee in his late thirties echoed: 'The Japanese nation was not as clearly demarcated from the military as the Germans were from the Nazis'.[57] Indeed, the fact that the nation has cooperated in the war with a belief, up to a point, in the good causes of their war will never be erased from the memory of the wartime generation. For them, it is difficult to detach themselves completely from the Tokyo Trial deep down.[58] This is why, an interviewee born in 1965 points out, there is right-wing criticism of the Tokyo Trial:

> If everybody is clear within themselves about the division between individual and collective responsibility, or the role played by the military and other nationals, there would be no backlash regarding the Tokyo Trial. If they think they were detached from the military, they can blame everything on the military. But that is not the case. Those right-wingers are claiming that our grandparents had done well. It shows that older generations are aware that they have cooperated with those executed as a result of the Trial.[59]

As examined earlier, people at the time could find an excuse in the Tokyo Trial for not facing their personal war responsibility. The point here, however, is that they were well aware of this. As the previous chapter found, a sense of guilt in the wartime generation is linked to the taboo of the Tokyo Trial and prevents people from facing the trial directly and sincerely. This is sensed by post-war generations. A man in his early forties stated:

> Those of the wartime generation who take the trial personally may feel guilty that they were also thinking and acting in the same way. But for those who were against the war, the trial may have been a matter of course.[60]

The silence over the Tokyo Trial becomes significant if it is a sense of 'collective guilt', or 'collective humiliation', that prevents the wartime generation from talking about it.[61] Japan, in the summer of 1945, experienced a radical change from an imperial state to a democracy introduced by GHQ, which engendered either voluntarily or forcefully various conversions at a personal level, from strong support of imperial Japan to support for peace-loving democracy. A man in his late sixties reflected: 'I was astonished to see how completely and immediately teachers at school changed their stance and opinion after the War'.[62]

While the Japanese at the time could not free themselves from a sense of collective responsibility, the form of *international* prosecution itself could not help giving the impression that the Tokyo Trial was trying the Japanese collectively. In the operation of international trials that excluded the Japanese from the process, Dower sees the Allies' logic assuming that 'virtually all Japanese bore some measure of responsibility for the war, and so none could be trusted to pursue the issue of war responsibility impartially where their compatriots were concerned'.[63] This logic of collective responsibility contradicts the trial's tactic to individualize responsibility. Whether the Allies themselves were conscious of this contradiction or not, the logic was sensed by the Japanese because the trial was conducted *externally*.[64] Kiyose Ichirō, Tōjō's defence counsel, expressed his ambivalent feeling as a defence lawyer in 1946:

> The Trial is entirely international in its character and therefore we have to explain to the world that those incidents and wars were not conducted with aggressive intentions and were not against the spirit of various treaties. ... If the trial was to pursue responsibility against the national, the attitude of we, the defence counsel, might have been different from what it is now. However, because the Trial is international in its character, I do my best to express to the world our country's past position.[65]

Sugawara Yutaka, another member of the defence counsel, also wrote: 'Let us remember that we are here as lawyers *for the defence of Japan* as well as for the twenty-eight defendants'.[66] These comments indicate recognition that what was on trial were not individual leaders but Japan herself. This sentiment is rather ironic given the Allies' intention, but nonetheless has been shared by many Japanese. This is well expressed by the fact that it has been widely held by the Japanese that the Tokyo Trial was 'victor's justice' against the 'vanquished'.

The scar of 'victor's justice'

As seen in previous chapters, the immediate reaction of the Japanese regarding the Tokyo Trial now and then is that it was 'victor's justice'. It is natural that this reaction is accompanied by frustration and a question: 'why was it that only Japanese leaders were prosecuted?' Yui Daizaburō, an historian, points out a sense of unfairness, which has been existing within the Japanese. This sense, he concludes, prevents people from accepting the trial's judgment unambiguously.[67]

'Victor's justice', especially problems regarding *ex post facto* legislation and unilateral prosecution, has been picked up enthusiastically by nationalists and revisionists to challenge the authenticity of the Tokyo Trial and deny its verdict.[68] Interestingly, most of them claim that it is the Japanese nation as a whole that was the direct target of the trial. Maeno Tōru argued: 'The Nuremberg Trial was targeting Nazi Germany but not Germans. In the case of the Tokyo Trial, it was a trial to judge Japan and the Japanese'.[69] Itō Shunya, the director of the film *Puraido*, which depicts Tōjō as a hero at the Tokyo Tribunal, claimed: 'Although it gave immunity to the Emperor and the Japanese people and put the blame on a handful of military men, the aim of the trial was to convict the Japanese completely'.[70]

Nationalists and right-wingers often depict the defeat and the occupation as 'an overwhelmingly humiliating epoch when genuinely free choice was repressed and alien models were imposed'.[71] This is a 'disgraceful' moment, and the Tokyo Trial for them is a symbol of disgrace and humiliation that unjustly branded the Japanese nation as war criminals. Many of these arguments claim that the aim of the Tokyo Trial was to destroy the culture, philosophy and national spirit of Japan, in order to achieve the mental remodelling of the vanquished nation. Tanaka Masaaki, an anti-Tokyo Trial polemicist, has been vocal on this point:

> People become servile once they become conscious that they have committed a crime. The Tokyo Trial has deliberately instigated this consciousness and concluded, by distorting the facts, that Japan's whole past was a crime. Indeed, it was one of the main aims of American occupation policy to weaken the Japanese people ... and, with the stern appearance of a military trial, it completely succeeded in weakening the Japanese nation.[72]

For the nationalist, the trial is a disgrace not only because an external trial was dishonourably imposed on Japan but also because the Japanese people themselves accepted and continue to accept such dishonour blindly. Some attribute the current 'moral decay' of the Japanese to the Tokyo Trial. Kase Toshikazu, the first Japanese ambassador to the UN, argued: 'Our nation was brainwashed by the victor's manipulation and still does not understand the truth of the trial. Without rectifying this, it is not possible to recover the mental independence of our people'.[73]

Not to share the nationalist and conservative view of the Tokyo Trial, the Japanese in general sense some significance, be it positive, negative or a mixture of both, in the intention of the Tokyo Trial's principal organizer, the United States, for having conducted such a trial. In other words, it is commonly perceived that the Tokyo Trial was not an ordinary trial but a 'political trial', pursuing ends other than simple justice. Intensive interviews and focus groups showed that the trial is now generally seen within the context of the post-war American occupation policy and the transformation of Japan and regarded as a necessary means for the post-war settlement. *Asahi Shimbun*'s opinion poll in May 2006 also showed that among those who knew about the Tokyo Trial to some extent (27 per cent), 48 per cent answered that 'with some problems, the Tokyo Trial still was necessary as a settlement'.[74]

Among present-day Japanese, the Tokyo Trial is often associated with Tōjō Hideki, who was the only person recognized by most interviewees. Tōjō being the icon of past Japanese militarism, and the military and militarism having been given a bad name in Japan since the end of the war, it is understood, even if only vaguely, that the trial worked to eliminate the military and militarism, which itself was good for a Japan in transition.[75] 'In the case of the Tokyo Trial, bad things were judged', stated an interviewee born in 1978: 'On building a new society, things that could have been an obstacle to the new era were eliminated. I see the Tokyo Trial as such a thing'.[76] This is echoed by many others.[77]

However, it is difficult to find unreserved praise for the Tokyo Trial. This is partly because the trial's contribution to the post-war transformation of Japan is often not very clear, mingled with the impact of other occupation policies. In the eyes of the Japanese, it is not the Tokyo Trial that symbolizes the demilitarization of Japan; it is the 1947 Constitution, which contains Article 9 renouncing war as a Japanese sovereign right, that symbolizes the new era of a peaceful Japan. The Tokyo Trial's role in demilitarization is overshadowed by the impact of the new constitution.

People's low evaluation of the trial, however, is to do with the fact that the Tokyo Trial was a 'political trial' based on the *victor's* politics. Kitaoka Shinichi, a scholar of Japanese diplomatic history, describes the politics of the Tokyo Trial as a way of reaching a settlement and a ritual for reconciliation. He argues that there is no point in seriously questioning its legality and ethics: 'The nature of the Tokyo Trial will never be understood without examining its effect on the big political turning point after the war'.[78] However, people are not quiet about questioning the legality and ethics of the trial. 'Japan at the time became too extreme and it was good that we were defeated. I have no feeling of remorse', stated an interviewee in his late twenties: 'But I cannot agree with the idea that only Japan should have been tried. The Tokyo Trial seems very hypocritical'.[79] Students in a focus group stated that the victor used the Tokyo Trial to eliminate the military because it was an obstacle to the US occupation policy: 'They wanted to make the occupation easier'.[80] Some others in the same group argued that Japan was stripped of its military power because the United States wished to subordinate Japan, or weaken it psychologically.[81]

Several interviewees saw that through the Tokyo Trial the victors imposed their own values and ideas. 'Perhaps the United States wanted to make Japan in its own image', a woman in her early thirties stated: 'and the trial was to transform Japan in a favourable way for the United States during its occupation'.[82] Another interviewee commented: 'The United States led the trial and imposed it on Japan with their own idea of building a new country. Japan was forced to change'.[83] There were even comments pointing to a racist element in the conduct of the Tokyo Trial. This is most 'moderately' expressed as follows: 'I know there was also a similar trial in the case of Germany. But I feel in Tokyo something more oppressive and forceful in the intention of the victor'.[84] No matter how good the intentions of the organizer or how positive the nature of the transformation, the fact that the trial was imposed externally and unilaterally harms its positive significance.

Despite all these views, most interviewees did not necessarily express specific hostility or frustrations towards the Tokyo Trial and its organizers. Of course, there is the passage of time, through which the Tokyo Trial is regarded by some merely as one event in history. More importantly, a common attitude of the majority of Japanese now and then, as seen in the previous chapters, is passive acceptance, which is based on the understanding that the Tokyo Trial was 'inevitable'.[85] A sense of inevitability shared by the Japanese at the time is still widely shared by the current generations; the term 'inevitable [*shikata ga nai*]' was repeatedly used by many interviewees when talking about the trial. The interviews clarified that this sense of inevitability consists of different elements. A number of interviewees commented that the trial was inevitable because what Japan had done was wrong and deserved a judgment: 'It was Japan who started the war and did bad things during it. I think it was a matter of course that the trial was held', stated an interviewee in his forties.[86] This commonly held view connotes two things. First, it is perceived as necessary to seek where the responsibility for the war lies; the responsibility for such a grave event needed to be pursued.[87] Second, there is an understanding that those defendants at the Tokyo Trial represented by Tōjō were 'bad guys' who deserved judgment.[88]

The inevitability of the Tokyo Trial, however, is more generally attributed to the defeat in the war: it was inevitable *because Japan lost the war*.[89] 'Victor's justice' has been accepted as the result of defeat, with the logic of might is right, which has been strongly embraced by the Japanese. 'After all, that is war', a man in his sixties said: 'The trial itself, as well as the way it was conducted, was based on the logic of the victor.... War trials after all are of such a nature'.[90] The fact that no examination has been conducted of America dropping atomic bombs was also understood in this context. 'The trial was never intended to try Hiroshima and Nagasaki from the beginning', said a woman from Hiroshima.[91] 'Being unilateral was a prerequisite, and there is no point in complaining about it. That was understood right from the beginning', stated another interviewee.[92]

No matter how much the trial itself was good in intention, and whether prosecuted leaders were popular or not, 'victor's justice' leaves in the mind of the people some ambivalence: the vague sense of war guilt at best, cynicism and passive acceptance in general, and reactionary nationalistic attitudes at worst. 'Victor's justice', although it has been accepted as inevitable, remains as a scar in the Japanese mind. This was well observed through an interview with a man in his late thirties, who was one of a few who tried to see positive and constructive aspects of the Tokyo Trial and its strategic purpose for current Japan. After having argued the positive aspects of the trial, he nonetheless expressed his ambivalent feeling regarding the trial: 'Having said that, *as a Japanese person*, I feel discomfort. I think people were convicted unilaterally by the victor. I have an image that it was not a fair but political trial, similar to a witch hunt'.[93] Other interviewees, who had shown some understanding of the Tokyo Trial, also said that 'as a Japanese', they had a negative feeling about the Tokyo Trial.[94] The fact that the trial was imposed externally *and* unilaterally evokes national, or nationalistic, pride, which leads to a sense of distaste, if not revulsion. A businessman saw the Tokyo Trial as 30 per cent positive but 70 per cent negative: 'In the short term, the Tokyo Trial was not necessarily bad; it worked to eliminate militarism. But in the long run, it was not good because it negated the good of old Japan'.[95] It is ironic that an international attempt to de-collectivize guilt and responsibility resulted in emphasizing collective guilt and, in some cases, being taken as collective humiliation.

Ara Takashi states that there could have been areas of agreement between those conducting the Tokyo Trial and the Japanese nation who held a certain sense of war responsibility at the time. However, he argues that because responsibility for the war was pursued forcibly by the Allies, the two came to be connected in an unnatural form.[96] Ōnuma Yasuaki states:

> The Tokyo Trial was the judgment by the Allies, as outsiders, and it was conducted with some unfairness that was maintained by the authority of the occupation army. This is why the Trial could not obtain universality and morality. In that sense, the Tokyo Trial may have been an obstacle to dealing with the issue of war responsibility without any distortion.[97]

These comments by Ara and Ōnuma were echoed by the businessman interviewed above, who concluded as follows: 'The problem was that the Japanese could not do it by themselves'.[98]

The desirability and feasibility of domestic trials

Regarding criticisms that Tokyo was 'victor's justice' and an internationally imposed trial, it can be argued that domestic rather than international trials might have been a better way to prosecute and punish Japan's war criminals. Domestic trials are also said to have endorsed the more active participation of the Japanese in war crimes prosecutions and thus 'strengthened popular acceptance of the idea that the Japanese, more than anyone else, had to take responsibility for their crimes'.[99]

Whether a legal procedure originating from the West is the best way for the Japanese to pursue responsibility is one of the points made regarding the pros and cons of the Tokyo Trial. Many non-Japanese as well as Japanese point this out. A number of interviewees wondered if the clarification of right and wrong was a suitable way to solve the problem for the Japanese, who prefer to leave things vague.[100] However, people were not necessarily against trials per se. The Japanese government was not silent over prosecuting war crimes by themselves. When MacArthur's first order for the arrest of war criminals was issued on 11 September 1945, the Higashikuni cabinet hastily discussed a basic policy for conducting 'voluntary trial [*jishu saiban*]'.[101] Reflecting people's strong resentment towards their wartime leaders, the media and commentators also raised, soon after the war, the idea of war crimes trials conducted by the Japanese people.[102] Interestingly, many of those who criticized the Tokyo Trial did not deny the necessity of pursuing war crimes prosecutions itself.[103]

The Japanese now as then see a war crimes trial after the war as necessary, appropriate or as a better option than others, including summary execution or doing nothing at all. What is not at all proper in their eyes is the fact of the victors conducting the trial. Having been asked about whether there should have been domestic trials conducted by the Japanese themselves, there was very little opposition to the idea among the interviewees. Domestic trials were regarded as desirable if they were conducted fairly and properly.[104]

Interestingly, however, almost all the interviewees immediately expressed strong scepticism about the feasibility of such trials. Japan, soon after the war, many thought, lacked the necessary infrastructure, organization and ability to conduct trials by themselves. The moral and ethical appropriateness of domestic trial was also seriously questioned. 'Who could stand on the side of the judge?' was a frequently raised point. 'The nation as a whole supported the movement towards the war. The negation of that war cannot be done except from outside', an interviewee argued: 'The external judgment is undoubtedly harsher, but you cannot judge your own past, can you?'[105] For this reason, another interviewee opposed domestic trials: 'If some people should be judged after the war, those who press for judgment should have raised their voice during the war. Everyone was involved in the war to some extent'.[106] Students majoring in the history of Japanese–American relations expressed even stronger scepticism:

> If there had been a revolution and a new government had been built, a domestic trial would have been reasonable. But without this, such a trial might have ended up in putting all the blame on the military or have resulted in mutual recrimination within the military. Domestic trials could have become even more flawed than the Tokyo Trial.[107]

Another stated: 'The Tokyo Trial was more of a symbolic settlement of the war. If it had been done by the Japanese, it would not have become a settlement; it might have become something completely different'.[108] Regarding the non-feasibility of domestic trials soon after the war, some commented that the Allies conducting the Tokyo Trial might have been appropriate.[109]

Whether domestic trials could have been conducted 'fairly' and 'properly', or whether such trials would have diminished the complex and ambiguous sense of war guilt and responsibility is not known. Yet, the public discourse and historical research of the late 1940s suggest that domestic trials at the time would not necessarily have been an ideal form of war crimes prosecution, especially with regard to fostering a better understanding of war responsibility on the part of the Japanese. Examining the policy of the Japanese government in the 1940s on war crimes issues, Dower concluded that trials by the Japanese would not have been significantly different from what actually took place under the Tokyo Tribunal: 'Loser's justice, like victor's justice, ultimately would have entailed arguing that Japan had been led into "aggressive militarism" by a small cabal of irresponsible militaristic leaders. Indeed, it would have involved a home-grown conspiracy theory'.[110] This is understandable given the public anger towards the military in the aftermath of the war. What is more, the government's intention behind 'voluntary trials' was to evade, through double jeopardy, the expected damage to be inflicted on ex-leaders by the Allies' future trials. The judgments of the earlier trials under the Japanese court martial also suggested that punishments meted out by domestic courts would have been too lenient.[111] And, undoubtedly, the Emperor would never have been prosecuted under a domestic legal procedure.

Kobayashi Shunzō, a member of defence counsel at Tokyo, looked back on the Tokyo Trial and stated:

> the responsibility of our leaders for having blindly headed towards defeat should be judged by their own nations. However, because we had no such autonomy and power, we had to accept submissively the victor's punishment, which was masked as a trial.[112]

This comment implies that what Kobayashi meant by 'domestic trial' is the pursuit of the 'responsibility for defeat' for one's own nation, not for waging aggressive wars and committing war crimes against other nations. This completely misses the logic of war crimes prosecutions. This comment is also symbolic in that it regards the Japanese people as the victim of the war, not the victimizer. A leftist academic, Inoue Kiyoshi, claimed during the occupation that, in order to break with the past, it was necessary to uproot the basis of the old militarist powers: 'The most important way of doing this is that the Japanese themselves thoroughly try those criminals who imposed this suffering on the nation'.[113] Again, this comment is based on the idea that people were the victim of the military, and implies that a domestic trial could have become a stage for quasi-revenge. Claims made by leftist intellectuals at the time had a serious limitation in that they failed to refer to the nation's war responsibility as well as their own.[114] Mochida Yukio remembers having heard liberal scholars vocally denouncing the Emperor, the military clique and *zaibatsu* for their war responsibility: 'but those commentators rarely pointed out that each Japanese person should bear war responsibility and war guilt'.[115]

In any case, calls for 'a people's court' and domestic trials could not attract the wider interest of the public. This is partly because of strict censorship by

GHQ, which suppressed and deleted academics' comments on the domestic trial for war crimes, such comments being regarded as anti-Tokyo Trial.[116] However, it was more to do with a lack of will on the part of the people. A lack of will may be because of the effects of the Tokyo Trial, where prosecution and punishment of Tōjō and other leaders marked a closure. It was also because people were suffering terribly from post-war poverty and were preoccupied with their everyday life. Kinoshita Junji, who wrote in 1970 a well-known play on the Tokyo Trial focusing on war crimes prosecutions and responsibility for the war, reflects: 'Soon after the war, I myself could not think about our pursuing Japanese war criminals by ourselves'.[117]

Collective responsibility perceived (II): the limitation of 'vertical' demarcation

While the Tokyo Trial could not successfully de-collectivize war responsibility and a sense of war guilt 'horizontally' in a real sense, it also failed to de-collectivize them 'vertically'; the issue of war responsibility and a sense of war guilt were passed on to future generations. In other words, the trial did not attain complete closure.

Buried responsibility

'Every Japanese sensed the issue of war responsibility vaguely', Funabashi Yōichi, the chief diplomatic correspondent for *Asahi Shimbun*, states: 'but they continued not to take it seriously and personally until around the 1980s'.[118] One of the issues that allowed this Japanese attitude is the development of the Cold War following the end of the Second World War. The relationship between Japan and the United States took an unexpectedly favourable turn during the occupation, as the latter came to regard the former as an important ally for the new era. As for the Asian countries who had suffered under Japanese colonial rule, many of them were too occupied with their domestic turmoil and civil and independent wars to pursue Japan's war responsibility. China, for example, had demanded extradition of several major war crimes suspects at the beginning but pulled out of the whole issue later on as its civil war became intense.[119] In addition, Japan's neighbouring states were in the process of development and thus still had very little say within the international community, especially against the United States, who was unwilling to react harshly towards Japan regarding war responsibility, especially after 1948.[120] Japan herself did not feel an immediate need to achieve reconciliation and create a friendly relationship with other Asian countries, especially China. China, turning itself into a communist country, became the enemy of the United States, with whom Japan was strengthening its strategic ties.

This is a critical difference between Japan and Germany; the latter had to renounce its past in order to survive the post-war world, coexisting with other fellow Europeans, who were former enemies and victims but who immediately became important political and economic partners in the new security environment in the region. But Japan did not sense such 'immediate' pressure from its neighbouring countries to solve the issue of war responsibility and reconciliation. This lack of pressure enabled the Japanese to leave the past behind, at least for a while. At the same time, an already existing Japanese victim consciousness was further strengthened by the devastation of Hiroshima and Nagasaki, the details of which became widely known to the public after the US occupation. Ever since, Hiroshima and Nagasaki have been the symbol of Japan's war experience, as the victim.[121]

Japan's past war crimes against its Asian neighbours became known to the Japanese public in the 1980s, through the textbook row with China and publications focused on war crimes conducted by the Japanese Imperial Army.[122] It is also during this period that schools, endorsing the so-called 'peace education' centring around the experience of Hiroshima and Nagasaki, started to teach children about the devastation inflicted not only on the Japanese but also by the Japanese army during the war. However, Japanese consciousness towards their past war crimes, especially those conducted under colonial rule, was still low during the 1980s.

The Tokyo Trial and 'post-war responsibility'

In the current generation, a view that the Tokyo Trial was a way of war settlement, or the 'ritual for demarcation', can be found. 'With the Tokyo Trial, Japan's war crimes were judged and Japan could start as a new country *without being bound by the war*', stated a woman in her fifties:

> Without the Tokyo Trial, we would not have been able to undertake *a precise summary of the war*... it was victor's justice and may not have been fair. But I think there were some positive meanings in the Trial for Japan to start its new life after the war.[123]

This view that the trial worked as a watershed with regard to an era of militarism echoes the newspaper editorials in 1948. However, currently, such a watershed is seen not only in a practical sense but also in a psychological sense, that is, in terms of war guilt and responsibility. As the above quoted opinion poll in 2006 shows, the majority of those who knew about the Tokyo Trial saw it as necessary as a settlement. This was also suggested by many people during interviews in 2003 through their usage of terms, such as purification (*misogi*), settlement (*atoshimatsu*, *kejime*), closure (*shimekukuri*, *kugiri*), in describing their perception and image of the Tokyo Trial.

What is not well known among the Japanese, however, is the fact that the Tokyo Trial was not a stage to examine most of the war crimes committed against Asian civilians under Japanese colonial rule, which had been left untouched ever since.[124] By not having examined Japanese colonial rules and associated war crimes, the trial failed to become a forum of closure for Asian victims, even though Japan has 'officially' settled reparation through state-to-state bilateral negotiations. Takahashi Tetsuya argues that the fact that adequate punishment and compensation have not been exacted for the war crimes committed by the past Japanese Empire causes the current awareness of Japan's 'post-war responsibility [*Sengo Sekinin*]'. He points out that the Tokyo Trial enabled 'post-war responsibility' to be carried over to the present-day, rather than to have succeeded in detaching the current generation from collective responsibility and guilt over the country's past.[125]

Indeed, in the 1990s, it became clear that the de-collectivization of responsibility and the closure of the issue of war and war crimes were illusory; the voices of the long-silent victims in Asia, especially the former 'comfort women', became louder, stimulated by the end of the Cold War, the death of the wartime Emperor and the further development and democratization of Asian countries. While many of the Japanese felt sorry for those victims and showed some sympathy, they also expressed dismay and uneasiness towards victims' claims. Their ambivalence can be seen from the fact that while an opinion poll in 1994 showed that more than 70 per cent thought that the government 'has not adequately compensated the people of countries Japan invaded or colonized',[126] about five million signatures were gathered for a petition against a 1995 parliamentary resolution of apology.[127] According to a *Yomiuri*'s opinion poll in 2005, 47 per cent answered that 'it is necessary to keep on feeling responsible for Asian victims of the past war', while 45 per cent answered 'it is no more necessary to do so'.[128]

Interviews and focus groups showed that the general reaction to the concept of post-war responsibility is ambivalent in several ways. First, there are 'temporal' questions regarding war crimes of the past: '*How long* are we to take the blame for the past deeds?' A man in his mid-sixties stated: 'I want this matter to be settled. It is painful to hear these issues of war and responsibility indefinitely from our fellow Asian countries'.[129] An undergraduate student stated: 'For me, they are events that occurred long before I was born and it is not we who waged the war. I wonder how long the Chinese and Koreans will talk about the issues of the distant past'.[130] Several interviewees of the post-war generation said that current affairs and economic ties were more important than the issue of past war crimes.[131]

For many of the post-war generation, who have little awareness of their country's past, an immediate reaction is '*why now*?'[132] For them, the issue seems to have been brought up 'suddenly' more than half a century after the war. However, reactions to a 'why now' question differ from person to person. The diversity in views and emotions was observed in a focus-group interview with undergraduate students. One student claimed, 'If they are talking about compensation, they should have brought it up earlier. There is no need to bring it up now'. Another one responded: 'I understand what they are talking about, considering Hiroshima and Nagasaki. We still talk about them. In that sense, a complaint "why now" does not make sense'.[133]

Each person found a different answer to these 'how long' and 'why now' questions. Some blamed the government for not having acknowledged past crimes and compensated for them much earlier. Others, including those who expressed sympathy towards the victims' voices, complained that the victims, as well as the governments of China and Korea, are too persistent, pointing out the fact that the Japanese government has already apologized several times, that Japan has been paying China, since 1978, Official Development Aid, as a gesture of reconciliation and that history is used by the Chinese and South Korean governments as a tool for domestic politics.[134] An interviewee pointed out an economic element involving reconciliation: 'If we were poorer than they are, we would not have been blamed this much. Japan has become a big power and they may be feeling that this is based on their sacrifice'.[135] Many interviewees sensed that the issue of war crimes and responsibility was highly politicized, being attached to various issues – the economic and domestic politics of victim countries. Regarding the issue as political and also looking at it in terms of compensation, some interviewees believed this was a matter for the government, not for individuals.[136]

What is more difficult and serious is the second type of question: 'why me?' Several interviewees showed dismay and frustration towards the fact that they are blamed 'collectively' for past events, in which most of the current generation were not directly involved. A woman in her late twenties said: 'I do understand the feelings of the victims. For them things are not yet settled. But, it has nothing to do with what I have done'.[137] 'I as a Japanese person shoulder an historical responsibility', a man in his late thirties stated. However, he also poured out 'pent-up' feelings: 'I don't want to shoulder such a thing. But we cannot help it because I cannot stop being Japanese, and I should shoulder it. But it is unpleasant. What have our ancestors done!'[138] Such a frustration was expressed publicly in the diet by a young Politician: 'Regarding self-reflection of the Japanese nation as a whole, because I myself am not of the generation directly involved in the war, I am not self-reflecting, and I see no reason to be asked to be so'.[139] Her comment received criticism as well as sympathy.

It is to this kind of frustration that the nationalists' anti-Tokyo Trial arguments appeal. The nationalists as well as the revisionists claim that the view that Japan conducted aggressive war and committed terrible war crimes is a fabrication of the Tokyo Trial that targeted the Japanese nation as a whole, branded the nation collectively as a war criminal and burdened them with responsibility and a sense of guilt. Such an argument is even more appealing when people know very little about the Tokyo Trial.[140]

Although neo-nationalist and revisionist claims are not necessarily supported literally by the majority of the population, several interviewees expressed their understanding of the underlying emotion of such claims.[141] After all, those claims are the magnification of a 'pent-up feeling' within the Japanese, who, after more than half a century, seek 'a positive identity and role in the world appropriate to the global economic superpower Japan has become', but, at the same time, are dismayed and frustrated by the outcry for apology and compensation, which drags the current generation back to the dark past.[142]

Yasukuni shrine

The interesting combination of the current Japanese people's 'ignorance' and 'frustration' regarding the Tokyo Trial and war responsibility can be observed in the row over Prime Ministers' visits to the Yasukuni shrine, where the spirits of 14 Class A war criminals are enshrined, together with about 2.5 million Japanese war dead since the nineteenth century.[143] The row intensified under Prime Minister Koizumi, who annually visited the shrine while he was in office from 2001 until autumn 2006. 'I don't think the Yasukuni problem is difficult at all', an interviewee stated.

> It is not a bad thing to enshrine the spirit of the war dead. But the problem is that there are also the spirits of Tōjō and others who are war criminals. The Tokyo Trial, in that sense, demarcated those who dragged others into the war and those who were dragged into it. I think it is a problem that the Prime Minister visits the place where both of them are held.[144]

This is exactly the point that the Chinese and Korean governments are furious about. In the eyes of China, it is a total contradiction to express atonement for aggressive war on the one hand, and to visit the shrine where wartime leaders are enshrined on the other. Koizumi's act not only questioned the sincerity of Japan's atonement, it was also seen as a challenge by the Japanese government to the Tokyo judgment, which the government had officially accepted through the Peace Treaty.

However, the demarcation between war criminals and other war dead is not necessarily clear in the minds of many Japanese. 'What's wrong with visiting Yasukuni to pray for the war dead?' was expressed by several interviewees, who felt that it was unreasonable that the shrine is criticized this much.[145] According to an opinion poll conducted by *Asahi Shimbun* in May 2005, 51 per cent answered they 'cannot understand the fact that China problematize Yasukuni to this extent'.[146] To some, this reaction is based on a lack of awareness that the spirit of Class A war criminals are also held at the shrine.[147] Some students felt that the problem lies in the shrine's connection with the war: the *war* dead. This reaction reflects the Japanese tendency to regard all things to do with the war and the military negatively and to take the defensive stance that Japan will be criticized by China and South Korea whenever they find connections between present-day Japan and its past war.

Even for those with knowledge of the Tokyo Trial, a clear differentiation between war criminals and other war dead in Yasukuni is still difficult to maintain. This may be related to the Japanese culture and custom of regarding 'death [as] absolve[ing] all traces of guilt', which contrasts with the Chinese view that death is 'a symbol of eternal evil'.[148] Yasukuni becomes an even more delicate and complex matter because issues it entails are also legal, social, cultural, ethical and religious concerns and matters of custom.[149] This is why not a few

Japanese feel that criticisms made by Asian neighbours are an 'intervention' in the domestic affairs of Japan.

For some, Yasukuni is a symbol of wartime militarism that encouraged the idea of dying for the Emperor and the glorification of the war. For others, the shrine is rather a symbol of the reverence with which those who gave their lives for their country and future generations of their countrymen are held. It is here that the pros and cons of Yasukuni are caught in one kind of dualism that has been surrounding the Tokyo Trial: whether Class A war criminals were villains or patriotic war dead.[150] The removal from the shrine of the spirit of Tōjō and other convicted Class A war criminals has been debated in the Diet; however, a decision in favour has been blocked by the conservative faction in the Diet as well as the shrine itself. Building a new memorial has also been discussed by the government; however, this idea has also faced challenges. Hata Ikuhiko, an historian, argues that if those war criminals had been tried by a domestic court and found guilty, the spirit of the defendants would not have ended up being enshrined at Yasukuni. According to him, the Tokyo Trial 'purified the "crimes" of the accused and turned them into martyrs'.[151]

The complexity and delicacy of the issue can be seen from the fact that public opinion has been completely divided, as well as fluctuating, regarding Koizumi's visit to Yasukuni. On his first visit to the shrine in the summer of 2001, *Asahi Shimbun*'s opinion poll showed that 41 per cent supported his plan for the visit and 42 per cent had expected him to be 'cautious', expressing hesitation to support his visit.[152] In late November 2004, 38 per cent thought the Prime Minster 'should continue his visit', while 39 per cent thought 'he should stop'.[153] The opinion shifted towards opposition after a mass demonstration took place in China and diplomatic relations between the two countries worsened in spring 2005, showing that 52 per cent answered that Koizumi 'should stop his visit', while 36 per cent supported the visit.[154] However, in May 2006, 50 per cent supported his visit, while 31 per cent were against.[155] On Koizumi's most controversial visit on 15 August 2006, the day to commemorate the end of the Asian-Pacific War, opinion polls were conducted by various medias, each of which showed different results with regard to pros and cons. Koizumi having left office in autumn 2006, it is not known at the time of writing whether the row continues to be a critical matter for Japan both domestically and internationally.

The Yasukuni row surely was a catalyst for public interest and increasing media coverage of the Tokyo Trial in 2005 and 2006, at the highest level ever since 1983, or perhaps even higher than that year.[156] While the pros and cons of Yasukuni stimulated old debates surrounding the Tokyo Trial focusing on the righteousness of the trial, as well as of Japan's past war, through the Yasukuni row the Tokyo Trial finally came to be discussed in relation with the meaning of war responsibility and the significance of the Tokyo Trial for the pursuit of such responsibility. In this regard, *Yomiuri Shimbun* conducted extensive research on war responsibility, responsibility especially for the conduct of the war that had caused a great harm nationally and internationally, and re-examined the verdict of the Tokyo Trial and its account of each defendant's role and responsibility.[157]

The individualization of responsibility and post-war Japan's reconciliation and transformation

This last section analyses how the Japanese sense of war responsibility, examined above in relation to the Tokyo Trial, affects Japan's reconciliation with the victims and its own past. Reconciliation is not a unilateral process but requires a joint effort by both sides.[158] For reconciliation, especially for the victim, it is necessary that the victimizer acknowledges the crimes they have committed against the victim as well as certain responsibilities arising from those crimes. This is crucial for the victim to achieve 'closure' and move forward. The victim, for his/her part, needs to refrain from demonizing and blaming his/her adversaries collectively. According to the 'Nuremberg legacy', trials are expected to facilitate such a delicate and difficult process through individual criminal punishment. The Nuremberg legacy also suggests that trials are expected to de-collectivize war responsibility in such a way as to free the majority of the nation, or group, from the burden of the past and thus facilitate the transformation of the given society.

The opinion poll in 1991 conducted by *Asahi Shimbun* both in Japan and the United States showed that 48 per cent of Americans still had 'a feeling of antagonism [*wadakamari*]' towards Japan's attack on Pearl Harbor half a century before, and 59 per cent of the Japanese sensed that the event remained as 'a source of bad feeling' between the two countries.[159] Nonetheless, these national feelings do not come to the surface in such a way as to become an obstacle to friendly relations between Japan and the United States. Regarding the relationship between Japan and the United States, the Tokyo Trial may have worked as a *formal* 'ritual for a settlement'.[160] The Tokyo Trial, however, was not a stage for reconciliation for Japan and its Asian neighbours, especially Asian civilians. The trial, in the first place, focused very little on Japan's war crimes against Asian countries, except for the Nanjing massacre, and did not wholly examine war crimes conducted by the Japanese Imperial Army against civilians under colonial rule. The Japanese had remained uninterested in, or ignorant of, the issues, until they were brought up in the 1980s and became a cause of tension between Japan and its neighbours in the 1990s. Some may draw from this the conclusion that Japan has not been able to achieve reconciliation with its Asian victims because the Tokyo Trial did not examine these victims' sufferings, thus affirming the Nuremberg legacy. However, analysis undertaken in this chapter indicates that this is a little too simplistic a conclusion.

What this chapter has observed is the paradoxical attitude and perception expressed by the Japanese who faced the Tokyo Trial at the time. The Japanese detached themselves from the trial and did not examine its significance and war responsibility personally because the trial did not directly target each one individually; nonetheless they felt frustrated that they were being blamed at the Tokyo Trial as a nation. This trend is observed also in contemporary Japanese through their indifference and frustration towards the Tokyo Trial, as well as war responsibility. These paradoxical attitudes regarding the trial are problematic because they both relate to the ambivalent sense of war responsibility.

How the Japanese understand their war responsibility is crucial for their reconciliation with other nations. For the victims asking for official acknowledgement of past war crimes, an ambivalent sense of responsibility held not only by the Japanese government but also by the Japanese people is as infuriating as the minor but vehement voices that deny any war crimes. The gap, which existed until recently, in perception between the people in Japan and its neighbouring countries of the past is clearly seen in a joint opinion survey conducted by Japanese and South Korean newspapers in 1984. While about 40 per cent of Koreans raised the issue of '36-years of colonial rule' as an image of Japan, only 4 per cent of the Japanese raised colonial rule, including aggression and torture, in their images of South Korea; instead, for most, food and culture reminded them of that country.[161] Such a gap is also recognized by the younger generation who have gone abroad and have directly heard the voice of people from other countries. A woman in her early thirties stated that she recognized the difference in perception for the first time while she was studying abroad:

> Both Americans and other Asians were very curious about how the Japanese think about war responsibility and past aggression. But as a Japanese person, I could not respond to them well. I had nothing to tell them because I had not really been conscious of these issues.[162]

An opinion poll conducted by *Asahi Shimbun* in 2006 shows that 69 per cent thought that the 'Japanese themselves had not made enough effort to look closely into and elucidate why Japan has conducted that war'. The *Yomiuri* opinion poll in 2005 also showed that 58 per cent answered that the issue of war responsibility of political and military leaders has not been well debated in post-war Japan.[163]

The Japanese sense of collective war guilt and responsibility is not merely cultivated internally but also imposed externally. This can be examined through the Japanese reaction to the Yasukuni row. A number of interviewees stated that they regarded politicians' visits to the Yasukuni shrine as not right because it caused anger and criticism from China and South Korea. While there were interviewees who expressed frustration against the submissive and apologetic attitude that the Japanese were forced to adopt against outside criticism, some others expressed dismay about their ignorance of Japan's unsettled past, which they came to know through voices from outside. These attitudes are reflected in an opinion poll conducted in late June 2005, in which 52 per cent opposed the Prime Minister's visit to the shrine and 36 per cent supported it. A total of 72 per cent of those who opposed held their view out of 'consideration for neighbouring countries', while 13 per cent related it to the issue of Class A war criminals. At the same time, 39 per cent of those who supported the visit gave as their reason that they thought it 'wrong to stop the visit according to what outside people say', followed by 36 per cent who regarded Yasukuni 'as an appropriate place for expressing remorse'.[164]

Japanese ignorance of past war and war crimes tends to be exaggerated in China and South Korea, which adds to the already existing antagonism towards

Japan in both societies. An overly emotional pursuit of war responsibility on the part of the victim, however, is counterproductive for reconciliation. While the victims' claims elicit certain sympathy in Japan, the persistent voice of accusation stirs up the Japanese people's 'pent-up' feelings and frustration that they have been collectively targeted with excessive blame. There even emerges a sense that they are victimized for being overly accused of having been the victimizer. The problem here is a twisted sense of collective guilt, which is not merely internal but also imposed externally.

The perception of collective guilt and responsibility frames the identity of the nation; this is why the Japanese sense of collective responsibility has been attacked not only externally but also internally, both from leftist and rightist commentators: the former criticizes people for being too little aware of Japan's responsibility for the past; and the latter for being too aware. Ironically, the right-wing cannot claim that the issue of war responsibility and compensation was laid to rest with the Tokyo Trial because of their absolute denial of the trial, which, according to them, has imposed an excess sense of guilt that is still haunting Japanese society. As for the left, which is eager to pursue responsibility for Japanese war crimes and to criticize the militarist past, it is not easy to accept the Tokyo Trial wholeheartedly because of the trial's failure to examine the war responsibility of the Emperor and Japan's alleged war crimes committed against Asian civilians under colonial rule. Both the right and left are critical about the Tokyo Trial with regard to the issue of war responsibility in different ways. Being stuck in the middle, the majority of Japanese people remain silent.[165] They do not talk about the war crimes and responsibility and the Tokyo Trial, not necessarily because they do not care about them but because they are conscious, sometimes too conscious, about discomforting issues. Businessmen in a focus group said that they didn't want to touch the issue. 'I don't want to feel the war directly', one stated: 'I don't want to talk about it because it is still raw'. Another stated that during his business with a Chinese counterpart, the topic of the war was not raised: 'If it had been raised, I would have tried to change the subject'. This comment is intriguing as it was made by the same person who stated that the issue of war responsibility was already settled and that there was nothing specific to talk about regarding the Tokyo Trial.[166]

According to psychoanalytic studies of post-war Germans, Mark Osiel argues, 'societal self-analysis, however difficult to induce, is essential to restoring a nation's mental health and solidarity in the aftermath of administrative massacre'. What is indicated is the problem of an 'unmastered past'.[167] In that sense, the Japanese people's ambivalent attitude towards war crimes and responsibility, observed from their paradoxical attitudes towards the Tokyo Trial, are problematic, because either way – apathy and lack of interest by detachment from war crimes, and frustration deriving from collective responsibility imposed externally – active 'societal self-analysis' will not be achieved. This chapter, as well as the previous one, shows that Japanese society is still struggling to 'master the past', for which the Tokyo Trial is rather an unhelpful national experience.

Conclusion

By selecting a handful of symbolic figures for criminal punishment and appealing to people's strong anger and frustration towards their wartime leaders, the Tokyo Trial successfully cut off the rest of the population from the military clique, who were labelled as war criminals. What is more, the trial also cut off the Japanese nation from its war responsibility and past militarism, giving the impression that what was examined under the trial was all that mattered and allowing them to move forward as a peace-loving nation. In this sense, the Tokyo Trial contributed to the Allies' strategic purpose to demilitarize and democratize post-war Japan.

Yves Beigbeder states: 'One of the purposes of both the Nuremberg and the Tokyo Trials was to individualize punishment in order to avoid German or Japanese collective criminal responsibility. Has this aim succeeded too well in the case of the Japanese?'[168] An underlying assumption here is that, in the case of Japan, the individualization of criminal responsibility worked so well that it detached the Japanese from the overall issue of war and responsibility; the result has been national apathy and a self-righteousness attitude towards their past war crimes. Indeed, people in Japan now as then consider that the Tokyo Trial was a way of war settlement, and, until the 1980s, remained apathetic regarding the issue of war responsibility. However, as this chapter examined, this is only half of the story.

Close examination of Japanese perception as well as national apathy towards the Tokyo Trial reveal that the Japanese have never been freed from a sense of collective responsibility, which has been not merely cultivated from within but also imposed from outside. Such a sense has been present ever since and has become a part of the society. In spite of the Allies' intention to avoid pursuing collective responsibility, a number of Japanese felt, and still feel, that it was their nation as a whole that was judged under the Tokyo Tribunal. This impression is inevitable when their own leaders were prosecuted externally and unilaterally and the people were excluded from that process. 'Victor's justice' left the Japanese with a vague sense of war guilt at best, frustration in general and repellent nationalistic attitude at worst. What is more, regarding the war that was conducted in the name of the nation, people themselves are well aware that the responsibility of the nation cannot be de-collectivized totally. These reflections remain in the society as a 'pent-up' feeling, or scar.

The examination in this chapter has revealed paradoxical trends: while the Japanese at the time, because of passive acceptance and cynicism, remained as bystanders at the Tokyo Trial and did not take its significance actively and personally so as to cause them to reflect on their own responsibility for war cooperation, they, nonetheless, felt frustrated that the trial blamed them collectively as a nation. This Japanese perception indicates the complexity and delicacy of the issue of war responsibility and war crimes prosecutions, which the 'Nuremberg legacy' does not illustrate. The chapter set out the paradoxical combination of 'individual responsibility pursued' and 'collective responsibility perceived', which left the Japanese with an ambiguous and distorted sense of war responsibility and guilt, which is problematic not only in itself but also in terms of achieving reconciliation with their neighbours and a healthy social transformation in the long term. This chapter has challenged understanding of the promoter of international war crimes tribunals on whether and in what way individual criminal punishment affects societies in transition.

A complex relationship between war crimes prosecution and post-war society was also observed from the fact that while many interviewees would have favoured domestic trials after the war, they nonetheless felt, with the benefit of hindsight, that such trials would not have been feasible. This chapter has questioned what is assumed by promoters of international criminal justice as desirable and feasible for the society in the aftermath of armed conflicts.

Through the people's perception of the Tokyo Trial, it was observed that lack of interest, cynicism, dismay and frustration are all keys to understanding the Japanese people's sense of war guilt and responsibility, and that they have been embraced by the Japanese in a very complex form. The current generation is struggling with the fact that responsibility over past war crimes has stretched out vertically and horizontally, growing into a timeless collective responsibility. This is creating a rather distorted sense of collective guilt within the society. This is what the advocates of international criminal justice maintain ought to be avoided. It is ironic that the Tokyo Trial not only failed in this but also came to be attacked by some as the source of such overarching collective guilt. The experience of the Tokyo Trial illustrates that international war crimes prosecution can make the issue of war crime responsibility complex, especially in the long term; it can even distort people's sense of war guilt.

Conclusion

The creation of the UN ad hoc international criminal tribunals (ICTs) in the early 1990s was set against a background of developing approaches to international justice, where it was believed that lasting peace could be fostered by judicial means. Peace through justice was the theme. The operation of the ICTs was much discussed and generated great debate about their very existence, their nature and their effect. However, arguments in this extensive body of research and writing in the field of international was crimes tribunals tend to focus on the legal aspect of the tribunals or remain at a theoretical, or preference level. What is not addressed enough is exactly what is achieved by prosecuting war crimes: the *strategic purposes* of international war crimes tribunals. This study has sought to develop this concept and understanding of the effectiveness of the tribunals by focusing on the so-called 'Nuremberg legacy', which fostered the idea of peace through justice and examining the 'other' International Military Tribunal at the end of the Second World War, in Tokyo, which has not received significant attention compared with Nuremberg and which, as this research has argued, leads to less idealistic and clear-cut conclusions than the Nuremberg legacy would suggest. As a consequence, the overall understanding of what can be achieved by international judicial mechanisms needs to be reappraised.

The contemporary ICTs' ultimate aim is not war crimes prosecution per se. They are judicial bodies created by the UN Security Council as an enforcement measure to respond to threats to international peace, and their strategic purpose is to 'restore' and 'maintain' international peace. This point is vital for understanding and assessing the ICTs' strategy and effectiveness. As Chapter 1 confirmed, the ICTs were established in response to, and as part of, the new security environment that emerged after the end of the Cold War, in which the 'non-military' sources of instability existing 'within' a state came to be a matter of international concern. This new situation made the establishment of the ICTs both possible and necessary. The ICTs were given a mission to contribute to the critical transition from war to peace, where peace should not only be restored, but also maintained, once it had been established. Justice was expected to consolidate fragile peace by promoting transformation of societies that have experienced mass atrocities.

The idea of peace through justice, a key concept underpinning the ICTs' strategic purposes, and the establishment of an international war crimes tribunal were not new. What was significant about the ICTs, however, was that they were established half a century after the two International Military Tribunals (IMTs), Nuremberg and Tokyo, which had been created in the aftermath of Second World War. The experience of Nuremberg, especially, was closely borne in mind by those building the ICTY and the ICTR, in their early days. The experience of the IMTs was clearly significant in the context of post-Cold War international relations. Chapter 2 examined that in spite of states' affirmation of the Charter and judgment of Nuremberg and the remarkable development of international law thereafter, states were reluctant to resort to the Nuremberg precedent during the Cold War, which prevented any subsequent international tribunal from being established – primarily because there was a lack of political will, unsurprisingly in the Cold War context. However, as the definition of what constituted a 'threat to international peace' changed with the end of the Cold War, the Nuremberg experience came to be seen as a key instrument in international peace and security. Based on the experience of Nuremberg and the impact and effect this international war crimes tribunal was said to have had on post-conflict German society, promoters of the ICTs believed strongly in the positive impact of international war crimes tribunals on post-conflict society, especially in terms of social transformation and reconciliation in the context of the former Yugoslavia, Rwanda and other post-conflict societies. However, as noted, the experience of the Tokyo Trial and post-war Japan can tell a different story about the impact and effect of such a tribunal.

Through empirical research, including interviews and focus groups, this study has analysed the impact of the Tokyo Trial, both in the short and the long term, by examining how people in Japan have reacted to the trial over time. That 'the Tokyo Trial was "victor's justice"' was a view widely held by the Japanese at the time, and one that remained 60 years later. The creation and operation of the Tokyo Trial served the strategic purposes of the Allies, really the United States, to demilitarize and democratize the vanquished nation: Japan. Although the unfairness and political nature of the trial, especially its *ex post facto* legislation and unilateral trial, were felt strongly, the Japanese accepted, and ever since have continued to accept, the Tokyo Trial with the understanding that it was 'an inevitable consequence of defeat'. Their passive acceptance, in fact, is close to apathy. Considering Japanese attitudes towards the Second World War, war crimes and the issue of war responsibility, revealed in the present research, it is evident that the Tokyo Trial had little 'visible' effect, or no 'positive' impact, on Japan. However, the silence of the Japanese is highly vocal, in a sense.

The Japanese view of the Tokyo Trial consists of a complex mixture of lack of interest, cynicism, sense of 'collective guilt' or 'collective humiliation' and frustration. These complex and ambivalent perceptions are not irrelevant to the 'unique' nature of the Tokyo Trial. As seen in Chapter 3, in spite of the fact that the Tokyo Trial was modelled on the Nuremberg Tribunal, with a similar impact expected by the organizers, there are several critical differences between the two tribunals, related to differences in the background and context of the defeat of the two countries, as well as to the different degree of initiative taken by the United States. The disputes over the Emperor's responsibility and unsettled responsibility for the victims in Asia, notably the issue of 'comfort women', are problems of kinds that were absent in the case of Nuremberg and post-war West Germany, and can be attributed to the unique nature of or specific 'shortcomings' of the Tokyo Trial. Some commentators have argued that the Japanese reaction is due to the unique character of Japan, its people and cultural and historical background. Cultural context will always be an important factor in particular situations, a factor relevant to the general understanding of strategic purpose in international war crimes prosecutions. However, it is the application and operation of the judicial instrument – and its limitations – that must be addressed, and that informs understanding not only of what happened in Japan, but of the general utility of international judicial mechanisms, and what can be expected of them. It is for this purpose that this author examined the Tokyo Trial and post-war Japan.

Rather than focus on the peculiarity of the case, therefore, this study has examined Japanese perceptions and reactions in terms of the tribunal's two key devices: the creation and presentation of an historical record of the event; and the pursuit of individual responsibility. These devices are key because the 'Nuremberg legacy', reiterated in the context of the ICTs, suggests that they determine the utility of war crimes tribunals. The historical record created through legal procedures, the advocates of international tribunals emphasize, is 'authoritative' and contributes not only to discrediting leaders responsible for mass atrocities, but also to cultivating collective memory and national identity. Individual criminal punishment is regarded as vital for the de-collectivization of responsibility, which promotes the detachment of those leaders most responsible from the majority of the population, the de-collectivization of hatred held by the victims, and the endorsement of social transformation of the nation by freeing them from the burden of guilt and the traumatic past. In these ways, international war crimes tribunals are expected to contribute to the social transformation of a war-torn society and to reconciliation within it. This understanding of international war crimes tribunals, however, cannot be treated as universal, or realistically achievable, as the impact of the Tokyo Trial on post-war Japan reveals.

Chapter 5 examined the Tokyo Trial's historical record, the first principal device of international prosecution, and its impact on post-war Japan. The Tokyo Trial's account of the war had a significant impact on the Japanese, at the time, by telling them the facts and judging the criminality of the war. Importantly, the account of the tribunal was accepted by the nation at the time. In one aspect, this is natural, regarding the fact that the Tokyo Trial itself was accepted as inevitable, following the logic of 'might is right'. What is more, the trial's account of the war was 'comfortable' for the people at the time. By focusing on the role of a military clique, the Tokyo Trial pointed the finger at who should be blamed for war, defeat and misery, and by doing so, it freed the majority of the population from the burden of war guilt. The Tokyo Trial had a symbolic effect.

Not only did it detach the wartime leaders, the military, from their angry and frustrated people, but it also gave people a setting in which to bury the militarist past and start from scratch as a peace-loving nation. Overall, this was an initial response not incompatible with the peace and justice theory embraced by advocates of the Nuremberg approach.

The view that Japan conducted aggressive wars recklessly led by the military and militarists is still held by the majority in Japan. However, it is difficult to point out the explicit impact of the Tokyo Trial on this Japanese historical view. The positive impact of the 'authoritative' account of the tribunal, at least, is not appreciated in society. People's general attitude to the Tokyo Trial is characterized by ignorance and indifference. At the same time, the 'authoritativeness' of the trial's account of the war has been severely attacked by nationalists and conservatives, and, recently, by revisionists, who put forward the 'affirmative view' of the war. Criticisms are made regarding both the content of the account and the fact that such an account was the outcome of 'victor's justice'. They further claim that the current Japanese view of history and war is the result of the verdict of the Tokyo Trial, which imposed a 'wrong' historical view. How to perceive the nature of the war is an issue that is still unsettled among the Japanese and has been debated politically, ideologically and emotionally. The Tokyo Trial is involved in this because it itself offered a specific account of the war. As the results of intensive interviews and focus groups showed, these ideological and emotional debates surrounding the trial scare the majority of the population away from thinking and talking in a casual and frank manner about the trial and war crimes. The very problem of the Tokyo Trial and the Japanese is that the trial is either talked about emotionally and ideologically within a limited circle, or simply ignored by the majority of the population. This is strongly related to the general perception that the Tokyo Trial is a national taboo. Interviews and focus groups strongly confirmed this perception. A sense of taboo is an important element, together with indifference and cynicism, that constitutes a national silence, or 'historical amnesia'.

Chapter 5 showed that the Tokyo Trial's authoritative historical record *did not* contribute to settling the history of a traumatic experience and a controversial period in Japan's past. The present-day Japanese still hold an ambiguous and unsettled view of the war, and have not successfully come to terms with their past. What is worse, regarding the historical perspective, the Tokyo Trial's verdict can be said to have stimulated nationalist and revisionist zeal, on the one hand, and contributed, unintentionally, to the majority's 'apathy' on the other. This passive attitude of the Japanese regarding the past is an obstacle to reconciliation not only with its victims but also with its own past, because it angers and irritates the Chinese and Koreans and harms the cultivation of healthy national identity and the true social transformation of Japan. Even after half a century, like F. Scott Fitzgerald's boats against the current, the Japanese are borne back ceaselessly into the past. This all suggests that the Tokyo Trial's account of the war has been rather counterproductive in terms of reconciliation and social transformation.

Chapter 6 illustrated that the Tokyo Trial's individualization of responsibility has also left an ambivalent perception and understanding of war guilt and responsibility within the Japanese. The criminal punishment of wartime leaders had a symbolic impact, at the time, because it successfully detached the Japanese people from the defendants who were labelled as war criminals, as well as from war crimes and responsibility. This gave the nation a setting in which to start from scratch. The side effect of this, however, was that the Japanese became bystanders to the Tokyo Trial. They did not examine the trial and its verdict actively and personally, so as to reflect on their own responsibility as a people. The Tokyo Trial facilitated people's self-justification, as well as self-immunization from responsibility by putting blame solely on the defendants at the trial.

At the same time, however, many of the Japanese felt, and still feel, paradoxically, frustration that it was their nation, as a whole, that was judged collectively by the Tokyo Trial. The view that the Tokyo Trial was 'victor's justice' imposed on the vanquished nation continues to be widely shared among the Japanese, with a bitter feeling. In spite of the Allies' intention to avoid pursuing collective responsibility, this impression is inevitable when their own leaders were prosecuted externally and unilaterally, and when people were excluded from that process. This point has been especially emphasized by nationalist and right-wingers, who question the fairness and justice of the trial.

Japanese acceptance of the Tokyo Trial's pursuit of responsibility of individual leaders, on the one hand, and their perception deep down of collective responsibility pursued under the trial, on the other, are paradoxical trends. Nonetheless, each of them, or a mixture of them, is an important indication of the differential, delicate and complex impact of the individual criminal punishment in the aftermath of war and conflict. What is more, regarding the war, as well as the large-scale atrocity that was conducted in the name of the nation or a social group, people themselves are well aware that their responsibility cannot be de-collectivized totally. The Tokyo Trial could not erase senses of 'collective guilt' in the Japanese; in some cases the trial itself became a 'collective humiliation'. In other words, individual criminal punishment under the Tokyo Trial left the Japanese with an ambiguous and ambivalent sense of war responsibility and guilt, which has been embedded in them ever since and remains repressed in society as a 'pent-up' feeling.

Opinion polls as well as intensive interviews and focus groups showed that the current generation is struggling to recognize and understand the meaning of contemporary Japan's responsibility for the war and for war crimes. While recognizing a sense of collective guilt, the post-war generation is dismayed and frustrated by the fact that responsibility for the past has grown into a timeless collective responsibility. A sense of collective responsibility has been not merely cultivated within, but also imposed without. This fact gives some Japanese a sense of frustration. It is based on this frustration that nationalist and conservative claims that the Tokyo Trial instigated the Japanese with a sense of guilt appeal. After all, their claim is a magnified version of a pent-up feeling suppressed by the

Japanese, who hold a rather distorted sense of collective guilt, or even a feeling of being victimized by enduring accusations of having been the victimizer. Excessive collective responsibility is what the advocates of international criminal justice believe that a war crimes tribunal should help to avoid. It is ironic, therefore, that the Tokyo Trial not only failed to achieve this, but also came to be attacked by some as the source of an overarching collective guilt.

Through analysis of Japanese perception and values, this study has argued that the Tokyo Trial left a mixed legacy in Japanese society. It played an important role in Japan's immediate demilitarization and democratization process, which was the Allies' original strategic purpose for conducting the Tokyo Trial. However, from the perspective of social transformation and reconciliation, which are the perceived (or received) strategic purposes of current international war crimes tribunals, the impact of the Tokyo Trial on post-war Japan is rather problematic. The Tokyo Trial, ironically, became a cause – not *the* cause – that endorsed the Japanese people's understanding of the war and sense of war responsibility to be twisted and distorted. What is more, as rows over textbooks and the Yasukuni shrine show, the Tokyo Trial clouds Japanese reconciliation with their Asian neighbours, as well as with their own past.

The historical perception of the war and a sense of war responsibility are very important issues for post-war reconciliation and social transformation. In this research, I have shown through the case of the Tokyo Trial and post-war Japan that international war crimes tribunals can cause an impact on historical perception and the sense of war responsibility in a society, possibly in ways that are different from, or even opposite to, those proposed by advocates of the Nuremberg legacy. In the worst cases, they can complicate the issue of war crimes responsibility, and even twist a people's sense of war guilt in the long run. This study raised a question of whether an international tribunal's historical record and its pursuit of individual responsibility is a useful means of encouraging peace, or a hindrance to the difficult processes of reconciliation and transformation that a society in transition has to go through.

I would not wish to maintain that the findings here are the *real* legacy of war crimes tribunals. Just as the experience of Tokyo and Nuremberg show, a 'one size fits all' is a simplistic approach, with which the present analysis has engaged critically throughout. Each international war crimes tribunal is different in its appearance, procedures and, thus, impact, based on the way an armed conflict ends and on the direction to which post-conflict society moves. This is clear from the continuing international war crimes tribunals in the former Yugoslavia, Rwanda and the hybrid court in Sierra Leone. However, in some respects, the 'Tokyo legacy' seems more relevant to the experience of other international tribunals and societies than its Nuremberg counterpart. Some of the limitations and side effects of the trial's account of events, described and analysed in the present study, have also been noted by others, particularly some legal scholars, with regard to the ICTs and cases in Latin America. Among scholars and practitioners of transitional justice, it is non-judicial mechanisms, such as truth commissions, that are increasingly regarded as appropriate for post-conflict truth seeking. Some reports of the Serbian reaction to the Milosevic trial at the ICTY note views and frustrations that the international tribunal is an 'anti-Serb' institution or a political court that tries Serbia as a whole, confusion over whether The Hague tribunal strictly distinguishes between the individual and the collective, and a pragmatic perception that the tribunal is a condition the country has to meet in order to gain financial and political support from the international community.[1] This ambivalent, or paradoxical, trend, if correct and confirmed by research, is in line with the findings and thesis presented in this study regarding the Tokyo Trial and Japan.

The Japanese people's attitude towards the war crimes tribunal and war responsibility has been influenced by the fact that the Tokyo Trial was an 'internationally imposed' institution. The scar of 'victor's justice' remains in the Japanese collective memory, which leads to a vague sense of war guilt at best, a repellent nationalistic attitude at worst, and frustration in general. The fact that the trial was 'victor's justice' degraded any positive significance that the trial might have had. What is more, the passive Japanese attitude towards, or 'silence' over, the issue of reflecting on the war and the war crimes legacy can be attributed to the fact that it was an international tribunal that has given a judgment on Japan's war. The Japanese could cling to the internationally given judgment, rather than re-examining the painful events and experiences by themselves. In this sense, the international tribunal deprived the Japanese the opportunity, and perhaps the will, directly to confront the past. This leads to general indifference about the war, war crimes and the Tokyo Trial itself. All these question the perceived positive impact of international tribunals and raise the importance of local ownership, which is highlighted by those who work in the field of transitional justice. Interestingly, however, the result of intensive interviews and focus groups showed that, although many Japanese think – with the benefit of hindsight – that domestic trials after the war would have been ideal, in theory, most of them are very sceptical about the feasibility of such trials. They pointed out the lack of necessary infrastructure so soon after the war and, more importantly, showed awareness of an ethical question about who could serve as a judge to try an event in which the whole nation had been involved. This suggests the dilemma in desirability and feasibility of local ownership in post-conflict societies. More importantly, this study shows a need to focus more on how people regard and accept war crimes trials and thus the importance of outreach programmes attempted along ongoing tribunals. For war crimes tribunals to be effective, justice needs to be done as well as to be seen to be done.

Half a century from the Nuremberg Trial, the ICTs became a new part of its legacy. In their turn, they too became the catalyst for a further development in the domain of international criminal justice, the emergence of the International Criminal Court. It is in this context, that the Tokyo Trial becomes an important case to research, because the experience of the Nuremberg Tribunal has been emphatically invoked with certain key assumptions about its impact on the subsequent peace and security. The Tokyo Trial has been little researched and appreciated, in comparison, but it remains the only public international war crimes tribunal, other than Nuremberg, that has operated and completed its cases. This fact alone shows that greater attention should be paid to the significance as well as impact of the Tokyo Trial, both in the short and the long term.

The case of the Tokyo Trial and post-war Japan brings into question prominent and popular beliefs among proponents of international criminal justice about the positive impact of war crimes prosecutions, especially concerning the two devices of individual criminal punishment and the creation of an authoritative account of the war. This work has offered research with which to examine the short-term and long-term impact of these two principal devices, which were considered and applied both at Tokyo and Nuremberg, and are currently regarded as important and effective tools by ad hoc international criminal tribunals and other post-Cold War international war crimes tribunals to promote social transformation. Strictly speaking, the strategic purposes of the post-Second World War International Military Tribunals and the post-Cold War international criminal tribunals are not precisely the same, as the former aimed at the denazification and democratization of post-war Germany and the demilitarization and democratization of Japan, whereas the post-Cold War tribunals have broader purposes. Nonetheless, the positive impact of international prosecution in the context of post-conflict nation building and transitional justice in the 1940s, especially the experience of Nuremberg, was emphasized in the subsequent discussion of the topic and was a key part of the discourse surrounding the more recent international judicial bodies. Moreover, certain assumptions about Nuremberg's impact on the subsequent peace and security crucially informed the creation of the ad hoc courts.

The experience of the Tokyo Trial and post-war Japan, as shown above, demonstrates that the impact and effect of international war crimes tribunals and their two principal devices are not necessarily wholly positive, nor are they straightforward. They may not only be complex, subtle and multifaceted, but also counterproductive and harmful by distorting the perpetrator people's sense of responsibility, guilt and historical perception. Such an impact is not at all welcomed when the strategic purpose of an international war crimes tribunal is to promote the healthy social transformation and true reconciliation, which are vital for the achievement of long-lasting peace in post-conflict society. The critical assessment this study has undertaken of the Nuremberg legacy based on research about the Tokyo Trial and its impact on post-war Japan suggests a need to re-examine the strategy of international war crimes tribunals and to question the understanding held by advocates of international tribunals regarding what international criminal justice can achieve and what outsiders can and cannot do to transform a war-torn society and promote reconciliation within it. Strategy of international war crimes tribunals cannot be developed without clear strategic purposes; and strategic purposes need to be set realistically, taking into consideration a context in which justice is pursued.

Appendix

Table A.1 Intensive interviews

Interviewee	*Born*	*Sex*	*Date of interview*	*Place of interview*
A	1959	Male	10 August 2003	London, UK
B	1974	Female	8 October 2003	Kyoto, Japan
C	1978	Female	17 November 2003	Kyoto, Japan
D	1938	Male	19 November 2003	Kyoto, Japan
E	1961	Male	21 November 2003	Kyoto, Japan
F	1974	Female	25 November 2003	Kyoto, Japan
G	1965	Male	2 December 2003	Kyoto, Japan
H	1949	Female	3 December 2003	Kyoto, Japan
I	1972	Female	6 December 2003	Kyoto, Japan
J	1959	Female	6 December 2003	Kyoto, Japan
K	1945	Female	13 December 2003	Kyoto, Japan
L	1972	Female	21 December 2003	Tokyo, Japan
M	1935	Male	12 January 2004	Kyoto, Japan
N	1935	Female	12 January 2004	Kyoto, Japan
O	1975	Male	10 July 2003	London, UK
P	1944	Female	17 November 2003	Kyoto, Japan
Q	1974	Female	9 July 2003	London, UK
R	1979	Female	12 August 2003	London, UK
S	1955	Male	15 October 2003	Kyoto, Japan

Note
The other two interviewees were: Andō Nisuke, Professor of International Law, Doshisha University, 13 November 2003, Kyoto, Japan and Asada Sadao, Professor of International History, Doshisha University, 15 January 2004, Kyoto, Japan.

Table A.2 Focus groups

A	Undergraduate students at the Faculty of Commerce, Doshisha University	3 males and 1 female (early 20s)	8 December 2003, Kyoto, Japan
B	Undergraduate students at the Faculty of Commerce, Doshisha University	8 males (early 20s)	25 November 2003, Kyoto, Japan
C	Postgraduate students at the Department of English, Doshisha University	1 male and 2 females (mid-20s)	18 November 2003, Kyoto, Japan
D	Postgraduate students at the Faculty of Law (majoring US–Japanese diplomatic history), Doshisha University	3 males and 1 female (mid to late 20s)	10 December 2003, Kyoto, Japan
E	Businessmen, graduated from Doshisha University	3 males (late 40s)	15 October 2003, Kyoto, Japan

Table A.3 Defendants at International Military Tribunal for the Far East (the Tokyo Trial)

Name	*Pre-war and wartime official position/s*
Araki Sadao (1877–1966)	General; Minister of War; Minister of Education
Doihara Kenji (1883–1948)	General; Commander, Kwantaung Army; Supreme War Council
Hashimoto Kingorō (1890–1957)	Colonel; various commander of artillery regiments
Hata Shunroku (1879–1962)	Field Marshal; Commander, China Expeditionary Force; Minister of War
Hiranuma Kiichirō (1867–1952)	Privy Council; Prime Minister
Hirota Kōki (1878–1948)	Ambassador to the Soviet Union; Foreign Minister; Prime Minister
Hoshino Naoki (1892–1978)	Director of General Affairs (chief civilian officer), Manchukuo; Minister Without Portfolio
Itagaki Seishirō (1885–1948)	General; Chief of Staff, Kwantung Army; Minister of War
Kaya Okinori (1889–1977)	Minister of Finance; President of North China Development Company
Kido Kōichi (1889–1977)	Minister of Education; Minister of Welfare; Minister of Home Affairs.
Kimura Heitarō (1888–1948)	General; Vice-Minister of War; Supreme War Council; Army Commander in Burma
Koiso Kuniaki (1880–1950)	General; Governor-general, Korea; Prime Minister
Matsui Iwane (1878–1948)	General; Commander, China Expeditionary Force
Matsuoka Yōsuke (1880–1946)	Japan's chief delegate, League of Nations; Foreign Minister
Minami Jirō (1874–1955)	General; Minister of War; Commander, Kwantung Army; Governor-general, Korea
Mutō Akira (1892–1948)	Vice-Chief of Staff, China Expeditionary Force; Director, Military Affairs Bureau
Nagano Osami (1880–1947)	Admiral; Navy Minister; Navy Chief of Staff
Oka Takasumi (1890–1973)	Chief, Naval Affairs Bureau; Vice-Minister of the Navy
Ōkawa Shūmei (1886–1957)	Intellectual behind the rise of the Japanese militarists in the 1930s
Ōshima Hiroshi (1886–1975)	Military Attaché in Germany; Ambassador to Germany
Satō Kenryō (1895–1975)	Chief, Military Affairs Bureau
Shigemitsu Mamoru (1887–1957)	Career diplomat; Ambassador to China, to the Soviet Union, to Great Britain; Foreign Minister
Shimada Shigetarō (1883–1976)	Admiral; Navy Minister; Supreme War Council
Shiratori Toshio (1887–1949)	Ambassador to Italy; Adviser to the Foreign Minister
Suzuki Teiichi (1888–1989)	President, Cabinet Planning Board; Adviser to the Cabinet
Tōgō Shigenori (1882–1950)	Career diplomat; Ambassador to Germany, to the Soviet Union, Foreign Minister
Tōjō Hideki (1884–1948)	General; Chief of Staff, Kwantung Army; Minister of War; Prime Minister
Umezu Yoshijirō (1882–1949)	General; Commander, Kwantung Army; Army Chief of Staff

Note

Created by the author with reference to Minear (1971) Appendix 3; and Ushimura (2004) p. 16.

Table A.4 Verdicts and sentences at the International Military Tribunal for the Far East (the Tokyo Trial)

Count	*1*	*27*	*29*	*31*	*32*	*33*	*35*	*36*	*54*	*55*	*Sentence*
ARAKI	G	G	A	A	A	A	A	A	A	A	Life imprisonment
DOIHARA	G	G	G	G	G	A	G	G	G	O	Hanging
HASHIMOTO	G	G	A	A	A				A	A	Life imprisonment
HATA	G	G	G	G	G		A	A	A	G	Life imprisonment
HIRANUMA	G	G	G	G	G	A	A	G	A	A	Life imprisonment
HIROTA	G	G	A	A	A	A	A		A	G	Hanging
HOSHINO	G	G	G	G	G	A	A		A	A	Life imprisonment
ITAGAKI	G	G	G	G	G	A	G	G	G	O	Hanging
KAYA	G	G	G	G	G				A	A	Life imprisonment
KIDO	G	G	G	G	G	A	A	A	A	A	Life imprisonment
KIMURA	G	G	G	G	G				G	G	Hanging
KOISO	G	G	G	G	G			A	A	G	Life imprisonment
MATSUI	A	A	A	A	A		A	A	A	G	Hanging
MINAMI	G	G	A	A	A				A	A	Life imprisonment
MUTO	G	G	G	G	G	A		A	G	G	Hanging
OKA	G	G	G	G	G				A	A	Life imprisonment
OSHIMA	G	A	A	A	A				A	A	Life imprisonment
SATO	G	G	G	G	G				A	A	Life imprisonment
SHIGEMITSU	A	G	G	G	G	G	A		A	G	7 years imprisonment
SHIMADA	G	G	G	G	G				A	A	Life imprisonment
SHIRATORI	G	A	A	A	A						Life imprisonment
SUZUKI	G	G	G	G	G		A	A	A	A	Life imprisonment
TOGO	G	G	G	G	G			A	A	A	20 years imprisonment
TOJO	G	G	G	G	G	G		A	G	O	Hanging
UMEZU	G	G	G	G	G			A	A	A	Life imprisonment

Source: Reprinted by permission of the publisher from 'The Tokyo Trial', in *International Conciliations*, by Solis Horwitz (New York; Carnegie Endowment for International Peace, 1950), p. 584. Available online at: www.carnegieendowment.org.

Notes
Count
1: the overall conspiracy.
27: waging war against China.
29: waging war against the United States.
31: waging war against the British Commonwealth.
32: waging war against the Netherlands.
33: waging war against France.
35: waging war against the USSR at Lake Khassan.
36: waging war against the USSR at Nomonhan.
54: ordering, authorizing or permitting atrocities.
55: disregard of duty to secure observance of and prevent breaches of Laws of War.
Blank: Not indicated on the count
G: Guilty
A: Acquitted
O: Charged but no finding made by the Tribunal.

Notes

Introduction

1 Remarks by the President at the opening of the commemoration of '50 years after Nuremberg: human rights and the rule of law', 15 October 1995. Available online at: http://clinton6.nara.gov/1995/10/1995–10–15-president-at-50-years-after-nuremberg-symposium.html (accessed 5 January 2004).
2 Shklar (1964) p. 180.
3 Key Figures of ICTY Case. Available online at: www.un.org/icty/glance-e/index.htm (accessed 16 October 2006).
4 ICTR Detainees – Status on 25 September 2006. Available online at: http://69.94.11.53/default.htm (accessed 16 October 2006).
5 See Romano *et al.* (2004).
6 See Press Briefing by White House Press Secretary, Ari Fleischer, on 11 October 2002. Available online at: www.whitehouse.gov/news/releases/2002/10/20021011–5.html (accessed 12 December 2003).
7 See Schabas (2001).
8 There is not enough space here to raise all the important works in this developing field. The importance and popularity of this field of study can be seen from the fact that *Journal of International Criminal Justice* was launched in 2002 and has been very successful, currently publishing five volumes per year.
9 UN Doc. S/RES/827 (1993), 25 May 1993, para. 11 (2).
10 Article 24 (1) of the UN Charter.
11 UN Doc. S/RES/827 (1993), para. 6.
12 UN Doc. S/RES/955 (1994), 8 November 1994. Resolution 955 stated that the tribunal was for

> the sole purpose of prosecuting persons responsible for genocide and other serious violations of international humanitarian law committed in the territory of Rwanda and Rwandan citizens responsible for genocide and other such violations committed in the territory of neighbouring States, between 1 January 1994 and 31 December 1994.

13 Kerr (2000), p. 17.
14 Kelsen (1951), p. 13.
15 Preamble, para. 1 of the UN Charter.
16 Howard (1993), pp. 64–5.
17 See Chapter 1 for a further analysis of peace, justice and international security.
18 As of July 2005, regarding Chapter VII enforcement measures, the phrasing the 'restoration and maintenance' of peace is repeated only in resolutions with regard to the ICTs. For example, UN Doc. S/RES/1165 (1998), 30 April 1998; UN Doc. S/RES/1166 (1998), 13 May 1998; UN Doc. S/RES/1329 (2000), 5 December 2000.

19 Paul Williams and Michael Scharf, for example, raise five issues as 'the function of justice': establishing individual responsibility; dismantling institutions and discrediting leaders responsible for atrocities; establishing an accurate historical record; victim catharsis; and deterrence. Williams and Scharf (2002), pp. 16–22. As the present study argues, the first and third 'function' are justice as a 'means', which can bring 'impacts' such as the second, fourth and fifth. They need, therefore, to be analysed at a different conceptual level.

20 See three different approaches to international justice explored in Snyder and Vinjamuri (2003/04), pp. 5–44.

21 See for example the statement of UK Ambassador to the UN, Sir David Hannay, at the Security Council. UN Doc. S/PV 3217 (1993), 25 May 1993.

22 How great a deterrent effect the ICTY actually had on the ground is arguable. The one thing that can be said, however, is that the massacre in Srebrenica conducted by the Serbs against more than 7,000 Muslims occurred in July 1995, when the ICTY had already started issuing indictments.

23 D'Amato (1994), p. 500.

24 Anonymous (1996), p. 258.

25 D'Amato (1994), pp. 500–1. He attempted to solve this dilemma *theoretically* by 'put[ting] the tribunal in play as an explicit bargaining chip in the peace negotiations', pp. 503–4.

26 Holbrooke (1998), p. 338; Kerr (2004), p. 187.

27 Schuett (1997), p. 110.

28 For a detailed analysis on the role of 'institutions of justice' in the process of peace negotiations and the conflicting relations between the two, see Williams and Scharf (2002). They argue that the relatively limited impact of the ICTY on the peace process was result not of the role of norms and the institution of justice per se but of the misapplication of those institutions by the most important peace builders and the Office of Prosecutor at the ICTY.

29 Alfred Rubin, for example, argues that attempts at international criminal tribunals are not based on a realistic understanding of the international legal order, which is confused by supporters of tribunals with moral order. He is also concerned about international tribunals seeking to determine the meaning of 'justice', on which there is no universal agreement. A. P. Rubin, 'The International Criminal Court: a skeptical analysis', in Schmitt (2000), pp. 421–38.

30 Cassese (1998), p. 11.

31 Article 9 (2) of the ICTY Statute and Article 8 (2) of the ICTR Statute.

32 Scheffer (1996); Kerr (2000).

33 Colson (2000), p. 51.

34 Quoted in Morris and Scharf (1995), p. 334.

35 Colson (2000), pp. 51–3.

36 See Chapter 1 for the idea of 'peace through justice'.

37 See tribunals' core achievements, raised by the ICTY. Available online at: www.un.org/icty/glance-e/index.htm (accessed 10 December 2005).

38 See for example Goldstone (1996b), pp. 485–503.

39 Annual Report of the International Tribunal for the Prosecution of Persons Responsible for Serious Violations of International Humanitarian Law Committed in the Territory of the former Yugoslavia since 1991, 29 August 1994, para. 16. Available online at: www.un.org/icty/rappannu-e/1994/AR94e.pdf (accessed 18 October 2002).

40 'Transitional justice' is a concept as well as a field of study, which has been growing rapidly over the past two decades. However, as Alex Boraine, President of International Center for Transitional Justice, states, 'the definition of transitional justice is still disputed and debated'. In a Report of the Secretary-General to the Security Council, 'The rule of law and transitional justice in conflict and post-conflict societies' (S/2004/616), the notion of transitional justice is set as to comprise 'the full

range of processes and mechanisms associated with a society's attempts to come to terms with a legacy of large-scale past abuses, in order to ensure accountability, serve justice and achieve reconciliation'. Defined as such, it includes various means, ends and actors. Recently, scholars and practitioners of transitional justice seem to distance themselves from judicial mechanism, especially international tribunals. Still, many of what is seen as main areas of transitional justice raised by Boraine – prosecution, truth-telling, reconciliation, reparation and institutional reform – coincide with strategic purposes and impact expected by the ICTs. This study uses the term 'transitional justice' to emphasize this aspect of international war crimes tribunals. See A. Boraine, 'Transitional justice as an emerging field' presented at the 'Repairing the Past: Reparations and Transitions to Democracy' symposium, Ottawa, Canada, 11 March 2004; Kritz (1995); Teitel (2000); Bassiouni (2002).

41 See Chapter 1.

42 Morris and Scharf (1995), p. 332, emphasis added.

43 See Chapter 2.

44 See Chapter 2.

45 Paskins and Dockrill (1979), p. 266.

46 See Chapter 2. The effect of deterrence is difficult to assess as it is only when the deterrence has failed that it can be recognized that the deterrence had been working. Still, it can be argued that Nuremberg may have reduced potential violations of *jus in bello*, by endorsing the development of the laws of war and enhancing the better understanding of the constraints on the method of warfare. And, surely, Nuremberg as well as the Tokyo Trial had a deterrent effect on post-war Germany and Japan, turning them away from war. On post-war Japan, see Chapters 5 and 6.

47 See for example Maguire (2001); Burchard (2006).

48 The Tokyo Trial, as Philip Piccigallo argues, was 'a constituent part of the entire Allied Eastern war crimes operation', and thus it is important not to ignore other minor war crimes trials held in Yokohama and other places outside Japan by each member of the Allies and their impact on Japan. Piccigallo (1979), p. 32. However, the present research is limited to the Tokyo Trial, i.e. an international military tribunal, because of its symbolism; as such it had a 'symbolic' impact on people.

49 Pritchard (1981), p. xxxi.

50 Minear (1971); Röling (1993). See also Horwitz (1950); Hosoya *et al.* (1986); Brackman (1987); Piccigallo (1979); Maga (2001). Some scholars examine the Tokyo Trial within the context of the US occupation of Japan. See Dower (2000), pp. 443–521; Harries and Harries (1987); Takemae (2002). See also Welch (2001).

51 Only a few studies have an equal focus on Tokyo and Nuremberg. See for example Beigbeder (1999); Ball (1999); Clark (1997), pp. 171–87. An exception is the trial of General Yamashita Tomoyuki, which can be found in many studies on this topic as an archetype for war crimes prosecution and principle of superior responsibility. See for example Walzer (1992), pp. 319–22. Although it is often dealt with under the heading of the Tokyo Trial, the case involved traditional military justice. General Yamashita was tried by an American court martial in Manila, well before the Tokyo Tribunal was established.

52 Simpson (1997), pp. 8–9.

53 Robertson (2002), p. 240.

54 One of the exceptions is Hosoya *et al.* (1986), the record of an International Symposium on the Tokyo War Crimes Trial held in Tokyo on 28–29 May 1983.

55 Taylor (1950), p. 473.

56 Awaya (1989), pp. 274–5.

57 Watt (1981), p. viii. The complete volumes of hectographed transcripts of proceedings, *Record of Proceedings of the International Military Tribunal for the Far East* are held by Bodleian Japanese Library at University of Oxford, together with Daily Index of Motions, Arguments, Decisions, Objections in Open Court,

Proceedings in Chambers, Index of Exhibits, Narrative Summary of Record and Analysis of Documentary Evidence. The British Library of Political and Economic Science in London also holds most, but not all, volumes of hectographed transcripts of proceedings, *Trial of the Major Japanese War Criminals before the International Military Tribunal for the Far East held at Tokyo*.

58 Watt (1981), p. xx.
59 Dull and Umemura (1957).
60 Watt (1981), p. viii.
61 Awaya (1989), p. 12.
62 Röling and Rüter (1977).
63 Pritchard (1981), p. xxxviii. Since 1998, Pritchard has been annotating, compiling, and editing a new edition of the complete transcripts of the Tokyo Trial: *The Tokyo Major War Crimes Trial: the Records of the International Military Tribunal for the Far East with an Authoritative Commentary and Comprehensive Guide: a collection in 124 volumes*. Lewiston, NY: Edwin Mellen Press for the Robert M.W. Kempner Collegium.
64 Kyokutō Kokusai Gunji Saibansho (1968).
65 Distribution of English stenographic records to news agencies was stopped during the trial on the grounds of reducing the burden of the US taxpayers, who had been paying for paper used for the trial. Asahi Shimbunsha Chōsa Kenkyūshitsu (1953), pp. 3–4.
66 Asahi Shimbun Hōtei Kishadan (1962), p. 2.
67 Röling (1993), p. 81.
68 Dower (2000), pp. 453–4.
69 Comment by K. Awaya, in Hosoya *et al.* (1986), p. 116.
70 See Chapter 4.
71 Comment by Y. Yoshida in Ōnuma *et al.* (2003). As a result, Yoshida argues, the Japanese government's attitude and policy regarding the Tokyo Trial have not yet wholly elucidated.
72 Shklar (1964), p. 179. The influence of Ruth Benedict's work cannot be ignored. She argues that Japanese culture is based on Confucian 'shame culture', which is different from Christian 'guilt culture'. Benedict (1946).
73 Röling (1993), pp. 35–6.
74 John Dower, a scholar of Japanese history, points out: 'Although all peoples and cultures set themselves apart (and are set apart by others) by stressing differences, this tends to be carried to an extreme where Japan is concerned'. Dower (2000), p. 29.
75 Buruma (2002), p. 164.
76 See Chapter 2.
77 See Shklar (1964), p. 180.
78 See Chapters 5 and 6.
79 See Chapter 4.
80 The International Symposium on the Tokyo War Crimes Trial, held in Tokyo in 1983, was the first occasion for public academic discussion on the multifaceted significance of the tribunal. The record of the symposium is available as Hosoya *et al.* (1986).
81 One such difference is that Japanese society after the Second World War faced very little need to achieve reconciliation among people in the society, as most of alleged war crimes of the Japanese army were conducted outside Japan, against non-Japanese.

1 The international criminal tribunals and international peace and security: theory and practice

1 See Introduction for the concept of 'strategic purposes'.
2 The academic interest in crossing the disciplinary boundary between international law and international politics has been increasing recently, and several works have been conducted on the role of international law in international politics, and their relations in the international arenas. See Byers (2001); Reus-Smit (2004).

3 Waltz (1959), p. 238.
4 Morgenthau (1967), p. 298.
5 See Keohane (1989).
6 Wight (1991), p. 239.
7 See, for example, Forsythe (1997), pp. 5–19.
8 See Owen (1992); Tisdall *et al.* (1992).
9 Neier (1998), p. 112. See also Ciechanski (1996), pp. 95–6.
10 See, for example, Chesterman (2001b), pp. 149–50.
11 See Meron (1998a); Cassese (1998), pp. 2–17.
12 Slaughter *et al.* (1998), p. 389.
13 Goldstone (1997), p. 108.
14 For example, deputy prosecutor Graham Blewitt stated: 'To me, the best measure of success is if it can achieve the prosecution of individuals fairly, *regardless of whether they are convicted or acquitted*'. Quoted in Scharf (1997), p. 220, emphasis added.
15 See Fox (1997), pp. 435–9.
16 Kerr (2004), p. 9.
17 Ibid., p. 3.
18 For such research, see Snyder and Vinjamuri (2003/04), pp. 5–44; Chesterman (2001b). See also the work of Chuter (2003).
19 Slaughter (1995), p. 503.
20 Under Article 39 of the UN Charter, the Security Council is authorized to determine the existence of any 'threat to the peace', 'breach of the peace' or 'act of aggression'. It should be emphasized that a 'threat to the peace' is neither a descriptive concept nor a fixed standard. While stating that it can be *objectively* characterized as a situation with a 'destabilizing and potentially explosive' character, Bernd Martenczuk argues that 'The term "threat to the peace" is sufficiently flexible and dynamic to include all major forms of serious international misconduct'. See Martenczuk (1999), p. 544. What is regarded as 'a threat' reflects not only the actual type of conflicts breaking out in the world but also the *perception* or *interpretation* of events, which includes the conjecture of actual harm in the future. In that sense, it can be said 'a threat to the peace is whatever the Security Council says is a threat to the peace'. See Akehurst (1987), p. 219. For 'subjective political judgment' of the Council, see Goodrich *et al.* (1969), pp. 293–4. The question of whether the Security Council has unlimited discretion or not was raised in the Lockerbie case. See Martenczuk (1999). Nonetheless, it is important to examine the Council's determination of a 'threat to the peace' for two reasons. First, it is such a determination that provides a legal basis for any enforcement measures taken by the Security Council under Chapter VII, which binds every member state. Second, the Council's determination embodies what international society, or strictly speaking Great Powers, perceives as a threat to the peace. What matters more on examining how the international community reacts *practically* to the situation is how states perceive incidents rather than what those incidents actually are. It is the former that directly evokes states' incentive for reaction.
21 Kelsen (1951), p. 930.
22 The civil war in the Congo (Resolution 161 (1961) of 21 February 1961, S/4741), the racist regime in Southern Rhodesia (Zimbabwe) (Resolution 217 (1965) of 20 November 1965) and the system of apartheid in South Africa (Resolution 418 (1977) of 4 November 1977). See Österdahl (1998), pp. 43–4.
23 Kelsen (1951), p. 19, emphasis added.
24 The Iraqi government's repression of its civilian population (SCR 688 of 5 April 1991); civil wars in Somalia (SCR 733 of 23 January 1992), in Liberia (SCR 788 of 19 November 1992), in Angola (SCR 864 of 15 September 1993); the humanitarian crisis in Rwanda (SCR 929 of 22 June 1994), in Zaire (SCR 1078 of 9 November 1996); the instability in Haiti (SCR 841 of 16 June 1993), in Burundi (SCR 1072 of

30 August 1996), in Sierra Leone (SCR 1132 of 8 October 1997) and in the Democratic Republic of the Congo (SCR 1291 of 24 February 2000). Three cases related to international terrorism, Libya (SCR 731 of 21 January 1992), Sudan (SCR 1054 of 26 April 1996) and Afghanistan (SCR 1267 of 15 October 1999), were also determined as a 'threat to international peace'. See Österdahl (1998), pp. 43–84. Whether civil war actually became more frequent in the post-Cold War era or whether each of the conflicts became more bloody than before can be argued. See for example Stedman (1993), pp. 7–8. However, for the current argument, this study regards, for reasons raised in Note 20, what the Council perceives as a threat to the peace matters.

25 Gow (2000), p. 304.

26 Secretary-General of the United Nations Report on the Work of the Organization, UN Doc. A/46/1, September 1991.

27 Report of the Secretary-General, 'An Agenda for Peace', 17 June 1992, UN Doc. A/47/277-S/24111, para. 17.

28 See for example, Mayall (1996); Ramsbotham and Woodhouse (1996).

29 Scheffer (1996), pp. 34–51; Kerr (2000), pp. 17–26.

30 S/23500 (1992), 31 January 1992.

31 On the traditional view of order/peace and justice, see Bull (1995); Bull (1984). See also Foot *et al.* (2003).

32 UN Doc. S/RES/808 (1993), 22 February 1993.

33 See Gow (2003); Kaldor (1999); Shaw (2003).

34 Goldstone (1996a), p. 19.

35 Akhavan (1998), p. 743, emphasis added.

36 The idea of 'peace through justice' corresponds to an argument made by Paul Van Zyl that transitional justice can contribute to post-conflict peace building and that in a number of ways the two are interrelated. See Van Zyl (2005), pp. 209–22.

37 See Paskins and Gow (2000), pp. 11–15. Some pointed out a tension between 'peace' and 'justice' in the structure of the United Nations itself, whose Charter declares its purpose as 'to maintain international peace and security' as well as 'to promote and encourage respect for human rights'. See Bailey (1994), pp. 1–10; Koskenniemi (1995), p. 327; Bratt (1999), pp. 63–5.

38 This point is exemplified in the work of Jack Snyder and Leslie Vinjamuri. They identify three approaches to international justice based on different logic regarding a choice of action taken: the logic of appropriateness – 'whether it follows right principles'; the logic of consequences – 'whether it leads to the right outcome'; and the logic of emotions – 'whether it feels right given the person's current emotional state'. Snyder and Vinjamuri associate themselves with the logic of consequences and argue that the strategy of the ICTs is not workable because they are based on the logic of appropriateness that places too much emphasis on the strength of norms and rule following, which are not effective in the deterrence of war crimes and crimes against humanity. However, the goals set out by each approach are not necessarily identical. As the authors themselves recognize, the focus of the logic of appropriateness is strengthening norms to change state behaviour, and of the logic of emotions is the role of international criminal justice as 'the emotional theatre of reconciliation', which are often regarded as important as the deterrence of future violence. Snyder and Vinjamuri (2003/04).

39 Bass (2000), p. 20.

40 Remarks by the President at the Opening of the Commemoration of '50 years after Nuremberg: Human Rights and the Rule of Law', 15 October 1995. Available online at: http://clinton6.nara.gov/1995/10/1995–10–15-president-at-50-years-after-nuremberg-symposium.html (accessed 5 January 2004).

41 See Snyder (2004), pp. 52–62.

42 Finnemore and Sikkink (1998), p. 916.

43 See Wendt (1999), pp. 313–69.

44 Gow (2005), p. 27.
45 Ibid., p. 29.
46 Ibid., p. 35.
47 See for example, Reus-Smit (2004).
48 Koh (1996/97), p. 2655.
49 Ibid.
50 See Finnemore and Sikkink (1998); Ruggie (1998).
51 Carr (1995), p. 164.
52 Klarin (1996), p. 35.
53 Ibid., emphasis added.
54 Human Rights Watch (1992), p. 5.
55 Ibid.
56 Neier (1998), p. 135. The news coverage itself was encouraged by previous news reports by Roy Gutman of *Newsday*. He also utilized the Holocaust analogy to describe the situation in Omarska. See Gutman (1993).
57 Owen (1992), emphasis added.
58 Tisdall *et al.* (1992).
59 Scheffer (1996), p. 35.
60 Bassiouni (1994a), p. 790, footnote 42.
61 UN Doc. S/PV.3175 (1993), 22 February 1993.
62 Ibid.
63 For a comparison of the Statutes of the International Criminal Tribunal for the former Yugoslavia and the IMTs, see Beigbeder (1999), pp. 152–4.
64 See O'Brien (1993), pp. 639–59. In the Security Council, state representatives emphasized that the Council was not creating new law but simply applying existing international law. See the statement of Venezuelan, Brazilian and Spanish Ambassadors in UN Doc. S/PV.3217 (1993), 25 May 1993.
65 See the ICTY Statute, Article 21. The trial in absentia, which was conducted by the Nuremberg Trial, is impermissible, and the right of appeal, which was ignored by the previous trial, is provided under the ICTY Statute.
66 See, for example, the statement of The President, Vorontsov, Russian Ambassador to the United Nations, at the Security Council. UN Doc. S/PV.3217 (1993).
67 Scharf (1997), pp. 214–15.
68 Mak (1995), pp. 550–3; Falk (1999), p. 711; Simpson (1997), pp. 5–8.
69 Mak (1995), p. 552; D'Amato (1994), p. 501.
70 Mak (1995), p. 552.
71 McCormack and Simpson (1997b), p. xix. Gary Bass states that to see, as many do, Nuremberg as 'an almost unique moment' for war crimes tribunals is incorrect: 'In fact, war crimes trials are a fairly regular part of international politics, with Nuremberg as only the most successful example'. Bass (2000), p. 5. In the aftermath of the First World War, there was a plan to prosecute leaders of the defeated nations before an international tribunal for personal responsibility for the war. International lawyers and diplomats at the United Nations War Crimes Commission set up in 1943 studied this precedent closely. See Willis (1982), pp. 173–4. However, the trial of the German Kaiser, Wilhelm II, ended in failure as he found asylum in the Netherlands that was not a contracting party of the Versailles treaty of Peace. The treaty also was not influential enough to force Germany to prosecute and punish its own war criminals severely; most of the national trials either ended up as shams or with very light sentences, or convicts were even allowed to escape after their trials. The Nuremberg Trial, on the contrary, successfully prosecuted Nazi leaders, while establishing important and innovative principles. The significance of the Nuremberg Trial lies in the fact that it established those principles at the same time as it demonstrated the feasibility of an international tribunal's prosecuting individuals, including state leaders, based on those principles. It is because of this that Nuremberg is different

from any other past international war crimes prosecution and has been treated as epoch-making and the model, not merely as 'only the most successful example'.

2 The Nuremburg legacy: ideas and practices

1 See, for example, Ratner and Abrams (2001); Fox (1993), pp. 194–7; Alvarez (1996), pp. 245–64; Scharf (1997).
2 Taylor (1992), p. 626.
3 Luban (1994), p. 343.
4 Falk (1999), p. 695, emphasis added.
5 Sprecher (1999), p. 1457.
6 Jackson (1947), p. xiv.
7 On the development of international law deriving from Nuremberg, see Meron (1998a); Bassiouni (1992).
8 General Assembly Resolution 95 (I), 11 December 1946.
9 The Principles also deny, as did the Nuremberg Tribunal, a defence based on an official position and on the existence of superior orders (Principles III and IV). The Principles also affirm the right of the accused to a fair trial under international law (V). See *Yearbook of the International Law Commission*, 1950, Vol. II, pp. 374–8.
10 Common Article 49/50/129/146 of the four Geneva Conventions of 1949.
11 Meron (2000), p. 263.
12 Beigbeder (2002), p. 3.
13 Judgment of the International Military Tribunal for the trial of German Major War Criminals (with the dissenting opinion of the Soviet member), Nuremberg, 30 September and 1 October 1946, presented by the Secretary of State for Foreign Affairs to Parliament by command of His Majesty, London: HMSO, 1946 (as judgment hereafter), p. 38.
14 For the arguments soon after the Nuremberg Trial, see Kelsen (1947), pp. 153–71; and articles in the *American Journal of International Law*, vol. 41, 1947.
15 Malanczuk (1997), p. 354.
16 Willis (1982), p. 170. Yoram Dinstein argues that none of those international instruments during the interwar period proclaiming the criminality of aggressive war was legally binding. See Dinstein (2001), pp. 106–7.
17 Kelsen (1947), p. 155.
18 'Crimes against humanity' in itself was not an entirely new concept. The term, covering 'inhumane acts committed by a government against its own subjects', was first used in 1915 by the governments of France, Great Britain and Russia to denounce the massacre of the Armenian population. However, the term was used in a 'non-technical' sense. See the United Nations War Crimes Commission (1948), pp. 188–9. In 1919, the Commission on Responsibility in charge of inquiring into the responsibilities relating to the First World War found the specific juxtaposition of 'war crimes' and 'crimes against humanity'. However, the Versailles Treaty did not refer to the 'laws of humanity' nor 'crimes against humanity'. Again, 'crimes against humanity' was used in the context of the Treaty in a 'non-technical sense'. Ibid., pp. 35–6, 45.
19 In general, it is positively accepted that with the concept of 'crimes against humanity', the Charter extended the jurisdiction of the Nuremberg Tribunal 'to include those who committed other serious crimes that fall outside the ambit of traditional war crimes, such as crimes where the victim is stateless, has the same nationality as the perpetrator, or that of a state allied with that of the perpetrator'. Opinion and judgment, Prosecution vs Dusko Tadic, IT-94–1, 7, May 1997, para. 619.
20 See Roberts and Guelff (2000), p. 3
21 Beigbeder (1999), p. 44.
22 Judgment, p. 41.
23 Luban (1994), pp. 337–9.

24 Whether obedience to superior orders can be used to defend war crimes is such a difficult issue that states could not agree, even after Nuremberg, the content of a Nuremberg principle regarding obedience to orders. See Dinstein (1965), pp. 228–41. See also Green (1976), for national and international approach to the problem of the defence of superior orders.

25 Judgment, p. 42.

26 The British had held that there were no laws relevant to such crimes against humanity. Wells (1984), p. 84. On the preparation of the draft of the Charter, French legal professionals questioned the criminality of launching a war of aggression under international law. Even an American jurist was doubtful about the idea that a violator of international law should suffer criminal penalties, unless such penalties were specified in the law concerned. Beigbeder (1999), p. 42.

27 Paskins and Dockrill (1979), p. 271. See also Shklar (1964), p. 164.

28 Kittichaisaree (2001), p. 16.

29 Shklar (1964), p. 149.

30 See Article 1 and 2 of the Charter of International Military Tribunal.

31 Beigbeder (1999), p. 40. The chief prosecutor for the US, on the other hand, argued: 'The worldwide scope of the aggressions carried out by these men has left but few real neutrals'. International Military Tribunal for the Trial of Major German War Criminals, 'The Trial of the Major German War Criminals before the International Military Tribunal, Nuremberg, 14 November 1945 to 1 October 1946' (as *Trial* hereafter), Vol. II, Proceedings, 14 November to 30 November 1945, p. 101. The International Criminal Tribunal for the former Yugoslavia (ICTY) sees the Nuremberg as well as Tokyo tribunals as '*multinational* in nature, representing only part of the world community'. Opinion and judgment, Prosecution vs Dusko Tadic, IT-94–1, 7 May 1997, para. 1, emphasis added.

32 Luban (1994), p. 361.

33 Paskins and Dockrill (1979), p. 277

34 Morris and Scharf (1995) vol. 1, p. 14.

35 Meron (2000), p. 243.

36 Common Article 49/50/129/146 of the four Geneva Conventions of 1949 made it the state's obligation to search for persons responsible for grave breaches and noted that the state shall bring such persons before its own courts, or extradite them to another state that has made out a *prima facie* case.

37 On the difference between 'vertical' and 'horizontal' mechanisms, Antonio Cassese argues that the extradition of accused persons to a state and surrender to an international jurisdiction are 'two totally different and separate mechanisms'. Cassese (1998), p. 13. Yoram Dinstein wrote in 1975 that without the existence of a permanent international criminal court, the distinction between 'real international offenses [*sic*]' and 'national offences originating in international treaties' is difficult to draw. Dinstein (2000), p. 136.

38 Borch (2003), pp. 52–4. See also Taylor (1971), pp. 123–53.

39 Wells (1984), p. 89.

40 Roberts (2003), p. 74.

41 See Wheeler (2000), pp. 55–110. Tanzania's intervention in Uganda was tacitly approved based on the fact that it had overthrown the barbaric regime of Idi Amin. However, as Nicholas Wheeler points out, the approval was possible because 'Tanzania had been attacked first' and her intervention 'did not touch on vital superpower interests, as in the case of Vietnam'. Ibid., p. 136.

42 Falk (1999), p. 708

43 Jackson's Opening Statement for the prosecution, in *Trial*, Vol. II, p. 154. This idea was also shared by Telford Taylor who saw the Nuremberg Trial and the United Nations as 'twin offspring of the Allied negotiations and agreements with respect to the peace that would follow victory'. Taylor (1971), p. 78.

44 Jackson's Opening Statement, in *Trial*, Vol. II, p. 154.

45 Ibid., p. 150.

46 Interestingly, although the importance of punishing the defendants for 'crimes against peace' was emphasized by the organizers and participants of Nuremberg, actual sentences given to the defendants show a slightly different story. Among 22 defendants, 16 were charged for 'crimes against peace' and 12 were found guilty, while 18 defendants were charged for 'crimes against humanity' and 16 were found guilty. Among 12 defendants who were sentenced to death, no one was hanged for 'crimes against peace' alone, while four were sentenced to death for war crimes and 'crimes against humanity', and one hanged only for the charge of 'crimes against humanity'. As B. V. A. Röling, a judge at the Tokyo Trial, sees, sentences given for 'crimes against peace' may be too lenient considering the fact that the tribunals called crimes against peace 'the supreme international crime'. See Chapter 3. This discrepancy in what was publicized at the beginning, the outcome of the Nuremberg judgment and the following public view and image of Nuremberg as 'the trial to end all wars' may point to an interesting aspect of 'legacy', which, as noted at the beginning of this chapter, is often based on teleological interpretation, not necessarily on the rigid fact.

47 Dinstein (2001), pp. 112–13.

48 General Assembly Resolution 3314 (XXIX), 14 December 1974.

49 Dinstein (2001), p. 115.

50 Bassiouni, 'Historical survey: 1919–1998', in Bassiouni (1998), pp. 11–15. The Rome Statute of the International Criminal Court adopted in 1998 includes the crime of aggression within the jurisdiction of the Court. However, Article 5 of the Statute notes that 'The Court shall exercise jurisdiction over the crime of aggression once a provision is adopted in accordance with Articles 121 and 123 defining the crime'. Judging from Articles 121 and 123, such a procedure does not seem to take place immediately. See Broomhall (2003), pp. 46–7.

51 Bassiouni (1998), p. 15.

52 Wells (1984), p. 103.

53 Davidson (1973), p. 2.

54 Ibid., p. 291.

55 Meron (2000), pp. 243–4.

56 Roberts (1995), p. 80. Roberts states that this view of the laws of war 'does have the merit of concentrating attention on what is practically achievable within our own societies and their armed forces'. Ibid.

57 Meron (2000), p. 243.

58 General Assembly Resolution 488 (V), 'Formulation of the Nuremberg Principles', 12 December 1950.

59 Roberts (1995), p. 29, emphasis added.

60 Paskins (1981), p. 76.

61 Eric Norden quoted in Taylor (1971), p. 96. The title of Taylor's book, *Nuremberg and Vietnam: An American Tragedy*, itself is a good example of the normative application of Nuremberg to examine Vietnam.

62 Bush (1993), p. 2066.

63 Ibid., pp. 2066–7.

64 Vincent (1986), p. 125.

65 Robertson (2002), p.xiii.

66 Ratner and Abrams (2001), pp. 343–4. They argue that the Nuremberg Trial married two trends: international law which directly mandates individual criminal accountability for violations of the laws of war; and the evolution of international human rights law, which 'seeks to guarantee the rights of persons vis-à-vis their own government'. See, Ibid., pp. 5–10.

67 Crocker (2001), p. 271.

68 See for example the case in Argentina: Zalaquett (1995a), p. 204.

69 Kritz (1995b), p. xx; Zalaquett (1995b), p. 6.

70 Falk (1999), p. 718.
71 Teitel (2000), p. 31.
72 Ibid., p. 29.
73 Ibid.; See also Kritz (1995b), p. xxi.
74 Zalaquett (1995b). Other countries in Latin America also experienced the same kind of tension between punishment and impunity during their transition and finally selected the latter. In El Salvador, the National Assembly approved a government-backed amnesty and thus prevented further investigation and punishment of the perpetrators. In Chile, an amnesty law created under the Pinochet government in 1978 was applied to those who committed human rights violations in the name of political objectives, and, accordingly, only a few human rights violators were actually punished. See Beigbeder (1999), pp. 107–15.
75 A number of researches on transitional justice compares and contrasts prosecution and its alternatives – amnesty, clemency or truth commission – and examines their effect on post-totalitarian society. See Kritz (1995a); Minow (1998); Bassiouni (2002); Snyder and Vinjamuri (2003/04).
76 Crocker (2001), p. 272.
77 See the cases of Czechoslovakia, Germany (after communism), Hungary, Bulgaria and Russia, in Kritz (1995a) Vol. II.
78 Teitel (2000), p. 31. Currently, practioners and scholars of transitional justice put less emphasis on judicial mechanism. Instead, it is claimed that transitional justice is a range of procedures that includes various components such as prosecution, truth telling, reconciliation, reparations and so on. See Boraine (2004).
79 See Krause and Williams (1996), pp. 229–54.
80 Colson (2000), pp. 51–3.
81 Paskins and Dockrill (1979), p. 266.
82 The Allies' aims in establishing the International Military Tribunal were not necessarily clear nor coherent, and consisted of different factors, such as the creation of an international legal order examined above, as well as the transformation of post-war Germany examined below. The aim of this study is not to complete the whole picture of Nuremberg. On examining the 'legacy' of Nuremberg, the author believes it important to highlight certain aspects of the Allies' intention because they are often referred to by those who talk about Nuremberg in the context of the ICT's policy.
83 Herz (1982b), pp. 17–18. Herz insists on adding to the four 'd's another 'd': democratization.
84 Maguire (2001), p. 284, emphasis added.
85 Jackson's Opening Statement, in *Trial*, Vol. II, p. 102.
86 Ibid., p. 104.
87 Mark Osiel, however, argues that the prosecutor's usage of the concept of a 'criminal organization' is one of several positions taken by Nuremberg which 'appear to have entailed a commitment to elusive and illiberal notions of collective responsibility, distressingly similar to those the Nazis themselves employed'. Osiel (2000), pp. 124–5. His point indicates a potential difficulty in drawing the line between those who are responsible and not responsible for war crimes. See Chapter 6 for a detailed analysis of this point in the case of the Tokyo Trial.
88 Smith (1981), p. 8.
89 Document 13: From Henry L. Stimson to Henry Morgenthau, Jr, 5 September 1944, in Smith (1982), p. 30.
90 Osiel (1997), p. 167.
91 Smith (1982), p. 9.
92 The initial pressure for post-war trials came from the German-occupied nations. In January 1942 in London, representatives of the nine governments-in-exile organized themselves as the Inter-Allied Commission on the Punishment of War Crimes, and issued the St James Declaration requiring the United States and the United Kingdom

to 'place among their principal war aims the punishment, through the channel of organised justice, of those guilty of or responsible for these crimes, whether they have ordered them, perpetrated them or participated in them'. Punishment for War Crimes: the Inter-Allied Declaration Signed at St James's Palace London on 13 January 1942, and relative documents, A Document issued by The Inter-Allied Information Committee, London, His Majesty's Stationery Office, 1942, p. 4.

93 Shklar (1964), p. 158.

94 Ibid.

95 Herz explains that denazification meant

> not only to destroy every remnant of the Nazi party and affiliated organizations and institutions and to repeal all Nazi types of laws ... but also to remove all non-nominal Nazis from positions of influence and responsibility as well as to bring to justice all those who had participated in war crimes and atrocities.

Herz (1982b), p. 19. In this sense, it is difficult to analyse the impact of the Nuremberg Trial separately from all those subsequent trials following the IMT, conducted by Britain, France, the Soviet Union and the United States in their own military occupation zones. These trials covered a wide range of people including industrialists, diplomats and doctors, which had accompanied purges. This, Herz points out, created confusion between purge and punishment, and thus widespread feelings of resentment that the process of denazification was 'punishment for collective guilt and thus was considered unfair'. Ibid., p. 17. Herz's argument is an important clue for re-examining the Nuremberg legacy through re-examining the experience of Nuremberg and Germany. For the purposes of this study, this chapter focuses only on the IMT.

96 Jackson's Opening Statement, in *Trial*, Vol. II, p. 103.

97 Maguire (2001), pp. 145–6. Gary Bass relates the Allies' attempt at war crimes prosecution to their liberal political culture. See Bass (2000).

98 Meron (1998a), p. 198.

99 Report to the President of the United States by Robert H. Jackson, Chief of Counsel for the United States, 7 June 1945 in Jackson (1947), p. 8.

100 Jackson's Opening Statement, in *Trial*, Vol. II, p. 102.

101 Document 18: The letter of the Secretary of War (Stimson) to the Secretary of State (Hull), 27 October 1944 in Smith (1982), pp. 40–41.

102 Document 13, in Smith (1982), p. 30.

103 As to conspiracy, Article 6 of the IMT Charter notes: 'Leaders, organizers, instigators and accomplices participating in the formulation or execution of a common plan or conspiracy to commit any of the foregoing crimes are responsible for all acts performed by any person in execution of such plan'.

104 Quoted in Smith (1981), p. 76.

105 Shklar (1964), pp. 155–6, emphasis added.

106 Maguire (2001), p. 13.

107 Smith (1981), pp. 250–1.

108 Document 14: Secretary of War (Stimson) to the President, 9 September 1944, in Smith (1982), p. 31.

109 Osiel (1997), p. 82.

110 Statement of Sir Hartley Shawcross on 4 December 1945 in *Trial*, Vol. III, p. 92, emphasis added.

111 Quoted in Taylor (1992), p. 626.

112 See Chapter 1.

113 Annual Report of the International Tribunal for the Prosecution of Persons Responsible for Serious Violations of International Humanitarian Law Committed in the Territory of the former Yugoslavia since 1991, 29 August 1994 [as ICTY Report hereafter], para. 15. Available online at: www.un.org/icty/rappannu-e/1994/AR94e.pdf (accessed 18 October 2002).

114 Ibid.
115 Ibid., para. 16. See also Introduction.
116 Van Zyl (2005), pp. 209–22.
117 See Chapter 1.
118 Cassese (1997), p. 269.
119 Richard Goldstone quoted in Taylor (1995). See also Meron (1998a), p. 200.
120 Goldstone (1996b), p. 488.
121 ICTY Report, para. 16.
122 Goldstone (1996a), p. 19; Cassese (1997), p. 269.
123 Akhavan (1998), p. 753.
124 See Akhavan (2001), pp. 7–31.
125 UN Doc. S/PV.3217 (1993), 25 May 1993.
126 Akhavan (1998), p. 741.
127 See, for example, Mamdani (2001), for examination of the role of a radio station, which developed genocidal propaganda.
128 Cassese (1997), p. 269, emphasis added. Theodor Meron sees the historical record prepared by the tribunal as 'analogous to the report of a truth commission'. Meron (1997), p. 8.
129 Against this popular view and practice, some legal scholars point out limitations and problems in the legal process with regard to 'fashioning national identity through cultivation of collective memory'. See Osiel (1997); Teitel (2000), pp. 69–117.
130 Alvarez (1998), p. 2034.
131 UN Doc. S/PV.3217 (1993).
132 Akhavan (1998), p. 765.
133 Ibid., p. 767. Jose Alvarez also posits that the model of closure – 'emotionally cathartic closure' – is inspired by the Nuremberg Trials. Alvarez (1998), pp. 2032–3.
134 Unlike the truth commissions established in Latin America, the Truth and Reconciliation Commission in South Africa is a unique case, which attempts to combine criminal procedure and truth-telling. The Commission is given power to grant amnesty to those who have made 'total disclosure' of their violation of human rights. This, however, is not automatic, as each case is strictly examined under criteria for amnesty, given only for an act associated with a political objective.
135 Scharf (1997), p. 215.
136 Ibid., p. 216. See also Cassese (1997), p. 269.
137 UN Doc. S/PV.3217 (1993).
138 Robertson (2001), emphasis added.
139 Goldstone (1996b), pp. 499–501.
140 Mark Osiel points out: 'At Nuremberg, there was little testimony by surviving victims of the concentration camps and entirely nothing about their felt experience of life there or its emotional aftermath'. Osiel (1997), p. 103. The difference may be related to the difference in the jurisdictions between the ICTs and Nuremberg. The ICTs set at their centre 'crimes against humanity' and other war crimes conducted especially against civilians. Nuremberg was more focused on 'crimes against peace', which the ICTs did not even include in their jurisdiction.
141 O'Brien (1993), p. 659.
142 Goldstone regards the Truth and Reconciliation Commission in South Africa as a 'political compromise' between doing little and Nuremberg style trials. Goldstone (2000), p. 66. Chapters 3 and 4 of the book show how he developed his belief in the ICTs through his experience in post-apartheid South Africa.
143 Falk (1999), p. 716.
144 Robertson (2001).
145 The 'pedagogic' impact of Nuremberg on the German people, or such an attempt on the part of the Allies, is questioned by various scholars pointing out the negative attitude of the Germans towards Nuremberg. See Maguire (2001); Taylor (1992),

pp. 233–5. Jonathan Bush states that Nuremberg had more success as a history lesson for the Allies: 'For the next fifteen years, the Nuremberg legacy was essentially retrospective: it was a definitive historical text, especially for British and American audiences, verifying the evil of the Third Reich'. Bush (1993), pp. 2062–3.

3 The Tokyo Trial: an overview and purposes of the trial

1 Interestingly, the Japanese government, for its part, had difficulty in determining what the Allies were trying to do. The Japanese Ministry of Health and Welfare wrote in 1955:

> Even though there was the precedent of post-war Germany and its war trials, bearing in mind differences between Japan and Germany with regard to the circumstances surrounding the surrender, national characteristics and so on, the Japanese government could not easily grasp the character, content and sphere of the trials noted by Article 10 of the Potsdam Declaration.
>
> Kōseishō (2000), p. 127.

2 The characteristic aspect of the US occupation of Japan was indirect occupation, exercising the authority of the SCAP through the existing Japanese government via SCAP directives. For an analysis of the intricate relationship between the US and the Japanese government as well as the Japanese people during the occupation, see Dower (2000).
3 The responsibility for arrest was subsequently delegated to the Japanese government.
4 'Minor war criminals' having conducted conventional war crimes and crimes against humanity were called 'Class-B' and 'Class-C' war criminals. Under the Nuremberg Charter, Class B war crimes are categorized as conventional war crimes, and Class C as 'crimes against humanity'. In the Tokyo Trial, B and C were dealt with in the same category of 'conventional war crimes and crimes against humanity'. In the case of Japanese war criminals, some see Class B as referring to actual perpetrators of war crimes and C as the superior officers responsible for planning and giving orders, or failing to prevent, war crimes; or vice versa. Piccigallo (1979), p. 33. This, however, was difficult to determine under the Japanese military command structure. Instead of treating the two separately, trials dealt with minor war criminals as 'Class B and C war criminals'. Tōkyō Saiban Handobukku Henshū Iinkai (1989), p. 84. The term 'Class B and C war criminals' is now commonly used in Japan to refer to war criminals other than those prosecuted and punished under the Tokyo Tribunal. Suspects of Class B and C war crimes were prosecuted under special national military courts organized by the United States, Britain, Australia, France, Holland, the Philippines and China, in their own occupied territory previously dominated by Japan, based on their own laws and in their own jurisdiction. For details of trials conducted by each country, see Piccigallo (1979). The Soviet Union also conducted Class B and C war crimes trials, details of which are still not known.
5 See Appendix, Table A.3.
6 Prosecution opening statement presented by Joseph Keenan, 4 June 1946, in Pritchard and Zaide (1981) [as *Transcripts* hereafter], vol. 1, p. 435.
7 For a concise summary of each phase, see Horwitz (1950), pp. 503–25.
8 A motion on the jurisdiction of the tribunal, on 13–14 May 1946. *Transcripts*, vol. 1, pp. 119–232.
9 Ibid., p. 319.
10 Horwitz (1950), p. 526.
11 The Japanese government decided, as early as 12 September 1945, the supreme principle of defence was: (1) to avoid any responsibility being placed on the Emperor; (2) to defend the state; and (3) to defend individuals within the sphere of (1) and (2). Defence lawyers agreed to the first principle, but could not reach consensus on the prioritization of the state or individuals in their defence. The defence opening statement, written by Kiyose Ichirō, associate chief of the Japanese defence section,

was based on the defence of the state and therefore was not approved fully by some of his staff. Tōkyō Saiban Handobukku Henshū Iinkai (1989), p. 25.

12 General Headquarters Supreme Commander for the Allied Powers, Civil Information and Education Section and Public Information Section, Press Release: 'Summary of the Final judgment International Military Tribunal for the Far East', Summary no. 1, p. 2, reprinted in Bix *et al.* (2000), pp. 3–4.

13 See Appendix, Table A.4.

14 The judgment of the tribunal, *Transcripts*, vol. 20, p. 48437.

15 All the separate opinions are available in *Transcripts*, vol. 21.

16 Justice Jaranilla in fact was a survivor of the Bataan Death March, a notorious example of Japanese maltreatment of POWs. Some argue that this questions his objectivity as a judge at the tribunal.

17 His opinion was published as Pal (1953).

18 *Transcripts*, vol. 1, pp. 387–8.

19 Ibid., pp. 384, 389.

20 Ibid., p. 384, emphasis added. Based on Keenan's opening statement, the Tokyo Trial came to be understood by the Japanese as 'civilization's justice' (*Bunmei no Sabaki*), together with 'victor's justice'.

21 Politico-Military Problems in the Far East: United States Initial Post-defeat Policy Relating to Japan (SWNCC150/4/A), 21 September 1945, p. 1.

22 Ibid., pp. 3–4.

23 Demilitarization in this context is not mere disarmament. This research adopts Meirion and Susie Harries' definition of demilitarization encompassing 'both the eradication of the symptoms of militarisation, and the creation of a democratic state'. Harries and Harries (1987), p. xxxiv. It is militarism, 'the spirit that pervades militarised states', not the actual arms, that the Tokyo Trial was directly targeting. Demilitarization was also attempted through purges of thousands of officers, bureaucrats and industrialists conducted in the first two years of the occupation. See Takemae (2002).

24 The Apprehension and Punishment of War Criminals (Japan) (SWNCC57/3), 12 September 1945, Appendix B, para. 2.

25 Apprehension, Trial and Punishment of War Criminals in the Far East, Far Eastern Commission (FEC007/3), 29 March 1946. Higurashi Yoshinobu argues that FEC007/3 had a legal effect to give retroactively an 'international authority' to the Tokyo Tribunal. Higurashi (2002), p. 205. The Far Eastern Commission was established in February 1946 and consisted originally of 11 countries – Australia, Canada, China, France, Great Britain, India, the Netherlands, New Zealand, the Philippines, the Soviet Union and the United States.

26 SWNCC 57/3 stated:

> The advantages of an international military tribunal or tribunals for the trial of major criminals charged with offenses [... 'crimes against peace'], and of organizations whose members are collectively charged with criminal acts, for example, the Japanese Army and Navy General Staffs of recent years and the leading ultra-nationalistic societies, are as apparent in the case of Japan as in the case of Germany.
>
> SWNCC57/3, Appendix B, para. 3.

27 Harries and Harries (1987), p. xxix, emphasis added.

28 *Transcripts*, vol. 1, p. 468.

29 In reply to an invitation to the ceremony in London to sign the St James Declaration identifying the principal war aims against the European Axis as 'the punishment, through the channel of organised justice, of those guilty of or responsible for these crimes', the Chinese Minister to the Netherlands expressed his intention to 'apply the same principles to the Japanese occupying authorities in China when the time comes'. The Minister continued:

> The Chinese Government believes that the elementary principles of justice and morality cannot be vindicated unless the wrongs thus done to the Chinese people as those done to other peoples are equally righted and the guilty persons equally dealt with according to law.

Punishment for War Crimes: the Inter-Allied Declaration Signed at St James's Palace London on 13 January 1942, and relative documents, A Document issued by The Inter-Allied Information Committee, London, His Majesty's Stationery Office, 1942, p. 16.

30 'Our Relations in the Far East As They Appear in the International War Crimes Trial in Tokyo', an address prepared for delivery by Joseph B. Keenan, Chief of Counsel, International Prosecution Section, to be read at the meeting of the American Bar Association at Atlantic City, 29 October 1946, p. 40. RG-41, Box 4, Folder 4, MacArthur Archive.
31 Harries and Harries (1987), p. 103.
32 Röling (1993), p. 80. Röling points out that such a limited trial in Japan was 'effectively precluded' by the precedent of the Nuremberg Trial. Ibid.
33 Ginn (1992), p. 241.
34 See Dower (1986).
35 Quoted in Minear (1971), p. 126, footnote 3, emphasis added. Keenan also echoed this point shortly after the Tokyo Trial ended: 'I think that the foremost service they [the Tokyo Trial] rendered was to establish the facts authentically, particularly with the Japanese people'. Quoted in ibid.
36 The serial was published in major newspapers during 8 to 17 December 1945. *Asahi Shimbun* entitled its serial 'The History of the Pacific War: The Collapse of Truthless Militarist Japan – the Source Offered by GHQ' (*Taiheiyō Sensōshi: Shinjitsunaki Gunkoku Nihon no Hōkai, Rengōgun Shireibu Teikyō*); and *Yomiuri Shimbun* as 'The History of the Pacific War written by GHQ' (*Rengōgun Shireibu no Kijutsuseru Taiheiyō Sensōshi*).
37 Hosaka (1998), pp. 143–5.
38 Röling (1993), p. 79.
39 Maga (2001), p. 121. Takayanagi Kenzō, member of the defence counsel at the Tokyo Tribunal, writes that he as well as many Japanese were impressed by 'a spirit of fair play' at the tribunal, which, despite being a military tribunal, gave equal status to the defence and the prosecution and allowed the defence to challenge the legal logic of the prosecution. Takayanagi (1948), p. 5.
40 SWNCC 57/3, Appendix 'C', para. 5.
41 Elliott Thorpe quoted in Dower (2000), p. 452.
42 See Appleman (1954), p. 239. Having examined the Tokyo Trial's procedures, he concluded:

> it would seem essential that future bodies crystallize in advance the nature of evidence to be introduced, rules of procedure to be followed, and the respective duties owing by counsel to the tribunal and by the tribunal to the counsel.
>
> Ibid., p. 264.

43 Dissenting judgment of the member from France of the International Military Tribunal for the Far East (Henri Bernard), p. 20, in *Transcripts*, vol. 21.
44 Excerpts taken from Hankey (1950), pp. 112–13. Dower points out that the tribunal's controls over acceptable evidence seemed reasonable considering the fact that it was a military tribunal. Special restrictions on the defence evidence were based on strong US concern that the trial might have been used by the defendants as a stage for propaganda. Dower (2000), p. 466.
45 Ibid., p. 467.
46 Pritchard (1987b), p. 17.

47 Pointing out through the transcript of proceedings that the insults to defence counsel were frequent in the court, Appleman argues that Webb's attitude towards the counsel was not consistent with the standards of US courts. Appleman (1954), pp. 243–4.
48 Watt (1981), p. xvii.
49 Röling (1993), p. 31.
50 See Appendix, Table A.4.
51 Kojima (1971), p. 179.
52 Minear (1971), pp. 31–2, footnote 24.
53 Higurashi (2002), pp. 528–39.
54 Mr Joseph B. Keenan to the Secretary General of the Far Eastern Commission (Johnson), 16 July 1948, in *Foreign Relations of the United States* [as *F.R.U.S.* hereafter], 1948, vol. VI, p. 833.
55 According to Horwitz, when witnesses were examined via translation, the speed of the trial was reduced to one-fifth of its normal pace. Horwitz (1950), p. 538. In March 1948, George Kennan, the first director of the State Department's Policy Planning Staff, expressed his strong scepticism regarding the ongoing trials of the Japanese war criminals, based on several reasons: the punishment of individual leaders of the defeated nation 'should take place as an act of war, not of justice'; too slow process of the ongoing trials is harmful by itself; that legal professionals are not up to political trials; and 'The spectacle of American lawyers defending the policies of past Japanese Governments … is absolutely preposterous in its impact on the Japanese'. He maintained that 'these trials were profoundly misconceived from the start and are working increasing injury to the Allied cause in Japan'. Explanatory Notes by Mr George F. Kennan, 25 March 1948, in *F.R.U.S.*, 1948, vol. VI, pp. 717–18.
56 Report by the National Security Council on Recommendations with Respect to United States Policy toward Japan, 7 October 1948 (NSC 13/2), para. 18.
57 Minear (1971), p. 173. A shift in American war crimes prosecution policy was not unique to the case of Japan. Peter Maguire illustrates that war crimes prosecutions in Germany, especially those trials after the international military tribunal, were influenced by changes in US Cold War strategy. Maguire (2001), p. 254.
58 Horwitz (1950), p. 483. The associate prosecutors, after having arrived in Japan, were given an opportunity to suggest revisions to the Charter.
59 Articles 2 and 3 of the IMTFE Charter. Eleven justices at the Tokyo Trial were appointed by the SCAP, one each from the nine signatories of the Instrument of Surrender – Australia, Canada, China, France, Great Britain, the Netherlands, New Zealand, the Soviet Union and the United States – and India and the Philippines.
60 Article 17 of the Charter allows the SCAP 'at any time [to] reduce or otherwise alter the sentence except to increase its severity'.
61 Röling (1993), p. 31.
62 The subordinate position of other Allies can be attributed to the fact that it was the US who had played the primary role in fighting and defeating Japan militarily. See Watt (1981), p. ix.
63 For details of Unit 731 and American policy, see Harris (2002).
64 Röling (1993), p. 48. In a German case, human medical experiments conducted by Nazi doctors and military surgeons were judged by the American military trial following Nuremberg.
65 Ibid., pp. 49–50. The conduct of Unit 731 was later judged by the Soviet court martial at Khabarovsk in December 1949. The trial, lacking most of the top leaders of the Unit who had been given immunity by GHQ, sentenced the defendants to a maximum of 20 to 25 years' imprisonment.
66 While Article 7 of the Nuremberg Charter, stating no immunity for defendants' official positions, clearly states 'whether as Heads of State or responsible officials in Government Departments', Article 6 of the Tokyo Charter simply mentions 'the official position, at any time, of an accused'. Although this does not preclude the pursuit

of Japan's head of state, the Emperor, the disappearance of the phrase 'Heads of State' is worth noting given that immunity was accorded to the Emperor.

67 In his well-known telegram to Eisenhower, the Chief of Staff of the US Army, on 25 January 1946, MacArthur strongly insisted that indicting the Emperor would cause 'a tremendous convulsion among the Japanese people', causing the nation to disintegrate into total chaos and disorder. As a result, 'It is quite possible that a minimum of a million troops would be required which would have to be maintained for an indefinite number of years'. General of the Army Douglas MacArthur to the Chief of Staff, United States Army (Eisenhower), 25 January 1946, in *F.R.U.S.*, 1946, vol. VIII, p. 396. The impact of MacArthur's view can be seen in a later telegram of the Secretary of State, who wrote on 18 February 1946 that 'This question [of position of Emperor as war criminals] has *far-reaching political implications involving also military security*'. The Secretary of State to the Ambassador in the United Kingdom, 18 February 1946, in ibid., p. 415, emphasis added.

68 Against the often claimed view that the Soviet Union and China insisted on indicting the Emperor, recent research based on new archival material shows that it was only Australia that firmly maintained the position of working to bring the Emperor to justice. According to research conducted by NHK (Japan Broadcasting Corporation), supervised by Awaya Kentarō, in spite of its people's zeal to punish the Emperor, Chian Kai-shek of China regarded him as a useful bulwark against the expansion of communism. Awaya and NHK Shuzaihan (1994), pp. 60–72. The Soviet Union's decision not to push for a prosecution of the Emperor was based on the consideration not to confront American policy directly. Awaya and NHK conclude that it can be understood in terms of Stalin's Cold War policy towards the Far East. Ibid., pp. 161–2.

69 Arai (1994), p. 193.

70 Dower (2000), pp. 470–1.

71 According to Higurashi, the reason why the number of counts went up to 55 was due to diplomatic bargaining and compromising among prosecutors, each one of whom tried to reflect in the indictment their country's own interests. Higurashi (1997), p. 74.

72 Awaya (1994), p. 86.

73 Separate opinion of the president of the tribunal, William Webb, p. 15, in *Transcripts*, vol. 21.

74 The result of this restriction was the exclusion from the process of selecting defendants members of the industrial group (*zaibatsu*), who had played a vital role in carrying out aggressive wars and mistreating POWs, but nonetheless could not be charged with the commission of 'crimes against peace'. Horwitz (1950), pp. 497–8.

75 Counts 1 to 5 charged the accused with conspiracy. Count 1 was the basic count charging that the defendants, between 1 January 1928 and 2 September 1945, participated together in formulating or executing a common plan or conspiracy. This was broken down into smaller conspiracies under counts 2 to 5: conspiracy to wage aggressive war against China, the United States, the British Commonwealth of Nations, France, the Netherlands, Thailand, the Philippines and the Soviet Union; and conspiracy with Germany and Italy to assist mutually in aggressive warfare. Counts 6 to 17 charged defendants with the planning and preparing of aggressive wars, and counts 18 to 26 with the initiation of such wars. Counts 27 to 36 charged defendants with waging aggressive war against named countries.

76 Counts 6 to 26 were regarded as charges that replicated Counts 1 to 5. Counts 39 to 52 were regarded as charges against killing that had *resulted from* the unlawful waging of war, thus could be incorporated in the charge against aggressive war. Counts 37, 38, 44 and 53 were dismissed for the reason that 'the Charter does not confer any jurisdiction in respect of a conspiracy to commit any crime other than a crime against peace'. *Transcripts*, vol. 20, pp. 48447–53.

77 Counts 2 to 4 were incorporated into Count 1, so was Count 28 into 27. Insufficient

evidence was found for judging Count 5. Count 30, wars of aggression waged against the Philippines, was not examined as they were regarded as 'being a part of the war of aggression waged against the United States of America'. Count 34, aggressive wars against the Kingdom of Thailand, was also not examined. *Transcripts*, vol. 20, pp. 49769–72.

78 Considering the fact that the tribunals called crimes against peace 'the supreme international crime', Röling argues that at both Nuremberg and Tokyo 'the sentences given for the crime against peace were more lenient than one would expect'. Röling (1993), p. 67.
79 Ibid., p. 87.
80 See Chapters 4 and 5.
81 Piccigallo (1975) p. 210.
82 Minear (1971), pp. x–xi.
83 See Chapter 2.
84 Ōnuma (1997), p. 10.
85 See Chapters 4, 5 and 6.
86 Minear (1971), pp. 22–3.

4 The Japanese perception of the Tokyo Trial, 1946–2006

1 Röling (1993), p. 84.
2 See Chapter 2.
3 When the defence offered, as evidence, a document on the American decision to use atomic bombs against Japan, British associate prosecutor, Arthur Comyns-Carr, claimed that 'the question of the choice of weapons on the Allied side in the war has no bearing upon any issue before this tribunal'. The tribunal subsequently rejected the document. Pritchard and Zaide (1981) [as *Transcripts* hereafter], vol. 8, pp. 17655–62.
4 Minear (1971), p. 169.
5 As some Japanese scholars rightly point out, the perception of the Tokyo Trial is strongly related to the issue of war responsibility, which has been debated and researched much more broadly and within greater dynamics. See Utsumi (1997). For the purpose of this research, however, the following analysis is focused on debates and research on the Tokyo Trial; debates on war responsibility in general will be examined when they are directly related to the trial.
6 Supreme Commander for the Allied Powers, Summation of Non-Military Activities in Japan, No. 8, May 1946, p. 242, para. 38.
7 The editorial, *Asahi Shimbun*, 13 November 1948.
8 Awaya (1994), pp. 117–18.
9 Dower (2000), p. 411.
10 For example, the report on the defence counsel's claims that 'conspiracy' would not be applied in the case of international law and that 'crimes against peace' and 'crimes against humanity' did not constitute a generally accepted concept of war crimes was deleted from the original drafts of the article for the 24 February 1947 edition of *Yomiuri Shimbun*, a popular daily newspaper together with *Asahi Shimbun* and *Mainichi Shimbun*. Also deleted was a report in *Yomiuri* on 24 October 1947 that *The Diary of Kido*, highly regarded evidence on the part of the prosecutor, was roughly translated and interpreted. Takakuwa (1984), pp. 130–1, 207. Having been asked by a newspaper agency to write on the Tokyo Trial in December 1948, Kiyose Ichirō, associate chief of the Japanese defence section, rejected the offer. He finally published a book on the trial in 1967 based on his critical view. Kiyose wrote:

> Had I accepted the offer [during the occupation] and written honestly [a critical view on the trial], the newspaper agency might have suffered suppression or

something even worse. However, if I had commented mildly, people would have taken it as the truth because of my official position at the tribunal. That is why I decided not to write on the trial during the occupation.

(Kiyose, 1966, pp. 276–7)

11 Tsurumi Shunsuke, on the other hand, sees that the media's role in conveying the story of the trial was very limited, because newspapers were printed on one sheet of paper, radios had been destroyed by bombings, and television was not yet available. Instead, he states, the Japanese people came to know about the Tokyo Trial mainly through 'gossip', which focused on four issues: the massacre of Nanjing and other atrocities conducted by the Japanese soldiers; the American chief prosecutor accusing Japanese leaders in the name of civilization; seven leaders being hanged; and the Emperor not being called to the court. 'It was these four things', Tsurumi argues, 'which remained in the memory of the Japanese people'. Tsurumi (1987), p. 14.

12 Ibid., p. 15. See also Chapters 5 and 6.

13 The MacArthur report stated:

The firm hand of General MacArthur was controlling and guiding the Japanese nation and the people seemed responsive and cooperative. The large task of demilitarization of factories and resources had begun. War criminals were being arrested and held for trial. Ammunition, weapons, and other military material were being moved to depots to be inventoried and eventually destroyed. All these things the Japanese people had initially accepted, and continued to accept *submissively, if not favorably*.

Reports of General MacArthur, MacArthur in Japan: the Occupation: Military phase, vol. 1 supplement, prepared by His General Staff, reprinted as GHQ Sanbō Dainibu (1998), p. 53, emphasis added.

14 Interview with a man born in 1935 (Interviewee M), 12 January 2004, Kyoto Japan.

15 See Chapters 5 and 6 for further examination of people's sense of 'having been deceived' by their leaders.

16 See Chapter 6.

17 The sentence of the Nuremberg Trial in October 1946 seems to have also encouraged the Japanese to think that their leaders, who had allied themselves with the Nazis, deserved the punishment. Nakamura (1997), p. 179.

18 Awaya (1994), p. 118.

19 Hirota's 'tragic' life was put into a well-read novel. For the English translation of the novel, *Rakujitsu Moyu*, see Shiroyama (1977).

20 Mainichi Shimbun Seijibu (2000), p. xx.

21 According to its database covering 1946 to 2000, *the Asahi Shimbun* newspaper issued 1,001 reports on the Tokyo Trial, out of which 934 were published between 1946 and 1948. Coverage dropped drastically in 1949, during which only four articles were published. Much of the coverage after 1952 up to 2000 are reviews of publications, films or symposiums on the Tokyo Trial and the news on the release and declassification of primary sources.

22 Dower (2000), p. 510. See also Yoshimi (1992), pp. 82–4.

23 Röling (1993), p. 34.

24 Yoshida (1995a), p. 212. This is based on his earlier article, Yoshida (1991). The following references are from his work in 1995.

25 For example, see *Chōryoū*, September 1948; *Hōritsu Jihō*, vol. 21, no. 2, 1949; *Rekishi Hyōron*, vol. 3, no. 6, 1948.

26 See articles by Inoue Kiyoshi, Gushima Kanesaburō and Kainō Michitaka in *Rekishi Hyōron*, vol. 3, no. 6, 1948. For a detailed analysis of academic debate during this period on the Tokyo Trial and war responsibility, see Yoshida (1995a).

27 Higurashi (2002), pp. 14–17.
28 Kyokutō Kokusai Gunji Saiban Kenkyūkai (1947–48).
29 Takayanagi (1948).
30 Yokota (1947), p. 5.
31 Ibid., pp. 5–7.
32 See a round-table talk, chaired by Kainō Michitaka and participated by Ukai Nobushige, Takano Yūichi, Tsuji Kiyoaki and Maruyama Masao, 'Tōkyō Saiban no jijitsu to hōri', *Hōritsu Jihō*, vol. 21, 1949, 61–76. Kainō and Maruyama have written several important articles on the Tokyo Trial. Maruyama's article, 'Gunkoku shihaisha no seishin keitai' written in 1949 is an important work on Japanese militarism and the Tokyo Trial. In this famous article, he analyses the pathology of Japan's 'structure' that had created unplanned and disorganized political power, which paved the way for the Pacific War. Through examining the statements and behaviour of the defendants at the Tokyo Tribunal, Maruyama observed an undeveloped sense of responsibility among the leaders and saw it as 'a manifestation of the way in which the system itself had decayed'. His arguments of 'the dwarfishness of Japanese fascism' and the 'system of irresponsibility' having the Emperor at the head of it reflected the widely shared view of people at the time. Considering the academic impact of the article, Maruyama's argument may have given logical justification to blame the wartime leaders for the war and defeat. The article is translated into English: Maruyama (1963), pp. 84–134. For Kainō's work, see Ushiomi (1977), pp. 271–84.
33 Kyokutō Kokusai Gunji Saiban Kenkyūkai (1947–48), vol. 1, p. 6.
34 Article 11 of the San Francisco Peace Treaty goes:

> Japan accepts the judgments of the International Military Tribunal for the Far East and of other Allied War Crimes Courts both within and outside Japan, and will carry out the sentences imposed thereby upon Japanese nationals imprisoned in Japan. The power to grant clemency, to reduce sentences and to parole with respect to such prisoners may not be exercised except on the decision of the Government or Governments which imposed the sentence in each instance, and on recommendation of Japan. In the case of persons sentenced by the International Military Tribunal for the Far East, such power may not be exercised except on the decision of a majority of the Governments represented on the tribunal, and on the recommendation of Japan.

35 Takigawa (1952), p. 4.
36 Asahi Shimbunsha Chōsa Kenkyūshitsu (1953), pp. 8–9. On the difficulty of criticizing the Tokyo Trial, see Chapter 5.
37 Takigawa (1952), pp. 258–9.
38 Takigawa (1978), vol. 1, pp. 38–9.
39 Sugawara (1961), pp. 8–9.
40 Kobori (1996), p. 90.
41 For the English version, see Pal (1953). Pal's judgment, together with other separate opinions, was not read at the trial. GHQ prohibited its publication at the time considering that it would have stimulated Japanese anger and harmed the occupation policy. 'Jo', in Tōkyō Saiban Kenkyūkai (1984), vol. 1, p. 4.
42 Pal (1953), p. 700. Some argue that Pal's opinion is not free from his political and ideological background. Ienaga Saburō, who is famous for his decades of legal battle with the government over the history textbook, criticized Pal's opinion on the basis of 'his vehement anti-Communist ideology'. Ienaga (1986), p. 169. In addition to his anti-communist stance, Dower attributed Pal's repudiation of the majority judgment to his 'anti-colonial consciousness as an Asian nationalist'. Dower (2000), p. 632, footnote 65.
43 Tanaka (1963).
44 Tsunoda (1984), pp. 199–202. This volume was originally published in 1966 by a group of academics, which later became a society for research of the Tokyo Trial.

45 In 1966, Pal was given by the Japanese government the Grand Cordon of the Order of the Sacred Treasure (*Kun Ittō Zuihō Shō*), and an emeritus doctorate from Nihon University.
46 Asahi Shimbunsha Chōsa Kenkyūshitsu (1953), p. 6, emphasis added.
47 Nakamura (1997), p. 186.
48 *Asahi Shimbun*, 17 May 1952. Among the positive things raised were complete democratization (13 per cent), agrarian reform (9 per cent), food imports (7 per cent), the improvement in the position of women (6 per cent), economic support (4 per cent), education reform (3 per cent) and others (13 per cent). As for negatives, educational reform, too much emphasis on freedom and agrarian reform were raised.
49 Awaya (1989), p. 276.
50 Quoted in Tōkyō Saiban Handobukku Henshū Iinkai (1989), p. 219. A fact which is not well known is that those indicted for Class B and C war crimes included 173 Formosans and 148 Koreans, who, as Japanese colonial subjects, were forced to work for the Japanese Imperial Army. More than 40 were executed. See Utsumi (1982).
51 In stark contrast to this shared view of Class B and C war crimes trials among Japanese academics, Piccigallo states that trials featured 'excellent and devoted defense counsel', 'sufficient procedural safeguards', 'fair-minded judges', 'extraordinary thorough and impartial review procedures in all theaters', 'adequate translation facilities' and 'accessible, complete records of the proceedings'. Piccigallo (1979), p. 214.
52 See *Seikino Isho*, Tokyo: Sugamo Isho Hensankai Kankō Jimusho, 1953.
53 See Kōseishō (2000), pp. 152–9.
54 Hashimoto (1959).
55 Asahi Shimbun Hōtei Kishadan (1962), vol. 1, p. 44. In addition to supreme order, some point out the culture and mentality of the Japanese Imperial Army, which regarded becoming a POW as a disgrace. Such a mentality was not irrelevant to the way they treated the Allies' POWs.
56 Tsurumi (1986), pp. 141–2. Indeed, both in public and private discourse as well as in some academic research, the Tokyo Trial and Class B and C war crimes trials have often been confused by incorporating the latter into the former.
57 Dower (2000), pp. 513–15.
58 Korean and Formosan war criminals living in Japan were not entitled to receive equal state assistance on war-led issues. See Tōkyō Saiban Handobukku Henshū Iinkai (1989), pp. 230–2.
59 Comment by A. Utsumi, in Ōnuma *et al.* (2003), p. 289. See also Hayashi (1998), p. 303.
60 Unlike other defendants, Shigemitsu was a figure who had been favourably regarded by British and American diplomats, and, in the words of Lord Hankey, 'was no criminal'. Lord Hankey together with his friends had tried to help Shigemitsu at his indictment and his conviction. In his *Politics, Trials and Errors* (1950), Hankey conducts a defence of Shigemitsu.
61 For a good summary and analysis of academic research during this period, see Awaya (1989), pp. 269–97; Higurashi (2002), pp. 17–19; Sumitani (1984), pp. 126–30.
62 Sumitani (1995), pp. 52–3.
63 Kinoshita, quoted in Awaya (1989), p. 271.
64 For an English translation of the script of the play, see Kinoshita (1979).
65 Ibid., p. 9.
66 Ibid., p. 4.
67 Asahi Shimbun Hōtei Kishadan (1962), vol. 1, p. 49.
68 See Chapter 2.
69 Tanaka (1963), p. 2.

70 Prosecution opening statement presented by Joseph Keenan, 4 June 1946, in *Transcripts*, vol. 1, p. 384.
71 Kiyose (1966), p. 219.
72 The term was used in the title of Hayashi Fusao's articles in *Chūō Kōron* from 1963 to 1965 in a rather sensational way: 'Daitoa senso kōteiron [Affirmation of the Greater East Asian War]'. He argued that Japan's war had been a part of a 100-year war against Western imperialism and emphasized Japan's role in liberating Asian countries.
73 GHQ prohibited the use in official writings of the term, together with other terms 'whose connotation in Japanese is inextricably connected with State Shinto, militarism, and ultranationalism'. SCAP Directive, 'Abolition of governmental sponsorship, support perpetuation, control, and dissemination of State Shinto', SCAPIN 448, 15 December 1945.
74 In addition to these terms, the term 'Asian-Pacific war' came to be used in the mid-1980s, which is now more generally used in public.
75 See Chapter 5 for a further examination of the Tokyo Trial's account of war and anti-'Tokyo Trial view of history' critics.
76 Awaya (1989), p. 270.
77 Minear (1971), p. ix.
78 Tanaka (1963), p. 5.
79 For example, Kiyose (1966); Sugawara (1961). Takigawa republished in 1978 his book published in 1952. These three were all members of the defence counsel. Kojima Noboru, the author of *Tōkyō Saiban* (1971), was a student at the time who attended the trial several times a week.
80 Sumitani (1995), p. 53.
81 See Asahi Shimbun Hōtei Kishadan (1962), vol. 1, pp. 30–1; Takigawa (1978), pp. 8–9.
82 See Chapters 5 and 6 for a detailed analysis of the nature of Japanese apathy.
83 Kojima (1971), vol. 1, p. iii. His book has been well read because it was a part of the popular paperback series of *Chūkō Shinsho*.
84 Ibid.
85 See Chapter 5.
86 See Chapter 3.
87 Andō (1983), p. 100.
88 Ibid.
89 Andō (1985), p. 217.
90 Ōnuma (1997), p. 55. First edition was published in 1985.
91 Ibid., pp. 45–6.
92 Awaya (1989).
93 A record of the symposium was published in 1984, which is available in English as Hosoya *et al.* (1986).
94 Comment by Ōnuma in Hosoya *et al.* (1986), p. 123.
95 Ibid., p. 56.
96 See ibid., pp. 58–9, 62.
97 Kobayashi (1983), pp. 64, 67. Kobayashi is a director who had been tackling various war films, in which he tried to 'express the horror, futility and foolishness of war'. He saw the Tokyo Trial as 'the historic heritage of the century that should be taken up by any of Japanese who take part in filming'. Kobayashi (1983b), p. 112.
98 Kobayashi (1983), p. 67.
99 Ibid.
100 Ōnuma (1997), pp. 156–7.
101 Ibid., p. 23.
102 Ibid.
103 The title of the book by Ezra F. Vogel, *Japan as Number One*, published in 1979 and also published in Japanese in the same year, was repeatedly referred to in Japan through the 1980s.

104 According to an opinion poll conducted by *Asahi Shimbun* in July 1985, 48 per cent answered that Japan's national power had become equal, or almost equal, to that of the US. *Asahi Shimbun*, 9 July 1985.
105 Maki (1988), p. 24.
106 Fujio (1986), p. 124.
107 Quoted in Nakamura (1997), p. 184.
108 The German Minister of Justice, Sabine Leutheusser-Scharrenberger, for example, commented in November 1995 publicly on Nuremberg:

> From this trial the German people learned of the complete scale of atrocities committed, in their name, by an unscrupulous clique of criminals.... The Nuremberg Tribunal was the first time a criminal system that breached all civilized values was given the correct responses.
>
> Quoted in Sprecher (1999), p. 1450.

109 According to the National Diet Library's database, 177 books, appearing under key words either '*Tōkyō Saiban* [the Tokyo Trial]' or '*Kokusai Gunji Saiban* [the International Military Tribunal]' excluding Nuremberg, were published between 1946 and 2004. Among them 23 books including court materials were published during the occupation (1946–51); 13 during the 1950s (1952–60); 14 in the 1960s; and 21 in the 1970s. The number suddenly went up in the 1980s, during which time 36 were published, out of which 33 were published after 1983, the year the film was released. In 1990s, there were 54 publications, and from 2001 up until 2004, there were 16. Nearly 60 per cent of the publications on the Tokyo Trial up until 2004 were published after 1983. In the 1980s, the variety of people conducting research on the Tokyo Trial increased, unlike previous periods when only a small number of regular members published and republished their works.
110 Tanaka (1998), p. 28.
111 See for example *Seiron*, no. 114 (December 1982), no. 163 (April 1986); *Asahi Jānaru*, vol. 25, no. 23 (1983); *Shokun*, vol. 15, nos 8, 9, 10 and 11 (1983); *Chūō Kōron*, vol. 98, no. 9 (1983); and *Shisō*, no. 719. (May 1984).
112 See Igarashi and Kitaoka (1997), as the record of the symposium.
113 Series of his articles became a monograph, Higurashi (2002).
114 The content of the documentary is published as Awaya and NHK Shuzaihan (1994).
115 The series of 52 volumes are entitled *Kokusai Kensatsukyoku Jinmon Chōsho* and published by Nihon Tosho Sentā. The International Prosecution Section's 'Evidentiary Documents' were also compiled and published in 28 volumes.
116 Tōkyō Saiban Shiryō Kankōkai (1995).
117 See Yoshimi (2001), originally published in Japanese in 1995. Yoshimi is the one who located wartime documents on the comfort women issue.
118 Takahashi (1999), pp. 31–2, 39–51.
119 See for example, ibid.; Ajia Minshūhōtei Junbikai (1995); Awaya *et al.* (1994); Ajia Minshūhōtei Junbikai (1998).
120 See Chapter 5 for details of the neo-nationalism and the textbook row.
121 'Japanese shrine visit angers Seoul', Monday 22 April 2002, BBC News. Available online at: http://news.bbc.co.uk/1/hi/world/asia-pacific/1942086.stm (accessed 7 March 2004). See Chapter 6 for details of the Yasukuni row.
122 Reactions of people with whom the author conducted intensive interviews and focus groups during the autumn and winter of 2003 also confirm this point. See chapters 5 and 6.
123 According to the database of the National Diet Library, in 1995 alone, 21 books on the Tokyo Trial, including eight volumes of compiled documents of the defence counsel, were published. They comprise about 40 per cent of the books published in the 1990s.
124 According to *Asahi Shimbun*'s database covering articles from 1985 to the present

day, the newspaper had 28 articles referring to the Tokyo Trial in 2004, but 90 in 2005 and 121 in 2006 (until September). According to the database of *Yomiuri Shimbun*, covering 1986 onwards, the newspaper had 20 articles referring to the trial in 2004, then 62 in 2005 and 55 in 2006 (until September). According to the database of the National Diet Library, 21 books were published in 2005 and 2006 (until August) on the Tokyo Trial.

125 *Yomiuri Shimbun*, 21 October 2005; *Asahi Shimbun*, 2 May 2006.

126 See Yomiuri Shimbun Sensō Sekinin Kenshō Iinkai (2006); and Asahi Shimbun Shuzaihan (2006). These volumes are based on two newspapers' series of special articles during 2005 and 2006, focusing on the war, war responsibility, collective memory and the significance of the Tokyo Trial to these issues.

5 The Tokyo Trial and the historical record of the war

1 See Chapter 3.

2 The judgment, in Pritchard and Zaide (1981) [as *Transcripts* hereafter], vol. 20, p. 49765.

3 Ibid.

4 Ibid., pp. 49, 592.

5 Summation by the prosecution, 11 February 1948, *Transcripts*, vol. 16, p. 38972.

6 Iokibe (1983), p. 109.

7 *Transcripts*, vol. 20, pp. 49768–9, emphasis added.

8 Quoted in Watt (1981), p. xviii.

9 Ibid. Unlike Nuremberg, in the Tokyo Trial there was no provision for trying 'criminal organizations', according to which the SA and the SS were tried under Nuremberg. This was because of the conclusion of preliminary studies of Japanese organizations that had 'failed to reveal any close parallel between the German organizational program and that of Japan'. Horwitz (1950), p. 487.

10 The indictment charged 26 defendants under Count 55: 'deliberately and recklessly disregarded their legal duty to take adequate steps to secure the observance and prevent breaches thereof, and thereby violated the laws of war'. Seven were found guilty.

11 General Matsui Iwane was sentenced to death only for the charge of negative criminality for the Nanjing massacre. Hirota Kōki was sentenced to death for counts including negative responsibility for the Nanjing massacre that occurred when he was the Minster of Foreign Affairs, while three defendants were sentenced to life imprisonment for exactly the same counts as Hirota except the conviction for negative criminality.

12 Minear (1971), p. 134. Other than the substantiation of conspiracy, Minear argues that the historical accuracy of the verdict is doubtful in narratives on relations between Japan and the Soviet Union and Japan and the Axis Alliance, and on the attack of Pearl Harbor. Ibid., pp. 125–59.

13 Dower (2000), p. 463.

14 *Transcripts*, vol. 20, p. 48513.

15 See Chapter 3.

16 Iokibe (1983), p. 111. Konoe committed suicide when GHQ started arresting. Matsuoka was one of 28 defendants of the Tokyo Trial but died immediately after the opening of the trial. Iokibe also saw the absence from the trial of Ishihara Kanji, a military officer and the mastermind of the Manchurian Incident, as significant. He concluded that the absence of these figures degraded the standard and accuracy of the tribunal's historical record. Ibid., p. 108.

17 Quoted in Nakamura (1997), pp. 181–2.

18 Asahi Shimbunsha Chōsa Kenkyūshitsu (1953), pp. 6–7.

19 Awaya (1989), pp. 269–70. The tribunal also ignored the defendants' claim that

Japan had been facing the threat of the rise of communism in the region, by rejecting the defendants' evidence as irrelevant to the issue. Tōkyō Saiban Shiryō Kankōkai (1995), vol. 1, p. 29.

20 Quoted in Yoshida (1995a), p. 248.
21 See Chapter 4.
22 Brackman (1987), p. 23.
23 Osiel (1997), p. 133.
24 Preface, in Hosoya *et al.* (1986), p. 8, emphasis added.
25 Pritchard (1987b), p. 50.
26 Minear (1971), p. 159. Regarding admissible evidence, see Chapter 3.
27 Watt (1981), p. xxii.
28 Sebald (1967), p. 151.
29 Awaya (1995), pp. 22–3; Ōnuma (1997), p. 150.
30 Iokibe (1983), p. 108.
31 Comments by I. Hata, in Hosoya *et al.* (1986), p. 103.
32 See Chapter 4.
33 See Chapter 3.
34 Gluck (1993), p. 66.
35 Quoted in Yoshimi (1992), p. 77.
36 According to the opinion poll conducted by *Yomiuri Shimbun* in August 1948, 68.5 per cent supported the Emperor maintaining his status, while 18.4 per cent wanted him to abdicate in favour of his son, 4 per cent wanted the abolition of the Emperor system and 9.1 per cent answered 'do not know'. Quoted in Tōkyō Saiban Handobukku Henshū Iinkai (1989), p. 233. Takeda Kiyoko points out, through examination of public opinion polls at the time, that people were 'favourable to the person of the emperor and not to an absolute and authoritarian emperor system'. Takeda (1988), p. 150.
37 Dower (2002), p. 233.
38 *Transcripts*, vol. 15, p. 36521.
39 Ibid., p. 36780.
40 See Hosaka (1998), pp. 142–50; Gluck (1993), pp. 66–70.
41 Fuji (1988), vol. 2, p. 542. This volume records the proceedings of the tribunal through the eyes of the author, who had attended most of the trial procedures.
42 Satō (1987), p. 71.
43 With regard to 'victor's justice', see Chapters 2 and 4.
44 Takigawa (1952), p. 3.
45 Fujioka and Yoshida (1997), p. 38.
46 Kobori (1988), p. 602, emphasis added.
47 Satō (1987), p. 67. Although the narrative of Nanjing under the Tokyo Tribunal shocked the Japanese people at the time, it soon went out of people's minds and was absent from people's consciousness until the 1970s, when the series of reports on the Nanjing massacre written by Honda Katsuichi appeared in *Asahi Shimbun*, one of the most popular daily newspapers in Japan. After his first series of 'Chūgoku no Tabi [Journey to China]', he wrote 'The Road to Nanjing', which appeared in serialized form in *Asahi Jānal* in 1984. See Honda (1998). Honda's report brought about a reactionary claim that 'the Nanjing massacre did not occur', raised by Suzuki Akira (1973). Honda has been attacked by right-wing activists for 'propagating the "Tokyo Trial view of history"', and has been harassed by extreme right-wingers because of his continuous research on the Japanese war crimes in China. Honda (1998), p. xxvi. Honda, for his part, calls people like Tanaka 'unprincipled hacks'. Tanaka's work is strongly criticized for misquoting the primary source in a way to justify his argument, ibid., p. 291. Most publications on the Nanjing massacre up to the present concentrate on the verification of the event: whether it was a 'massacre', an 'incident', or did not occur at all. Only a few of them, however, were based on rigid academic examination. The number of the massacre's victims is still under fierce debate even among

those who accept that the massacre occurred. In any case, the Nanjing massacre has been a cause of serious tension with China. See ibid., pp. vii–xiv.

48 See Chapter 4.

49 Quoted in Funabashi (2003b), p. 5.

50 Resolution to Renew the Determination for Peace on the Basis of Lessons Learned from History, House of Representatives, National Diet of Japan, 9 June 1995. Available online at: www.mofa.go.jp/announce/press/pm/murayama/address9506.html (accessed 15 October 2004).

51 Statement by Prime Minister Tomiichi Murayama, 'On the occasion of the 50th anniversary of the war's end' (15 August 1995). Available online at: www.mofa.go.jp/announce/press/pm/murayama/9508.html (accessed 15 October 2004).

52 The 1995 resolution in fact ended up being incoherent, reflecting conflicting attitudes towards the war and responsibility for it among political parties constituting the then coalition government.

53 For detailed analysis of the 'Fujioka phenomenon' and his approach, see McCormack (2000), pp. 53–73.

54 Fujioka and Yoshida (1997), p. 40.

55 Quoted in McCormack (2000), p. 60.

56 School textbooks in Japan have to go through the Ministry of Education's check and certificate process in order to be regarded as official textbooks. During this process, various forms of 'textbook row' have occurred especially with regard to history textbooks, which have often created tension between Japan and its Asian neighbours. For details of the textbook row which emerged before the 1990s, see Nozaki and Inokuchi (2000), pp. 96–126.

57 Available online at: www.tsukurukai.com/02_about_us/01_opinion.html (accessed 10 June 2002).

58 Ibid.

59 Quoted in Nakamura (1997), p. 184.

60 Kobayashi Yoshinori quoted in French 2001.

61 Kobayashi (1998).

62 Kobori (1996).

63 Maeno (2000), p. 23.

64 Nakajō (1998), p. 158.

65 Ibid., p. 161.

66 See Chapter 4.

67 'Ima naze Tōjō Hideki: Tōei eiga "Puraido Unmei no toki"', *Kyoto Shimbun*. Available online at: www.kyoto-np.co.jp/kp/event/geino/pride02.html (accessed 10 September 2002).

68 'Shuyaku Tsugawa Masahiko ha kataru', *Kinema Junpō*, no. 1257, 1998, 118.

69 Shūsen Gojushūnen Kokumin Iinkai (1996), p. 283.

70 This point was raised during the interview with Andō Nisuke, Professor of International Law, Doshisha University, on 13 November 2003, Japan. See also Chapter 6.

71 *Yomiuri Shimbun*, 5 October 1993, quoted in Dower (2002), p. 315, footnote 5.

72 For the 'contested memories' of the Japanese over the war and war crimes, see Dower (2002), pp. 217–41.

73 Among the generation in their seventies and beyond, those who regarded the war as 'inevitable' (45 per cent) exceeded those who saw it as 'wrong' (37 per cent). *Mainichi Shimbun*, 15 August 2005. This poll, just like *Yomiuri*'s, showed the generation gap in historical perception. However, a difference in the nuance of a question asked by the opinion poll of *Mainichi* and *Yomiuri* should be noted; the former used the term 'inevitable' and the latter 'aggressor'. More interestingly, to the *Mainichi*'s question, 26 per cent answered 'do not know'.

74 *Asahi Shimbun*, 23 August 1994.

75 See Appendix, Tables A.1 and A.2, for details of each interview and focus group.
76 *Asahi Shimbun*, 2 May 2006.
77 There was such a participant in Focus Groups A and B.
78 Interviewee H.
79 Focus Group C.
80 Interviewee L.
81 According to *Yomiuri*'s opinion poll in October 2005, 34.2 per cent answered that 'Both the war with China and the United States were aggressive war', and 33.9 per cent answered that 'The war with China was aggressive war but the war with the United States was not', while 10.1 per cent answered that the neither war was aggressive war. *Yomiuri Shimbun*, 27 October 2005.
82 Interviewees D, E, I, J and M.
83 See Chapter 3.
84 Brackman (1987), p. 27. His book was translated and published in Japan in 1991. The concern is also shared by Richard Minear. See below.
85 See Gluck (1993).
86 Paskins and Dockrill (1979), p. 266.
87 Interviewee G.
88 Interviewee A.
89 Focus Group E.
90 Focus Group C.
91 Interviewees D, I, L and O.
92 Focus Group C.
93 Higurashi (1997), p. 77; Ōnuma (1997), p. 27.
94 See Chapter 4. For some post-war generation it may be to do with ignorance as one interviewee replied: 'I cannot get resentful over things that I don't know much about'. Interviewee C.
95 Gushima (1948), pp. 30–2.
96 Ōhara in Takahashi *et al.* (1987), p. 67.
97 Interviewees I and J.
98 Focus Groups A, B and C.
99 Focus Group B.
100 Focus Group C.
101 Interviewee S.
102 Awaya (1994), p. 106.
103 Interviewee L.
104 Focus Group C. A similar view is also given by Interviewee F.
105 Interviewee H.
106 Interviewee L.
107 Interviewee G.
108 Focus Group B.
109 Focus Group B.
110 Interviewee F.
111 Interview with Asada Sadao, Professor of Diplomatic History, Doshisha University, 15 January 2004, Kyoto, Japan.
112 Interviewee J.
113 Focus Group A.
114 Ara (1984), pp. 19–20.
115 Kojima (1986), p. 77.
116 Ibid., p. 78. Little interest in the Tokyo Trial even among postgraduate students specializing in US–Japanese history, which was observed in Focus Group D, may be indicative.
117 Interviewee K.
118 Current secondary school textbooks contain critical information of the war, referring

to the Nanjing massacre and harsh colonial policies. Some researchers point out, however, that these depictions of Japan's war crimes tend to be 'elliptical': 'the textbooks themselves seem to seek an elusive middle ground that avoids explicit evaluation of the wartime past', Laura Hein and Mark Selden analyse: 'Their enigmatic comments can be used either to open debate about wartime attitudes and postwar responsibility or to dismiss the events in question as regrettable but unimportant facts, depending on the stance of the classroom teacher'. Hein and Selden (2000b), p. 11.

119 Interviewee H.
120 Interviewees D, H and L.
121 See Chapter 4.
122 Interview with Asada.
123 Interviewee B.
124 Interview with Asada.
125 Interviewee A.
126 Interviewee H.
127 See Chapter 3.
128 Interviewee D.
129 See Chapter 6 for the issue of the Emperor's responsibility and Japanese perceptions.
130 Utsumi (1995), p. 3. While the 'Second World War' and the 'Pacific War' are relatively neutral, the 'Fifteen-years war' and the 'Greater East Asia War' are burdened terms, which carry the political and ideological stance of those who utilize them: the former emphasizes the aspect of Japan as an aggressor towards its Asian neighbours, while the latter connotes the justification and glorification of the war as self-defence and the liberation of Asia. Recently, it has been pointed out that the term 'Pacific War' confines the historical view to that of America and ignore the Asian sphere of the war. Alternatively, since the mid-1980s, the term 'Asian-Pacific war' has become more popular in use.
131 As to the 1983 symposium, see Chapter 4.
132 Igarashi (1997), p. v.
133 Interview with Andō.
134 See Dower (2002), pp. 224–7.
135 Asahi Shimbunsha Chōsa Kenkyūshitsu (1953), pp. 8–9. See also Chapter 4.
136 Buruma (2002), p. 119.
137 Minear (1971), p. ix.
138 Minear (1972), pp. 5–6. The Tokyo Trial may be a taboo also for western academics. 'The objection may be raised that it is unwise to reopen now an issue that the Japanese people themselves never really protested', Minear wrote in 1971:

> there is some danger in denouncing the trial today. Japan today is only just emerging from her postwar political dependence on the United States; and denunciation of the trial may play into the hands of reactionary elements in Japanese politics.
>
> Minear (1971), pp. 176–7.

Similar concern is also expressed by Brackman on writing about the Tokyo Trial. See above.

139 Quoted in McCormack (2000), p. 63.
140 Pal (1953), p. 700.
141 Harries and Harries (1987), p. 170.
142 Interviewee B.
143 Focus Group C.
144 Interviewee D.
145 Interviewee S.
146 Interviewee H.
147 Focus Group B.

148 According to an opinion poll in August 2005 asking if Japan's war against the US and China was 'wrong' or 'inevitable', 34 per cent of those in their twenties responded 'do not know'. At the same time, it is this generation where the percentage of those who regarded the war as 'wrong' (36 per cent) was the lowest after the generation in their seventies and beyond. *Mainichi Shimbun*, 15 August 2005.
149 Interview with Andō.
150 Funabashi *et al.* (2003), p. 69.
151 See Cha (2003) and Yang (2003).
152 See Chapter 4.
153 See Chapter 6 for details of the Yasukuni row.
154 'Japan shrine visit angers China', BBC News, 15 August 2004. Available online at: http://news.bbc.co.uk/go/pr/fr/-/1/hi/world/asia-pacific/3567084.stm (accessed on 16 August 2004), emphasis added.
155 For example, Interviewee C, in her mid-twenties brought up in Hiroshima, remembered having learned about Japan's war crimes in China. The author of this study also has a memory of having been taught about the Nanjing massacre at primary school.
156 Interviewees C, D, E and F.
157 Focus Group C.
158 Interviewee I.
159 Focus Group B.
160 Focus Group D.
161 See Chapter 2.
162 Utsumi (1995), p. 5.
163 Mochida (1994), p. 5.

6 The Tokyo Trial and the individualization of responsibility

1 See Chapter 2.
2 See Chapter 3.
3 See Kitagawa (1995), pp. 163–201.
4 The Acting Political Adviser in Japan (Atcheson) to the Secretary of State, Telegram, 17 December 1945, in *The Foreign Relations of the United States*, 1945, vol. VI, p. 984.
5 Prosecution opening statement presented by Joseph Keenan, 4 June 1946, in Pritchard and Zaide (1981), p. 468.
6 Yoshida (1995b), pp. 80–1. During the occupation, the devastation of Hiroshima and Nagasaki was not yet known to the public in detail. Japanese victim consciousness at this stage, therefore, is slightly different from the victim consciousness based on the icon of Hiroshima, which came to be widely shared later on. For Japanese war memories and Hiroshima, see Buruma (2002), pp. 92–111.
7 See Chapter 5. The Allies' intention to appeal to the Japanese sense of 'having been deceived' can be observed also from Article 6 of the Potsdam Declaration in July 1945, which stated that those leaders to be eliminated 'have deceived and misled the people of Japan into embarking on world conquest'.
8 See Yoshimi (1992), pp. 76–8.
9 Dower (2000), p. 60. Nakajō Takanori reflects his experience as a student of a military academy, who, after the war, was jeered at as 'a war criminal' when he was wearing a school uniform. Nakajō (1998), pp. 76–7.
10 The editorial, *Asahi Shimbun*, 13 November 1948, emphasis added.
11 The editorial, *Mainichi Shimbun*, 5 November 1948, emphasis added.
12 For the Japanese sense of demarcation from the past, see Gluck (1993), pp. 64–95.
13 The editorial, *Mainichi Shimbun*, 13 November 1948.
14 The editorial, *Mainichi Shimbun*, 23 December 1948.

15 Yoshimi (1992), p. 74. For this reason, *Ichioku Sōzange* is criticized as the government's 'self-serving' campaign to extract from the leaders the burden of responsibility.
16 Ibid., pp. 86–9.
17 Ōnuma (1997), p. 56. See Chapter 3.
18 Quoted in Dower (2000), p. 490.
19 Ara (1984), p. 5.
20 Ōnuma (1997), p. 90.
21 See Yoshida (1995a), pp. 210–61.
22 Ara (1984), p. 6; Dower (2000), p. 505.
23 Quoted in Yoshida (1995a), pp. 256–7.
24 Yoshida Yutaka pointed out the risk that the pursuit of collective responsibility of the nation may have led to a nationalist approach to the issue or to 'the collective repentance of the hundred million' that obscured war responsibility as a whole. The fact that academics and commentators at the time, especially of the left, were aware of these points, Yoshida argues, was another reason why the debate on the nation's war responsibility did not develop during the occupation. Ibid., pp. 238–9, 256–7.
25 Gushima (1948), p. 26.
26 *Transcripts*, vol. 15, p. 36488.
27 Yoshida (1995a), p. 218.
28 See Chapter 4 for Class B and C war crimes trials.
29 Yoshimi (1992), pp. 91–3.
30 In parallel with this 'humanized Emperor', in post-war Japan there was the other conflicting view of the Emperor: 'authoritarian and inhumane' aspects of the Emperor and the absolute emperor system. As Takeda Kiyoko points out, this 'dual' image of the wartime Emperor remains 'part of the Japanese "mental structure" even today'. Takeda (1988), p. 152.
31 Tsurumi (1987), p. 16.
32 Ibid.
33 Buruma (2002), p. 259.
34 Dower (2000), p. 28.
35 Dower (2004), p. 75.
36 Interviewees D, H, I, K and L. See Appendix, Tables A.1 and A.2, for details of each interview and focus group.
37 Interviewee E.
38 *Asahi Shimbun*, 8 February 1989. Among female respondents, in every generation those who thought the Emperor was not responsible for the war exceeded those who thought he was.
39 Interviewee D.
40 See Chapter 5.
41 Awaya (1994), p. 93.
42 Interviewee H.
43 Ara (1984), pp. 3–4, emphasis added.
44 Karl Jaspers raises four different concepts of guilt: criminal, political, moral and metaphysical. Crime meets with punishment and political guilt with liability, both of which are pursued 'without'. Moral guilt requires inner development and the jurisdiction of metaphysical guilt rests with God, both of which are charged from 'within'. Although these four overlap and interrelate, Jaspers sees it as important to differentiate them in order to avoid 'the superficiality of talk about guilt that flattens everything out on a single plane'. Jaspers (1947), p. 33.
45 Yoshimi (1992), pp. 84–5.
46 Yoshida (1995a), pp. 219–20.
47 Yoshimi (1992), p. 99.
48 For details of Japanese 'apathy' towards the Tokyo Trial, see also chapters 4 and 5.
49 Röling (1993), p. 91.

50 See Chapter 3.
51 'War criminal list creates sensation: Unexpected names included puzzle Japanese; Konoye remains free', *Stars and Stripes*, 5 December 1945.
52 Tsurumi argues that the absence of the Emperor at the tribunal gave 'the War Crimes Trial the character of an offering of scapegoats to the altar of the conquerors in the view of the Japanese people both at the time and today'. Tsurumi (1987), p. 16. This point is raised also by several interviewees.
53 Interviewee K.
54 Asahi Shimbunsha Chōsa Kenkyūshitsu (1953), p. 5.
55 Takigawa (1952), pp. 3–4, emphasis added.
56 Interviewee D.
57 Interviewee G.
58 See Chapter 5.
59 Interviewee G.
60 Interviewee E.
61 See Chapter 5.
62 Interviewee M. This was echoed by other interviewees of the wartime generation.
63 Dower (2000), p. 475.
64 In early 1946, there existed among the Allies the view of appointing a Japanese prosecutor and judge to the international tribunal. This in part was to show the Japanese people that the trial was not the victor's revenge towards the vanquished. However, the idea was opposed by an American member of the prosecution counsel who claimed that the Japanese government had not officially shown a wish to participate in an international trial and that the vanquished's participation in the prosecutions would have set a confusing precedent for the future. Joseph Keenan also suggested that Japan might participate in the prosecution of the Japanese war criminals. This, according to Awaya, was based on an intention to prepare an attorney to protect the Emperor. Awaya (1994), pp. 82–4. Keenan's suggestion, however, was greeted in Allied circles with 'consternation' and never became a serious prospect. Pritchard (1987b), p. 28. Röling, with the benefit of hindsight, stated: 'the presence of a Japanese judge could have prevented many errors'. (1993), p. 87.
65 Quoted in Yoshida (1995a), p. 240
66 Quoted in Harries and Harries (1987), p. 156.
67 Yui (1997), p. 44.
68 See Chapter 5.
69 Maeno (2000), pp. 36–7.
70 An interview by *Kyoto Shimbun*. Available online at: www.kyoto-np.co.jp/ kp/event/geino/pride02.html (accessed 10 September 2002).
71 Dower (2000), p. 30.
72 Tanaka (1963), p. 199.
73 Shūsen Gojushūnen Kokumin Iinkai (1996), p. 1. See also Chapter 5.
74 Thirty-four per cent answered that 'it was an unjust trial conducted unilaterally by the victor on the vanquished', and 17 per cent answered 'it was a just trial'. *Asahi Shimbun*, 2 May 2006.
75 According to an opinion poll in 2005 with regard to war responsibility, 67.3 per cent answered that 'military leaders' were most responsible for starting the war and for the defeat. *Yomiuri Shimbun*, 27 October 2005.
76 Interviewee C.
77 Interviewees E and G. The view is also raised by participants in Focus Groups B and E.
78 Okazaki *et al.* (2002), p. 205.
79 Interviewee O.
80 Focus Group B.
81 Ibid.

82 Interviewee L.
83 Interviewee I.
84 Interviewee L. Several participants in Focus Group B, comprising undergraduate students, commented on racism as follows:

a 'When it comes to the war with Asians, they conducted a unilateral trial and treated us harshly. I think there was a racist element'.
b 'I don't think so, because there was Nuremberg'.
c 'But what about the complete demilitarization, which was not done in the case of Germany? I feel that they wanted the Asians to remain weak'.

85 Tsurumi relates this sense of inevitability to Japanese tradition and mentality: 'The trials were accepted like some unavoidable physical calamity. This does not mean, however, that the criterion of justice asserted in the trials was fully accepted'. Tsurumi (1987), p. 19.
86 Interviewee E. This point is also raised by Interviewees O and R.
87 Interviewees H, M and participants in Focus Group B.
88 Interviewees F, R and participants in Focus Groups B and C.
89 Interviewees M, O and participants in Focus Group E. See also chapters 4 and 5.
90 Interviewee D.
91 Interviewee C. A similar view was also expressed by Interviewee I.
92 Interviewee G.
93 Interviewee G.
94 Interviewees C and L.
95 Interviewee S.
96 Ara (1984), p. 7.
97 Ōnuma (1997), p. 160.
98 Interviewee S.
99 Dower (2000), p. 475.
100 Interviewees B, C, D and E.
101 The government policy noted that even if trials were to be conducted only by the Allies, Japan would conduct voluntary trials and send their results to the Allies in order to make the Allies' judgment fair and to treat defendants compassionately. Kōseishō (2000), p. 127. Within a week, Prime Minister Higashikuninomiya told foreign correspondents that the government intended to investigate and punish those who had committed atrocities against POWs and other war crimes. Although the plan was not accepted by the GHQ, the Japanese government tried, under court martial, eight individuals for war crimes conducted in Taiwan, Saigon and elsewhere. The voluntary trials continued until March 1946, when GHQ ordered a prohibition on the Japanese government to conduct further investigations and trials. This order closed the door, for the time being, for any future domestic trials of war crimes by the Japanese government.
102 *Asahi Shimbun* stated that Japan should prepare its own list of war criminals and many readers agreed. The idea of domestic trials was enthusiastically endorsed especially by left-wing intellectuals, who had been most resistant to the wartime government and had thus suffered most from the previous regime. Dower (2000), pp. 475–6. The Japanese communist party published a pamphlet, *Prosecuting War Criminals by the Hand of People*, emphasizing the inseparable relationship between the aggressive war and the Emperor system. Gushima wrote in 1948: 'it is a grave mistake to think that having not been tried under the Tokyo Trial means innocence. If the Japanese truly want to achieve the aim of the Tokyo Trial, the prevention of war, they by themselves should thoroughly pursue war crimes of those who were immunized by Tokyo'. He claimed that for Japan to achieve true democratization and transformation as a peaceful nation, the rapid prosecution of war criminals was indispensable. Gushima (1948), p. 32.
103 Sugawara Yutaka argues: 'On establishing an international tribunal, judges should

have been selected from third-party countries. And if the nationals of the victor nation were to participate, the nationals of the vanquished nation should have also been allowed to be involved'. Sugawara (1961), p. 318. He also claimed that 'The war trials should have been conducted with a cool mind after several years had passed from the end of the war, when the peace treaty had been concluded'. Ibid., p. 322.

104 Several interviewees questioned whether there had been, at the time, any international organization, like the United Nations, or a third party that could have conducted the trial instead. Interviewees I, J and M; Focus Group B.
105 Interviewee G.
106 Interviewee J.
107 Focus Group D.
108 Ibid.
109 Interviewees A, D and L.
110 Dower (2000), p. 480.
111 Ibid., p. 477.
112 Kobayashi (1978), p. 240.
113 Inoue (1948), p. 13.
114 Yoshida (1995a), pp. 229–30.
115 Mochida (1994), p. 10.
116 Yoshida (1995a), p. 245. Yoshida argues that the way censorship was conducted has distorted the Japanese view on war responsibility because it prevented people during the occupation from talking about the issue freely. Ibid., p. 248.
117 Kinoshita (1998), p. 13.
118 Funabashi *et al.* (2003), p. 50.
119 Awaya (1995), pp. 42–3.
120 See Chapter 3.
121 According to an opinion poll conducted by *Yomiuri Shimbun* in 2005, the most people raised peace and anti-war as a term that reminded them of the Asia-Pacific war. Terms related to atomic bombs came in second place. *Yomiuri Shimbun*, 27 October 2005.
122 Morimura Seiichi's bestseller in 1982 highlighted the notorious Unit 731 conducting human-body experiments in China. Morimura (1981). The research of Honda Katsuichi, a journalist who has been conducting detailed investigation on the Nanjing massacre, was first released on *Asahi Shimbun* in the 1970s and also in the 1980s in the *Asahi*'s magazine.
123 Interviewee H, emphasis added.
124 For the gap between the general knowledge of the Japanese and the facts of the Tokyo Trial, see Chapter 5.
125 Takahashi (1999), p. 21.
126 *Asahi Shimbun*, 23 August 1994.
127 Quoted in Osiel (1997), p. 189, footnote 74. For the 1995 resolution, see Chapter 5.
128 *Yomiuri Shimbun*, 27 October 2005.
129 Interviewee D.
130 Focus Group B.
131 Interviewees O, P and participants in Focus Group A.
132 Interviewees G and I.
133 Focus Group B.
134 See Yang (2003), pp. 66–73 for an analysis of the sources of the 'history problem' between Japan and China. He identified three major areas of explanation; 'China plays the history card', 'Japan has not faced the past' and bilateral dynamics and the international setting that has been influencing the problem.
135 Interviewee D.
136 Interviewees N and P.
137 Interviewee B.

138 Interviewee G.
139 The editorial of *Asahi Shimbun*, 18 March 1995.
140 During interviews, there are a few who, right from the beginning, expressed an interest in the Tokyo Trial. Interestingly, all of them stated that they had started to take an interest in the trial after having read neo-nationalist publications; and it may not be surprising that they were all very critical about the Tokyo Trial, echoing the neo-nationalist logic. See Chapter 5 for the neo-nationalist movement.
141 Interviewee G, and several students in Focus Group C.
142 McCormack (2000), p. 58.
143 For the Yasukuni row, see also chapters 4 and 5.
144 Interviewee H.
145 Interviewees L, P and participants in Focus Groups B and C.
146 *Asahi Shimbun*, 31 May 2005.
147 Focus Group A.
148 Yang (2003), p. 73. For details of the difference in two views, see Chiba and Xiang (2005), pp. 215–32.
149 See Takahashi (2005). One problematic aspect of the Prime Minister's 'official visit' to Yasukuni is that it may be against the Japanese constitution that upholds the principle of the separation of government and religion. This issue has been brought to court a number of times by several groups.
150 Ushimura Kei points out that what is missing in the current debate on Yasukuni is a recognition of who those enshrined Class A war criminals were and what role each of them actually played in the war. Ushimura (2004), p. 44.
151 Quoted in Buruma (2002), p. 163.
152 *Asahi.com*. Available online at: www.asahi.com/special/shijiritsu/ TKY200404190343. html (accessed 1 July 2005).
153 *Asahi.com*. Available online at: www.asahi.com/special/shijiritsu/ TKY200411290310. html (accessed 1 July 2005).
154 *Asahi Shimbun*, 28 June 2005.
155 *Asahi Shimbun*, 2 May 2006.
156 See Chapter 4.
157 Yomiuri Shimbun Sensō Sekinin Kenshō Iinkai (2006).
158 Funabashi (2003b), p. 17.
159 *Asahi Shimbun*, 18 November 1991.
160 Asada Sadao, a scholar of diplomatic history, points out that the Tokyo Trial had a symbolic effect that made the Americans recognize that Japan was no longer a militarist nation and, thus, it worked in a cathartic way, which opened the way for reconciliation. Interview with Asada Sadao, 15 January 2004, Kyoto, Japan. See also Chapter 3.
161 *Asahi Shimbun*, 26 November 1984. Little change can be observed in the result of another joint survey in 1988. *Asahi Shimbun*, 16 June 1988.
162 Interviewee L.
163 *Asahi Shimbun*, 2 May 2006; *Yomiuri Shimbun*, 27 October 2005.
164 *Asahi Shimbun*, 28 June 2005.
165 See Chapter 5 for a detailed analysis of the 'silence' of the Japanese.
166 Focus Group E.
167 Osiel (1997), p. 176.
168 Beigbeder (1999), p. 75.

Conclusion

1 Biljana Kovacevic-Vuco, 'Comment: Milosevic on Trial – the Serb View', *Tribunal Update*, No. 348, 15 March 2004. Available online at: www.iwpr.net/index.pl? archive/tri/tri_348_4_eng.txt (accessed 20 March 2004).

Bibliography

Abbott, K. W., 1999 'International relations theory, international law, and the regime governing atrocities in internal conflict', *American Journal of International Law*, vol. 93, 361–79.

Adam, H., 1998 'Trading justice for truth', *World Today*, January, 11–13.

Adibe, C. E., 1998 'Accepting external authority in peace-maintenance', *Global Governance: A Review of Multilateralism and International Organizations*, vol. 4, 107–22.

Adler, E., 1997 'Seizing the middle ground: constructivism in world politics', *European Journal of International Relations*, vol. 3, 319–63.

Ajia Minshūhōtei Junbikai (ed.), 1995 *Toinaosu Tōkyō Saiban* [Re-questioning the Tokyo Trial], Tokyo: Ryokufū Shuppan.

—— (ed.), 1998 *Jikō naki Sensō Sekinin: Sabakareru Tennō to Nihonjin, Zōho-ban* [Timeless war responsibility: Judging the Emperor and the Japanese], Tokyo: Ryokufū Shuppan.

Akazawa, S., 1989 *Tōkyō Saiban* [The Tokyo Trial], Tokyo: Iwanami Shoten.

Akehurst, M., 1987 *A Modern Introduction to International Law*, 6th edn, London: Routledge.

Akhavan, P., 1993 'Punishing war crimes in the Former Yugoslavia: a critical juncture for the new world order', *Human Rights Quarterly*, vol. 15, 262–89.

——, 1996 'The Yugoslav Tribunal at a crossroads: the Dayton Peace Agreement and beyond', *Human Rights Quarterly*, vol. 18, 259–85.

——, 1998 'Justice in The Hague, peace in the Former Yugoslavia? A commentary on the United Nations War Crimes Tribunal', *Human Rights Quarterly*, vol. 20, 737–816.

——, 2001 'Beyond impunity: can international criminal justice prevent future atrocities?', *American Journal of International Law*, vol. 95, 7–31.

Alvarez, J. E., 1996 'Nuremberg revisited: the *Tadic* case', *European Journal of International Law*, vol. 7, 245–64.

——, 1998 'Rush to closure: lessons of the Tadic judgment', *Michigan Law Review*, vol. 96, 2031–112.

——, 1999 'Crimes of states/crimes of hate: lessons from Rwanda', *Yale Journal of International Law*, vol. 24, 365–483.

Andō, N., 1983 'Tōkyō saiban towa nanika' [What is the Tokyo Trial], in Kōdansha (ed.), *Tōkyō Saiban: Shashin Hiroku*, Tokyo: Kōdansha.

——, 1985 'Yakusha atogaki tsuiho' [Afterword by the translator], in R. H. Minear (trans. N. Andō), *Tōkyō Saiban: Shōsha no Sabaki*, Tokyo: Fukumura Shuppan

Anonymous, 1996 'Human rights in peace negotiations', *Human Rights Quarterly*, vol. 18, 249–58.

Appleman, J. A., 1954 *Military Tribunals and International Crimes*, Indianapolis: The Bobbs-Merrill Company.

Ara, T., 1984 'Tōkyō saiban: sensō sekininron no genryū – Tōkyō saiban to senryōka no yoron' [The Tokyo Trial: the origin of the argument of war responsibility – the Tokyo Trial and public opinion during the occupation], *Rekishi Hyōron*, no. 408, 2–22.

Arai, S., 1994 'Sensō sekinin towa nanika: semarareru futatsu no sengo shori' [What is war responsibility: two post-war settlements], *Sekai*, February, 187–201.

Ariyama, T., 1996 *Senryōki Medhia-shi Kenkyū: Jiyū to Tōsei 1945nen* [History of the Media during the Occupation Period: Freedom and Control 1945], Tokyo: Kashiwa Shobō.

Asahi Shimbunsha Chōsa Kenkyūshitsu (ed.), 1953 *Kyokutō Kokusai Gunji Saiban Kiroku: Mokuroku oyobi Sakuin* [The Record of the International Military Tribunal for the Far East: Index], Tokyo: Asahi Shimbun Chōsa Kenkyūshitsu.

Asahi Shimbun Hōtei Kishadan, 1962 *Tōkyō Saiban* [The Tokyo Trial], 3 vols, Tokyo: Tōkyō Saiban Kankōkai.

Asahi Shimbun Tōkyō Saiban Kisha-dan, 1983 *Tōkyō Saiban* [The Tokyo Trial], 2 vols, Tokyo: Kōdansha.

Asahi Shimbun Shuzaihan, 2006 *Sensō Sekinin to Tsuitō* [War Responsibility and Mourning], Tokyo: Asashi Shimbunsha.

Awaya, K., 1989 *Tōkyō Saibanron* [On the Tokyo Trial], Tokyo: Ōtsuki Shoten.

——, 1994 'Tokyo saiban ni miru sengoshori' [Post-war settlement and the Tokyo Trial], in K. Awaya, H. Tanaka, K. Mishima, S. Hirowatari, Y. Mochida and Y. Yamaguchi (eds), *Sensō Sekinin, Sengo Sekinin: Nihon to Doitsu wa Dō Chigauka*, Tokyo: Asahi Shimbunsha,.

——, 1995 'Tōkyō saiban wo kangaeru' [Thinking about the Tokyo Trial], in Ajia Minshūhōtei Junbikai (ed.), *Toinaosu Tōkyō Saiban*, Tokyo: Ryokufū Shuppan, pp. 19–46.

—— and NHK Shuzaihan, 1994 *NHK Supesharu: Tōkyō Saiban e no Michi* [NHK Special: Road to the Tokyo Trial], Tokyo: Nihon Hōsō Shuppan Kyōkai.

—— Tanaka, H., Mishima, K., Hirowatari, S., Mochida, Y. and Yamaguchi, Y. 1994 *Sensō Sekinin, Sengo Sekinin: Nihon to Doitsu ha Dō Chigauka* [War Responsibility and Post-war Responsibility: The Difference between Japan and Germany], Tokyo: Asahi Shimbunsha.

Bailey, S. D., 1994 'Intervention: Article 2.7 versus Articles 55–56', *International Relations*, vol. XII, 1–10.

Ball, H., 1999 *Prosecuting War Crimes and Genocide: The Twentieth-Century Experience*, Lawrence: University Press of Kansas.

Bartov, O., Grossmann, A. and Nolan, M. (eds), 2002 *Crimes of War: Guilt and Denial in the Twentieth Century*, New York: The New Press.

Bass, G. J., 2000 *Stay the Hand of Vengeance: The Politics of War Crimes Tribunals*, Princeton, NJ: Princeton University Press.

Bassiouni, M. C., 1992 *Crimes against Humanity in International Criminal Law*, Dordrecht; Boston: M. Nijhoff Publishers; Norwell, MA: sold and distributed in the USA. and Canada by Kluwer Academic Publishers.

——, 1994a 'The United Nations Commission of Experts Established Pursuant to Security Council Resolution 780 (1992)', *American Journal of International Law*, vol. 88, 784–805.

——, 1994b 'Former Yugoslavia: investigating violations of international humanitarian law and establishing an international criminal tribunal', *Security Dialogue*, vol. 25, 409–23.

——, 1998 compiled, *The Statute of the International Criminal Court: A Documentary History*, New York: Transnational Publishers.

—— (ed.), 2002 *Post-Conflict Justice*, Ardsley, NY: Transnational Publishers.

Beigbeder, Y., 1999 *Judging War Criminals: The Politics of International Justice*, Basingstoke: Macmillan; New York: St Martin's Press.

——, 2002 *Judging Criminal Leaders: The Slow Erosion of Impunity*, The Hague: Martinus Nijhoff Publishers.

Beitz, C. R., 1999 *Political Theory and International Relations*, revised edn, Princeton, NJ: Princeton University Press.

Benedict, R., 1946 *The Chrysanthemum and the Sword: Patterns of Japanese Culture*, Boston: Houghton Mifflin.

Best, G., 1983 *Humanity in Warfare: The Modern History of the International Law of Armed Conflicts*, London: Methuen.

——, 1984 *Nuremberg and After: The Continuing History of War Crimes and Crimes against Humanity*, The Stenton Lecture 1983, Reading: University of Reading.

——, 1994 *War and Law since 1945*, Oxford: Clarendon Press.

Betts, R. K., 1994 'The delusion of impartial intervention', *Foreign Affairs*, vol. 73, no. 6, 20–33.

Bix H. P., Awaya, K. and Toyoda, M. (eds), 2000 *Tōkyō Saiban to Kokusai Kensatsukyoku: Kaitei kara Hanketsu made* [The Tokyo Trial and the International Prosecution section], Tokyo: Gendai Shiryō Shuppan, vol. 5.

Booth, K. and Smith, S. (eds), 1995 *International Relations Theory Today*, Cambridge: Polity Press.

Boraine, A., 2004 'Transitional justice as an emerging field' presented at the 'Repairing the Past: Reparations and Transitions to Democracy' symposium, Ottawa, Canada, 11 March.

Borch III, F. L., 2003 *Judge Advocates in Vietnam: Army Lawyers in Southeast Asia 1959–1975*, Kansas: US Army Command and General Staff College Press.

Brackman, A. C., 1987 *The Other Nuremberg: The Untold Story of the Tokyo War Crimes Trials*, New York: William Morrow and Company, Inc.

Bratt, D., 1999 'Peace over justice: developing a framework for UN peacekeeping operations in internal conflicts', *Global Governance: A Review of Multilateralism and International Organizations*, vol. 5, 63–81.

Broomhall, B., 2003 *International Justice and the International Criminal Court: Between Sovereignty and the Rule of Law*, Oxford: Oxford University Press.

Brown, C., 1992 *International Relations Theory: New Normative Approaches*, Hemel Hempstead: Harvester Wheatsheaf.

Bryder, A. and Hänggi, H. (eds), 2005 *Security Governance in Post-conflict Peacebuilding*, LIT Verlag: Geneva Centre for the Democratic Control of Armed Forces.

Bull, H., 1979 'The Universality of Human Rights', *Millennium: Journal of International Studies*, vol. 8, no. 2, 155–9.

——, 1984 *Justice in international relations*, Hagey Lectures, Ontario: University of Waterloo.

—— (ed.), 1984 *Intervention in World Politics*, Oxford: Clarendon Press.

——, 1995 *The Anarchical Society: a Study of Order in World Politics*, 2nd edn, Basingstoke: Macmillan.

——, Kingsbury, B. and Roberts, A. (eds), 1990 *Hugo Grotius and International Relations*, Oxford: Clarendon Press.

Burchard, C., 2006 'The Nuremberg Trial and its impact on Germany', *Journal of International Criminal Justice*, vol. 4, 800–29.

Buruma, I., 2002 *The Wages of Guilt: Memories of War in Germany and Japan*, paperback edn, London: Phoenix.

Bush, J. A., 1993 'Nuremberg: the modern law of war and its limitations', *Columbia Law Review*, vol. 93, 2022–85.

Buzan, B., 1993 'From international system to international society: structural realism and regime theory meet the English School', *International Organization*, vol. 47, 327–52.

Byers, M. (ed.), 2001 *The Role of Law in International Politics: Essays in International Relations and International Law*, Oxford; New York: Oxford University Press.

Carr, E. H., 1995 *The Twenty Years' Crisis 1919–1939: An Introduction to the Study of International Relations*, 2nd edn, London: Papermac.

Cassese, A., 1997 'Reflections on international criminal prosecution and punishment of violations of humanitarian law', in J. I. Charney, D. K. Anton and M. E. O'Connell (eds), *Politics, Values, and Functions: International Law in the 21st Century: Essays in Honor of Professor Louis Henkin*, The Hague: Kluwer Law International.

——, 1998 'On the current trends towards criminal prosecution and punishment of breaches of International Humanitarian Law', *European Journal of International Law*, vol. 9, 2–17.

——, 1999 'A follow-up: forcible humanitarian countermeasures and opinio necessitatis', *European Journal of International Law*, vol. 10, 791–9.

Cha, V. D., 2003 'Hypotheses on history and hate in Asia: Japan and the Korean Peninsula', in Y. Funabashi (ed.), *Reconciliation in the Asia-Pacific*, Washington, DC: United States Institute of Peace Press.

Chalk, F. R. and Jonassohn, K., 1990 *The History and Sociology of Genocide: Analyses and Case Studies*, New Haven: Yale University Press.

Charney, J. I., 1999 'Progress in international criminal law?', *American Journal of International Law*, vol. 93, 452–64.

——, Anton, D. K. and O'Connell, M. E. (eds), 1997 *Politics, Values, and Functions: International Law in the 21st Century: Essays in Honor of Professor Louis Henkin*, The Hague: Martinus Nijhoff Publishers.

Chesterman, S. (ed.), 2001a *Civilians in War*, Boulder, CO: Lynne Rienner Publishers.

——, 2001b 'No justice without peace? International criminal law and the decision to prosecute', in S. Chesterman (ed.), *Civilians in War*, Boulder, CO: Lynne Rienner Publishers.

Chiba, A. and Xiang, L., 2005 'Traumatic legacies in China and Japan: an exchange', *Survival*, vol. 47, no. 2, 215–32.

Chopra, J., 1999 *Peace-maintenance: The Evolution of International Political Authority*, London; New York: Routledge.

Chuter, D., 2003 *War Crimes: Confronting Atrocity in the Modern World*, Boulder, CO: Lynne Rienner Publishers.

Ciechanski, J., 1996 'Enforcement measures under chapter VII of the UN Charter: UN practice after the Cold War', *International Peacekeeping*, vol. 3, no. 4, 82–104.

Clark, R. and Sann, M. (eds), 1996 *The Prosecution of International Crimes: a Critical Study of the International Tribunal for the Former Yugoslavia*, New Brunswick: Transaction Publishers.

Clark, R. S., 1997 'Nuremberg and Tokyo in contemporary perspective', in T. L. H. McCormack and G. J. Simpson (eds), *The Law of War Crimes: National and International Approaches*, Boston, MA: Kluwer Law International, pp. 171–87.

von Clausewitz, C., 1976 *On War* (ed. and trans. by Michael Howard and Peter Paret), Princeton, NJ: Princeton University Press.

Colson, A. J., 2000 'The logic of peace and the logic of justice', *International Relations*, vol. 15, no. 1, 51–62.
Crocker, D. A., 2001 'Transitional justice and international civil society', in A. Jokic (ed.), *War Crimes and Collective Wrongdoing: A Reader*, Malden, MA: Blackwell Publishers.
Cryer, R., 2005 *Prosecuting International Crimes: Selectivity and the International Criminal Law Regime*, Cambridge: Cambridge University Press.
D'Amato, A., 1994 'Peace vs. accountability in Bosnia', *American Journal of International Law*, vol. 88, 500–6.
Dandeker, C., and Gow, J., 1997 'The future of peace support operations: strategic peacekeeping and success', *Armed Forces and Society*, vol. 23, 327–48.
Davidson, E., 1973 *The Nuremberg Fallacy: Wars and War Crimes Since World War II*, New York: The Macmillan Company.
Dillon, M., 1998 'Criminalising social and political violence internationally', *Millennium: Journal of International Studies*, vol. 27, 543–67.
Dinstein, Y., 1965 *The Defence of 'Obedience to Superior Orders' in International Law*, Leyden: Sijthoff.
——, 2000 'International criminal law', *Israel Yearbook on Human Rights*, vol. 55, 1975; reprinted in H. J. Steiner and P. Alston (eds), *International Human Rights in Context: Law, Politics, Morals*, 2nd edn, Oxford: Oxford University Press.
——, 2001 *War, Aggression and Self-Defence*, 3rd edn, New York: Cambridge University Press.
—— and Tabory, M. (eds), 1996 *War Crimes in International Law*, Boston: Martinus Nijhoff Publishers.
Donnelly, J., 1993 'Human rights, humanitarian crisis, and humanitarian intervention', *International Journal*, vol. 48, 607–40.
Douglas, L., 2001 *The Memory of Judgment: Making Law and History in the Trials of the Holocaust*, New Haven, CT: Yale University Press.
Dower, J. W., 1986 *War without Mercy: Race and Power in the Pacific War*, New York: Pantheon Books.
——, 2000 *Embracing Defeat: Japan in the Aftermath of World War II*, London: Penguin Books.
——, 2002 '"An aptitude for being unloved": war and memory in Japan', in O. Bartov, A. Grossmann and M. Nolan (eds), *Crimes of War: Guilt and Denial in the Twentieth Century*, New York: The New Press.
——, 2004 '"Bōryoku no rensa" wo tachikirutameni' [For cutting off the 'chain of violence'], *Ushio*, February, 72–85.
Duke, S., 1994 'The state and human rights: sovereignty versus humanitarian intervention', *International Relations*, vol. 12, no. 2, 25–48.
Dull, P. S. and Umemura, M. T., 1957 *The Tokyo Trials: A Functional Index to the Proceedings of the International Military Tribunal for the Far East*, Ann Arbor: University of Michigan Press.
Dunne, T., 1995 'The social construction of international society', *European Journal of International Relations*, vol. 1, 367–89.
Dupuy, R. J. (ed.), 1993 *The Development of the Role of the Security Council: Peace-Keeping and Peace-Building: Workshop, The Hague, 21–23 July 1992*, Dordrecht; Boston: M. Nijhoff; Norwell, MA: Distributed for the US and Canada, Kluwer Academic Publishers.
Elster, J., 2004 *Closing the Books: Transitional Justice in Historical Perspective*, Cambridge: Cambridge University Press.

European Commission, 1995 *Law in Humanitarian Crises Volume I: How Can International Humanitarian Law be Made Effective in Armed Conflicts?* Luxembourg: Office for Official Publications of the European Communities.

Falk, R., 1999 'Telford Taylor and the legacy of Nuremberg', *Columbia Journal of Transnational Law*, vol. 37, 693–723.

Farer, T. J., 2000 'Restraining the barbarians: can international criminal law help?', *Human Rights Quarterly*, vol. 22, 90–117.

Fein, H. (ed.), 1992 *Genocide Watch*, New Haven: Yale University Press.

Ferencz, B. B., 1998 'Make law not war', *World Today*, June, 152–3.

Finnemore, M., 1996 *National Interests in International Society*, Ithaca, NY: Cornell University Press.

—— and Sikkink, K., 1998 'International norm dynamics and political change', *International Organization*, vol. 52, 887–917.

Fishel, J. T. (ed.), 1998 *'The Savage Wars of Peace': Toward a New Paradigm of Peace Operations*, Boulder, CO: Westview Press.

Fisher, D., 1994 'The ethics of intervention', *Survival*, vol. 36, 51–9.

Foot, R., Gaddis, J. L. and Hurrell, A. (eds), 2003 *Order and Justice in International Relations*, Oxford: Oxford University Press.

Forbes, I. and Hoffman, M. (eds), 1993 *Political Theory, International Relations and the Ethics of Intervention*, Basingstoke: Macmillan.

Forsythe, D. P., 1994 'Politics and the International Tribunal for the Former Yugoslavia', *Criminal Law Forum: An International Journal*, vol. 5, 401–22.

——, 1997 'International Criminal Courts: a political view', *Netherlands Quarterly of Human Rights*, vol. 15, 5–19.

——, 2000 *Human Rights in International Relations*, Cambridge: Cambridge University Press.

Fox, H., 1993 'An international tribunal for war crimes: will the UN succeed where the Nuremberg failed?', *World Today*, vol. 49, no. 10, 194–7.

——, 1997 'The objections to transfer of criminal jurisdiction to the UN tribunal', *International and Comparative Law Quarterly*, vol. 46, 434–42.

Freedman, L. (ed.), 1994 *Military Intervention in European Conflicts*, Cambridge, MA: Blackwell.

——, 2004 *Deterrence*, Cambridge: Polity Press.

French, H. W., 2001 'Japan's resurgent far right tinkers with history', *New York Times,* 25 March.

Frey, R. G. and Morris, C. W. (eds), 1991 *Violence, Terrorism, and Justice*, Cambridge: Cambridge University Press.

Fuji, N., 1988 *Watashi no Mita Tōkyō Saiban* [The Tokyo Trial that I witnessed], 2 vols, Tokyo: Kōdansha.

Fujio, M., 1986 'Hōgen daijin ōini hoeru', *Bungeishunjū*, October.

Fujioka, N. and Yoshida, Y., 1997 'Koko ga okashii! Rekishi kyōkasho ronsō' [What is wrong with the textbook row], *This is Yomiuri*, March, 38–40.

Fujita, H., 1989 'Tokyō saiban no konnichiteki imi' [The Tokyo Trial's contemporary significance], *Hōritsu Jihō*, vol. 61, no. 9, 24–30.

Funabashi, Y. (ed.), 2003a *Reconciliation in the Asia-Pacific*, Washington, DC: United States Institute of Peace Press.

——, 2003b 'Introduction: why reconciliation?', in Y. Funabashi (ed.), *Reconciliation in the Asia-Pacific*, Washington, DC: United States Institute of Peace Press, pp. 3–17.

——, Mikuriya, T. and Mishima, K., 2003 '"Sensō sekinin" no chakuchiten wo motomete' [In search for the settlement of 'war responsibility'], *Chūōkōron*, no. 118, February, 47–71.

Gaer, F. D., 1997 'UN-anonymous: reflections on human rights in peace negotiations', *Human Rights Quarterly*, vol. 19, 1–8.

GHQ Sanbō Dainibu (ed.), 1998 *Makkāsā Repōto* [Reports of General MacArthur], vol. 2, Tokyo: Gendai Shiryō Shuppan (originally published in 1966 from Washington, DC: US GPO).

Ginn, J. L., 1992 *Sugamo Prison, Tokyo: An Account of the Trial and Sentencing of Japanese War Criminals in 1948, by a U.S. Participant*, Jefferson, NC: McFarland & Co.

Gluck, C., 1993 'The past in the present', in A. Gordon (ed.), *Postwar Japan as History*, Berkeley: University of California Press.

Goldstone, R. J., 1996a *Prosecuting War Criminals*, Occasional paper, no. 10, London: The David Davies Memorial Institute of International Studies.

——, 1996b 'Justice as a tool for peace-making: truth commissions and international criminal tribunals', *International Law and Politics*, vol. 28, 485–503.

——, 1997 'War crimes: a question of will', *World Today*, vol. 53, no. 4, 106–8.

——, 2000 *For Humanity: Reflections of a War Crimes Investigator*, New Haven, CT: Yale University Press.

Goodrich, L. M., Hambro, E. and Simons, A. P., 1969 *Charter of the United Nations: Commentary and Documents*, 3rd edn, New York: Columbia University Press.

Gordon, A. (ed.), 1993 *Postwar Japan as History*, Berkeley: University of California Press.

Gow, J., 2000 'A revolution in international affairs?', *Security Dialogue*, vol. 31, 293–306.

——, 2003 *The Serbian Project and Its Adversaries: A Strategy of War Crimes*, Montreal: McGill-Queen's University Press.

——, 2005 *Defending the West*, Cambridge: Polity Press.

Green, L. C., 1976 *Superior Orders in National and International Law*, Leyden: A. W. Sijthoff.

Greenwood, C., 1993a 'The relationship between jus *ad bellum* and *jus in bello*', *Review of International Studies*, vol. 9, 221–34.

——, 1993b 'Is there a right of humanitarian intervention?', *World Today*, vol. 49, no. 2, 34–40.

——, 1996 'International humanitarian law and the Tadic case', *European Journal of International Law*, vol. 7, 265–83.

Gushima, K., 1948 'Tōkyō saiban no rekishiteki igi' [The historical significance of the Tokyo Trial], *Rekishi Hyōron*, vol. 3, no. 6, 25–32.

Gutman, R., 1993 *A Witness to Genocide: The 1993 Pulitzer Prize-Winning Dispatches on the 'Ethnic Cleansing' of Bosnia*, Shaftesbury: Element Books.

Hankey, M. P. A., 1950 *Politics, Trials and Errors*, Oxford: Pen-In-Hand.

Harff, B. and Gurr, T. R., 1988 'Toward empirical theory of genocides and politicides: identification and measurement of cases since 1945', *International Studies Quarterly*, vol. 32, 359–71.

Harries, M. and Harries, S., 1987 *Sheathing the Sword: The Demilitarisation of Japan*, London: Hamish Hamilton.

Harris, I., 1993 'Order and justice in "The Anarchical Society"', *International Affairs*, vol. 69, 725–41.

Harris, S. H., 2002 *Factories of Death: Japanese Biological Warfare, 1935–1945, and the American Cover-up*, revised edn, New York: Routledge.

Hashimoto, S., 1959 *Watashi wa Kaini Naritai*, Tokyo: Gendaisha.

Hashizume, D., 2003 'Nihon kokumin ga hatasanakereba naranu sekinin towa' [The responsibility that the Japanese people need to meet], *Chūōkōron*, no. 118, February, 72–9.

Hayashi, H., 1998 *Sabakareta Sensō Hanzai: Igirisu no Tainichi Senpan Saiban* [Judged war crimes: Britain and its war crimes trials against Japan], Tokyo: Iwanami Shoten.

Hein, L. and Selden, M. (eds), 2000a *Censoring History: Citizenship and Memory in Japan, Germany, and the United States*, Armonk, NY: M.E. Sharpe.

——, 2000b 'The lessons of war, global power, and social change', in L. Hein and M. Selden (eds), *Censoring History: Citizenship and Memory in Japan, Germany, and the United States*, Armonk, NY: M.E. Sharpe.

Herz, J. H. (ed.), 1982a *From Dictatorship to Democracy: Coping with the Legacies of Authoritarianism and Totalitarianism*, Westport, CO: Greenwood Press.

——, 1982b 'Denazification and related policies', in J. H. Herz (ed.), *From Dictatorship to Democracy: Coping with the Legacies of Authoritarianism and Totalitarianism*, Westport, CT: Greenwood Press.

Higgins, R., 1994 *Problems and Process: International Law and How We Use It*, Oxford: Clarendon Press.

Higurashi, Y., 1997 'Kensatsu no ronri to saiban no tenkai' [The logic of the Prosecution section and the development of the trial], in T. Igarashi and S. Kitaoka (eds), *'Sōron' Tōkyō Saiban towa Nandattanoka*, Tokyo: Tsukijishokan, p. 74.

——, 2002 *Tōkyō Saiban no Kokusai Kankei: Kokusai Seiji ni okeru Kenryoku to Kihan* [International Relations of the Tokyo Trial: Power and Norm in International Politics], Tokyo: Bokutakusha.

Hill, S., 2000 'To prosecute or not', *World Today*, August/September, 35–7.

Hoffmann, S., 1995 'Thoughts on the UN at fifty', *European Journal of International Law*, vol. 6, 317–24.

Holbrooke, R., 1998 *To End a War*, New York: Random House.

Honda, K. (trans. K. Sandness; F. Gibney) (ed.), 1998 *The Nanjing Massacre: A Japanese Journalist Confronts Japan's National Shame*, Armonk, NY: M.E. Sharpe.

Horowitz, I. L., 1977 *Genocide: State Power and Mass Murder*, 2nd edn, New Brunswick, NJ: Transaction Books.

Horwitz, S., 1950 'The Tokyo Trial', *International Conciliation*, No. 465, 473–584.

Hosaka, M., 1998 'Dakara "Tōkyō saiban shikan" wo koerarenai' [This is why we cannot overcome the Tokyo Trial's view of history], *Shokun!*, January, 142–50.

Hosoya, C., Andō, N., Ōnuma, Y. and Minear, R. (eds), 1986 *The Tokyo War Crimes Trial: An International Symposium*, Tokyo: Kodansha; New York, NY: Distributed in the US by Kodansha International through Harper & Row.

Howard, M., 1993 'The historical development of the UN's role in international security', in A. Roberts and B. Kingsbury (eds), *United Nations, Divided World: The UN's Roles in International Relations*, 2nd edn, Oxford: Clarendon Press.

Human Rights Watch, Helsinki Watch Committee, 1992 *War Crimes in Bosnia-Herzegovina*, New York: Human Rights Watch.

Huntington, S. P., 1993 'The clash of civilizations?', *Foreign Affairs*, vol. 72, 22–49.

Ienaga, S., 1986 'The historical significance of the Tokyo trial', in C. Hosoya, N. Andō, Y. Ōnuma and R. Minear (eds), *The Tokyo War Crimes Trial: An International Symposium*, Tokyo: Kodansha; New York: distributed in the US by Kodansha International through Harper & Row.

Igarashi, T., 1997 'Hashigaki' [Preface], in T. Igarashi and S. Kitaoka (eds), *'Sōron' Tōkyō Saiban towa Nandattanoka*, Tokyo: Tsukijishokan, pp. iii–vi.

—— and Kitaoka, S. (eds), 1997 *'Sōron' Tōkyō Saiban towa Nandattanoka* ['Dispute' What was the Tokyo Trial], Tokyo: Tsukijishokan.

Ignatieff, M., 2000 *Virtual War: Kosovo and Beyond*, London: Chatto & Windus.

Inoue, H., 1990 'Wareware hitori hitori no sensō "mu"sekinin' [Our individual war irresponsibility], *Gekkan Asahi*, March, 98–101.

Inoue, K., 1948 'Hō no ronri to rekishi no ronri' [The logic of law and the logic of history], *Rekishi Hyōron*, vol. 3, no. 6, 1–13.

International Criminal Tribunal for Former Yugoslavia, 1996 *The Path to The Hague: Selected Documents on the Origins of the ICTY*, New York: ICTY.

Iokibe, M., 1983 '"Tōkyō saiban" ga sabaita hito to jidai' [People and the era that the Tokyo Trial judged], in Kōdansha (ed.), *Tōkyō Saiban: Shashin Hiroku*, Tokyo: Kōdansha.

Jackson, R. H., 1947 *The Nürnberg Case, as presented by Robert. H. Jackson, together with other documents*, New York: Alfred A. Knopf.

Jackson, R. H., 1993 'Armed humanitarianism', *International Journal*, vol. 48, 579–606.

Jaspers, K. (trans. E. B. Ashton), 1947 *The Question of German Guilt*, New York: The Dial Press.

Jokic, A. (ed.), 2001 *War Crimes and Collective Wrongdoing: A Reader*, Malden, MA: Blackwell Publishers.

Jones, J. R. W. D., 1996 'The implications of the peace agreements for the International Criminal Tribunal for the Former Yugoslavia', *European Journal of International Law*, vol. 7, 226–44.

Jorda, C., 2004 'The major hurdles and accomplishments of the ICTY: what the ICC can learn from them', *Journal of International Criminal Justice*, vol. 2, 572–84.

Jørgensen, N. H. B., 2000 *The Responsibility of States for International Crimes*, Oxford: Oxford University Press.

Kainō, M., 1948 'Sensōsaiban no hōritsuriron' [Legal theory of war crimes trials], *Rekishi Hyōron*, vol. 3, no. 6, 14–24.

—— and Ushiomi Toshitaka (eds), 1977 *Kainō Michitaka Chosaku-shū* [The Collection of Kainō Michitaka's Works], *Vol. 3, Saiban* [The Trial], Tokyo: Nihon Hyōron-sha.

——, Ukai, N., Takano, Y., Tusji, K. and Maruyama, M., 1949 'Tokyo saiban no jijitsu to hōri' [The fact and legal logic of the Tokyo Trial], *Hōritsu Jihō*, vol. 21, 61–76.

Kaldor, M., 1999 *New and Old Wars: Organized Violence in a Global Era*, Stanford, CA: Stanford University Press.

—— (ed.), 2000 *Global Insecurity*, London: Pinter.

Kaminski, M. M., Nalepa, M. and O'Neill, B., 2006 'Normative and Strategic Aspects of Transitional Justice', *Journal of Conflict Resolution*, vol. 50, 295–302.

Katzenstein, P. J. (ed.), 1996 *The Culture of National Security: Norms and Identity in World Politics*, New York: Columbia University Press.

Kelsen, H., 1947 'Will the judgment in the Nuremberg Trial constitute a precedent in international law?', *International Law Quarterly*, vol. 1, 153–71.

——, 1951 *The Law of the United Nations: A Critical Analysis of Its Fundamental Problems – with Supplement*, London: Stevens and Sons Limited.

Keohane, R. O. (ed.), 1986 *Neorealism and Its Critics*, New York: Columbia University Press.

——, 1989 *International Institutions and State Power: Essays in International Relations Theory*, Boulder, CO: Westview.

Kerr, R., 2000 'International judicial intervention: the International Criminal Tribunal for the Former Yugoslavia', *International Relations*, vol. 15, no. 2, 17–26.

——, 2004 *The International Criminal Tribunal for the Former Yugoslavia: An Exercise in Law Politics and Diplomacy*, Oxford: Oxford University Press.

King, C., 1997 *Ending Civil Wars*, Adelphi Papers 308, London: Oxford University Press.

Kingston, J., 2001 *Japan in Transformation, 1952–2000*, New York: Longman.

Kinoshita, J. (trans. E. J. Gangloff), 1979 *Between God and Man: A Judgement on War Crimes – A Play in Two Parts by Kinoshita Junji*, Tokyo: University of Tokyo Press.

——, 1998 'Tōkyō saiban ga kangaesasete kuretamono' [What I learned from the Tokyo Trial], in Ajia Minshū Hōtei Junbikai (ed.), *Jikō naki Sensō Sekinin: Sabakareru Tennō to Nihon, Zōhoban*, Tokyo: Ryokufū Shuppan. pp. 11–22.

Kitagawa, K., 1995 'Minshūni totteno haisen' [The meaning of the defeat of the people], in M. Nakamura, A. Amakawa, K. Yun and T. Igarashi (eds), *Sengo Nihon: Senryō to Sengokaikaku*, Tokyo: Iwanamishoten, vol. 1.

Kittichaisaree, K., 2001 *International Criminal Law*, Oxford: Oxford University Press.

Kiyose, I., 1966 *Hiroku Tōkyō Saiban* [Secret Notes: the Tokyo Trial], Tokyo: Yomiuri Shimbunsha.

Klarin, M., 1996 'Nuremberg now!', *Borba*, Belgrade, 16 May 1991, in *The Path to The Hague: Selected Documents on the Origins of the ICTY*, New York: ICTY, p. 35.

Kobayashi, M., 1983 'Watashi no "Tōkyō saiban"', in Kōdansha (ed.), *Tōkyō Saiban: Shashin Hiroku*, Tokyo: Kōdansha.

——, Uraoka, K. and Shinada, Y., 1983 'Tokushū Tōkyō saiban: Zadankai – Rekishi-teki shinjitsu wo kyakkantekini gurōbaruna shiten de' [Special feature the Tokyo Trial: roundtable: examining the historical truth objectively and globally], *Kinema Junpō*, no. 858, 61–7.

Kobayashi, S., 1978 'Takigawa Masajirō cho "Tōkyō saiban wo sabaku" no saikan nisaishite tōji wo kaisōsuru' [Afterword: Recollecting the Tokyo Trial], in M. Takigawa, *Tōkyō Saiban wo Sabaku*, Shinpan, vol. 2, Tokyo: Sōtakusha.

Kobayashi, Y., 1998 *Shin-Gōmanizumu Sengen Supesharu Sensō-ron* [On War], Tokyo: Gentōsha.

Kobori, K., 1988 'Kaisetsu' [Commentary], in N. Fuji, *Watashi no Mita Tōkyō Saiban*, vol. 2, Tokyo: Kōdansha. pp. 593–604.

——, (ed.), 1995 *Tōkyō Saiban Nihonno Benmei: "Kyakka Miteishutsu Bengogawa Shiryō" Bassui* [The Tokyo Trial and Japan's Defence: Selections from the Rejected and Non-Submitted Defence Materials], Tokyo: Kōdansha.

——, 1996 *Sai-Kenshō Tōkyō Saiban: Nihon wo Damenishita Shuppatsuten* [Re-examining the Tokyo Trial: the Starting Point that Ruined Japan], Tokyo: PHP Kenkyū-jo.

Kōdansha (ed.), 1983 *Tōkyō Saiban: Shashin Hiroku* [The Tokyo Trial: Secret Pictures], Tokyo: Kōdansha.

Koh, H. H., 1996/97 'Why do nations obey international law?', *Yale Law Journal*, vol. 106, 2599–659.

Kojima, N., 1971 *Tōkyō Saiban* [The Tokyo Trial], in two vol, Tokyo: Chūōkōron.

——, 1986 'Contributions to peace', in C. Hosoya, N. Andō, Y. Ōnuma and R. Minear (eds), *The Tokyo War Crimes Trial: An International Symposium*, Tokyo: Kodansha; New York: distributed in the US by Kodansha International through Harper & Row.

Kōseishō (ed.), 2000 *Zoku Hikiageengo no Kiroku, Fukkoku-ban*, Tokyo: Kuresu Shuppan (originally published in 1955).

Koskenniemi, M., 1995 'The police in the temple – order, justice and the UN: a dialectical view', *European Journal of International Law*, vol. 6, 325–48.

Kratochwil, F., 1989 *Rules, Norms, and Decisions: On the Conditions of Practical and*

Legal Reasoning in International Relations and Domestic Affairs, Cambridge: Cambridge University Press.

—— and Ruggie, J. G., 1986 'International organization: a state of the art on an art of the state', *International Organization*, vol. 40, 753–75.

Krause, K. and Williams, M. C., 1996 'Broadening the agenda of security studies: politics and methods', *Mershon International Studies Review*, vol. 40, 229–54.

Kritz, N. J. (ed.), 1995a *Transitional Justice: How Emerging Democracies Reckon with Former Regimes*, in three vols, Washington, DC: United States Institute of Peace Press.

——, 1995b 'The dilemmas of transitional justice', in N. J. Kritz (ed.), *Transitional Justice: How Emerging Democracies Reckon with Former Regimes, Vol.I, General Considerations*, Washington, DC: United States Institute of Peace Press.

Kyokutō Kokusai Gunji Saiban Kenkyūkai (ed.), 1947–48 *Kyokutō Kokusai Gunji Saiban Kenkyū* [Research of the International Military Tribunal for the Far East], in three vols, Tokyo: Heiwashobō.

Kyokutō Kokusai Gunji Saibansho (ed.), 1968 *Kyokutō Kokusai Gunji Saiban Sokkiroku* [The Stenographic Record of the International Military Tribunal for the Far East], Tokyo: Yūshodō Shoten.

Leifer, M. (ed.), 2000 *Asian Nationalism*, London: Routledge.

Luban, D., 1994 *Legal Modernism*, Ann Arbor: University of Michigan Press.

Lyons, G. M. and Mastanduno, M. (eds), 1995 *Beyond Westphalia?: State Sovereignty and International Intervention*, Baltimore MD: Johns Hopkins University Press.

McCormack, G., 2000 'The Japanese movement to "correct" history', in L. Hein and M. Selden (eds), *Censoring History: Citizenship and Memory in Japan, Germany, and the United States*, Armonk, NY: M.E. Sharpe, pp. 53–73.

McCormack, T. L. H. and Simpson, G. J. (eds), 1997a *The Law of War Crimes: National and International Approaches*, Boston, MA: Kluwer Law International.

——, 1997b 'Preface', in T. L. H. McCormack and G. J. Simpson (eds), *The Law of War Crimes: National and International Approaches*, Boston, MA: Kluwer Law International.

Maeno, T., 2000 *Sengo Rekishi no Shinjitsu: Waga Aisuru Magotachi e Tsutaetai* [Truth about Post-war History: For Our Dear Grandchildren], Tokyo: Keizaikai.

Maga, T., 2001 *Judgment at Tokyo: The Japanese War Crimes Trials*, Lexington: The University Press of Kentucky.

Maguire, P. H., 2001 *Law and War: An American Story*, New York: Columbia University Press.

Mainichi Shimbun Seijibu (ed.), 2000 (directed by A. Utsumi and H. Nagai) *Shimbun Shiryō ni miru Tōkyō Saiban, BC-kyū Saiban* [Media Coverage of The Tokyo Trial and Class B and C War Crimes Trials], vol. 1, Tokyo: Gendaishiryō Shuppan.

Mak, T. D., 1995 'The case against an International War Crimes Tribunal for the Former Yugoslavia', *International Peacekeeping*, vol. 2, 536–63.

Maki, T., 1988 *Nakasone Seiken 1806 nichi* [The Nakasone administration 1806 days], vol. 2, Tokyo: Gyōken Shuppankai, p. 24.

Malanczuk, P., 1993 *Humanitarian Intervention and the Legitimacy of the Use of Force*, Amsterdam: Het Spinhuis.

——, 1997 *Akehurst's Modern Introduction to International Law*, 7th revised edn, London and New York: Routledge.

Mamdani, M., 2001 *When Victims Become Killers: Colonialism, Nativism, and the Genocide in Rwanda*, Princeton, NJ: Princeton University Press.

Martenczuk, B., 1999 'The Security Council, the International Court and judicial review: what lessons from Lockerbie?', *European Journal of International Law*, vol. 10, 517–47.

Maruyama, M., 1963 'Thought and behaviour patterns of Japan's wartime leaders', in I. Morris (ed.), *Thought and Behaviour in Modern Japanese Politics by Masao Maruyama*, London: Oxford University Press.

Matsumoto, K., 1998 'Senpan towa nandattanoka' [What were war criminals?], *This is Yomiuri*, October, 38–45.

Mayall, J. (ed.), 1996 *The New Interventionism 1991–1994: United Nations Experience in Cambodia, Former Yugoslavia and Somalia*, Cambridge: Cambridge University Press.

Méndez, J. E., 1997 'Accountability for past abuses', *Human Rights Quarterly*, vol. 19, 255–82.

Meron, T., 1997 'Answering for war crimes: lessons from the Balkans', *Foreign Affairs*, vol. 76, no. 1.

——, 1998a *War Crimes Law Comes of Age: Essays*, Oxford: Clarendon Press; New York: Oxford University Press.

——, 1998b 'Is international law moving towards criminalization?', *European Journal of International Law*, vol. 9, 18–31.

——, 2000 'The humanization of humanitarian law', *American Journal of International Law*, vol. 94, 239–78.

Mikuriya, T., 2005 'Tōkyō saiban minaoshiga motomeru "kokkaron"' [Re-examination of the Tokyo Trial and the theory of the state], *Chūōkōron*, October, 244–9.

Minear, R. H., 1971 *Victors' Justice: The Tokyo War Crimes Trial*, Princeton, NJ: Princeton University Press.

——, 1972 (trans. N. Andō) *Shōsha no Sabaki: Sensō Saiban, Sensō Sekinin towa Nanika* [Victor's Justice: What is War Trial and War Responsibility?], Tokyo: Fukumura Shuppan.

——, 1985 (trans. N. Andō) *Tōkyō Saiban: Shōsha no Sabaki* [The Tokyo Trial: Victor's Justice], Tokyo: Fukumura Shuppan.

Minow, M., 1998 *Between Vengeance and Forgiveness: Facing History after Genocide and Mass Violence*, Boston, MA: Beacon Press.

Mochida, Y., 1994 '"Sensō sekinin, sengo sekinin": Mondai no suiiki' [War responsibility and post-war responsibility], in K. Awaya, H. Tanaka, K. Mishima, S. Hirowatari, Y. Mochida and Y. Yamaguchi (eds), *Sensō Sekinin, Sengo Sekinin: Nihon to Doitsu wa Dō Chigauka*, Tokyo: Asahi Shimbunsha. pp. 3–18.

Monshipouri, M. and Welch, C. E., 2001 'The search for international human rights and justice: coming to terms with the new global realities', *Human Rights Quarterly*, vol. 23, 370–401.

Morgenthau, H. J., 1967 *Politics among Nations: The Struggle for Power and Peace*, 4th edn, New York: Alfred A. Knopf.

Morimura, S., 1981 *Akuma no Hōshoku: 'Kantongun Saikinsenbutai' Kyōfu no Zenbō! Chōhen Dokyumento* [The Devil's Gluttony], Tokyo: Kōbunsha.

Morris, I. (ed.), 1963 *Thought and Behaviour in Modern Japanese Politics by Masao Maruyama*, London: Oxford University Press.

Morris, V. and Scharf, M. P., 1995 *An Insider's Guide to the International Criminal Tribunal for the Former Yugoslavia: A Documentary History and Analysis*, in two vols, Irvington-on-Hudson, NY: Transnational Publishers.

Nakajō, T., 1998 *Ojīchan Sensō no Koto wo Oshiete: Magomusume karano Shitsumon-Jō*

[Granddad, Tell Me about the War: Questionnaires from the Granddaughter], Tokyo: Chichi Shuppansha.

Nakamura, M., 1997 'Shōwashi kenkyū to Tōkyō saiban' [A study of the Shōwa era and the Tokyo Trial], in T. Igarashi and S. Kitaoka (eds), *'Sōron' Tōkyō Saiban toha Nandattanoka*, Tokyo: Tsukijishokan, pp. 178–92.

——, Amakawa, A., Yun, K. and Igarashi, T., 1995 *Sengo Nihon: Senryō to Sengokaikaku* [Post-war Japan: Occupation and Post-war Reformation], six vols, Tokyo: Iwanamishoten.

Neier, A., 1998 *War Crimes: Brutality, Genocide, Terror, and the Struggle for Justice*, New York: Times Books.

Newman, E., 2002 '"Transitional Justice": the impact of transnational norms and the UN', *International Peacekeeping*, vol. 9, 31–50.

Nish, I. (ed.), 1989 *Japan and the Second World War*, International Studies, Pamphlet, IS/89/197, London: London School of Economics and Political Science. Suntory Toyota International Centre for Economics and Related Disciplines.

—— (ed.), 1991a *The Occupation of Japan 1945–52*, International Studies, Pamphlet, IS/91/224, London: London School of Economics and Political Science. Suntory Toyota International Centre for Economics and Related Disciplines.

—— (ed.), 1991b *Aspects of the Allied Occupation of Japan, Part II*, International Studies, Pamphlet, IS/91/229, London: London School of Economics and Political Science. Suntory Toyota International Centre for Economics and Related Disciplines.

Nozaki Y. and Inokuchi, H., 2000 'Japanese education, nationalism, and Ienaga Saburo's textbook lawsuits', in L. Hein and M. Selden (eds), *Censoring History: Citizenship and Memory in Japan, Germany, and the United States*, Armonk, NY: M.E. Sharpe, pp. 96–126.

O'Brien, J. C., 1993 'The international tribunal for violations of international humanitarian law in the former Yugoslavia', *American Journal of International Law*, vol. 87, 639–59.

O'Brien, W. V., 1990/91 'The Nuremberg precedent and the Gulf War', *Virginia Journal of International Law*, vol. 31, 391–401.

Okazaki, H., Kitaoka, S. and Sakamoto, T., 2002 'Kingendaishikara miru 21-seiki "Nihonmaru" no kōkaizu' [The navigation of twenty-first century Japan: from the perspective of modern history], *Shokun!*, July, 160–226.

Olonisakin, F., 1997 'An international war crimes tribunal for Africa: problems and prospects', *African Journal of International and Comparative Law*, vol. 9, 822–35.

——, 2000 'Peace and justice in Africa: post-Cold War issues', *International Relations*, vol. 15, no. 1, 41–50.

Ōnuma, Y., 1997 *Tōkyō Saiban kara Sengo Sekinin no Shisō e* [From the Tokyo Trial to a Sense of Post-war Responsibility], 4th edn, Tokyo: Tōshindō.

——, Utsumi, A., Yoshida, Y. and Hosaka, M., 2003 'Renzoku tōron 1: Tōkyō Saiban to sensō sekinin' [Discussion 1: The Tokyo Trial and war responsibility], *Sekai*, January, 277–91.

Osiel, M., 1997 *Mass Atrocity, Collective Memory, and the Law*, New Brunswick, NJ: Transaction Publishers.

——, 2000 'Why prosecute? Critics of punishment for mass atrocity', *Human Rights Quarterly*, vol. 22, 118–47.

Österdahl, I., 1998 *Threat to the Peace: The Interpretation by the Security Council of Article 39 of the UN Charter*, Uppsala: Iustus Forlag.

Owen, D., 1992 'When it is right to fight', *The Times*, 4 August.

Pal, R. B., 1953 *International Military Tribunal for the Far East: Dissentient Judgment*, Calcutta: Sanyal & Co.

Paskins, B., 1981 'Prohibitions, restraints and scientists', in N. A. Sims (ed.), *Explorations in Ethics and International Relations: Essays in Honour of Sydney D. Bailey*, London: Croom Helm.

—— and Dockrill, M., 1979 *The Ethics of War*, London: Duckworth.

—— and Gow, J., 2000 'The creation of the international tribunals from the perspectives of pragmatism, realism and liberalism', *International Relations*, vol. 15, no. 3, 11–15.

Pease, K. K. and Forsythe, D. P., 1993 'Human rights, humanitarian intervention, and world politics', *Human Rights Quarterly*, vol. 15, 290–314.

Pfaff, W., 1995 'A new colonialism? Europe must go back into Africa', *Foreign Affairs*, vol. 74, no. 1, 2–6.

——, 2000 'Judging war crimes', *Survival*, vol. 42, no. 1, 46–58.

Piccigallo, P. R., 1979 *The Japanese on Trial: Allied War Crimes Operations in the East, 1945–1951*, Austin: University of Texas Press.

Popovski, V., 2000 'The International Criminal Court: a synthesis of retributive and restorative justice', *International Relations*, vol. 15, no. 3, 1–10.

Pritchard, R. J., 1987a 'Preface', in R. J. Pritchard and S. M. Zaide (eds) and Project Director: D. C. Watt, *The Tokyo War Crimes Trial: Index and Guide in Five Volumes*, vol. I, New York and London: Garland Publishing Inc.

——, 1987b *An Overview of the Historical Importance of the Tokyo War Trial*, Nissan Occasional Paper Series, No. 5, Oxford: Nissan Institute of Japanese Studies.

—— and Zaide, S. M. (eds) and Project Director: D. C. Watt, 1981 *The Tokyo War Crimes Trial: The Complete Transcripts of the Proceedings of the International Military Tribunal for the Far East in Twenty-two Volumes*, New York and London: Garland Publishing Inc.

—— (eds) and Project Director: D. C. Watt, 1981–87 *The Tokyo War Crimes Trial: Index and Guide*, in five vols, New York and London: Garland Publishing Inc.

Ralph, J., 2005 'International society, the International Criminal Court and American foreign policy', *Review of International Studies*, vol. 31, 27–44.

Ramsbotham, O. and Woodhouse, T., 1996 *Humanitarian Intervention in Contemporary Conflict: A Reconceptualization*, Cambridge: Polity Press.

Ratner, S. R. and Abrams, J. S., 2001 *Accountability for Human Rights Atrocities in International Law: Beyond the Nuremberg Legacy*, 2nd edn, Oxford: Oxford University Press.

Reus-Smit, C. (ed.), 2004 *The Politics of International Law*, Cambridge: Cambridge University Press.

Roberts, A., 1993 'Humanitarian war: military intervention and human rights', *International Affairs*, vol. 69, 429–49.

——, 1995 'The laws of war: problems of implementation in contemporary conflicts', in European Commission, *Law in Humanitarian Crises Volume I: How Can International Humanitarian Law be Made Effective in Armed Conflicts?* Luxembourg: Office for Official Publications of the European Communities.

——, 1999 'Willing the end but not the means', *World Today*, May, 8–12.

——, 2003 'Order/justice issues at the United Nations', in R. Foot, J. L. Gaddis and A. Hurrell (eds), *Order and Justice in International Relations*, Oxford: Oxford University Press.

—— and Guelff, R., 2000 *Documents on the Laws of War*, 3rd edn, Oxford: Oxford University Press.

—— and Kingsbury, B. (eds), 1993 *United Nations, Divided World: The UN's Roles in International Relations*, 2nd edn, Oxford: Clarendon Press.

Robertson, G., 2001 'Opinion: the court is on trial too', *Guardian*, 30 June.

——, 2002 *Crimes Against Humanity: The Struggle for Global Justice*, 2nd edn, London: Penguin Books.

Röling, B. V. A., 1993 (edited by A. Cassese) *The Tokyo Trial and Beyond: Reflections of a Peacemonger*, London: Polity Press.

—— and Rüter, C. F. (eds), 1977 *The Tokyo Judgment: The International Military Tribunal for the Far East (IMTFE), 29 April 1946–12 November 1948*, Amsterdam: University Press Amsterdam.

Romano, C. P. R., Nollkaemper, A. and Kleffner, J. K. (eds), 2004 *Internationalized Criminal Courts: Sierra Leone, East Timor, Kosovo, and Cambodia*, Oxford: Oxford University Press.

Roy, D., 2005 'The sources and limits of Sino-Japanese tensions', *Survival*, vol. 47, no. 2, 191–214.

Rubin, A. P., 1996/1997 'Dayton, Bosnia, and the limits of law', *National Interest*, Winter, 41–6.

——, 1997 *Ethics and Authority in International Law*, New York: Cambridge University Press.

Rudolph, C., 2001 'Constructing an atrocities regime: the politics of war crimes tribunals', *International Organization*, vol. 55, 655–91.

Ruggie, J. G., 1998 'What makes the world hang together? Neo-utilitarianism and the social constructivist challenge', *International Organization*, vol. 52, 855–85.

Safferling, C. J. M., 2001 *Towards an International Criminal Procedure*, New York: Oxford University Press.

Satō, K., 1987 *Kenpō Kyūjō, Shinryaku Sensō, Tōkyō Saiban* [Article 9 of the Constitution, Aggressive War and the Tokyo Trial], Tokyo: Hara Shobō.

Schabas, W. A., 2001 *An Introduction to the International Criminal Court*, Cambridge: Cambridge University Press.

Scharf, M. P., 1997 *Balkan Justice: The Story Behind the First International War Crimes Trial Since Nuremberg*, Durham, NC: Carolina Academic Press.

Scheffer, D. J., 1996 'International judicial intervention', *Foreign Policy*, no. 102, 34–51.

Schmitt, M. N. (ed.), 2000 *International Law Across the Spectrum of Conflict: Essays in Honour of Professor L.C. Green on the Occasion of His Eightieth Birthday*, Newport, RI: Naval War College.

Schrag, M., 2004 'Lessons learned from ICTY experience', *Journal of International Criminal Justice*, vol. 2, 427–34.

Schuett, O., 1997 'The International War Crimes Tribunal for Former Yugoslavia and the Dayton Peace Agreement: peace versus justice?', *International Peacekeeping*, vol. 4, no. 2, 91–114.

Sebald, W. J., 1967 *With MacArthur in Japan: A Personal History of the Occupation*, London: Cresset Press.

Sewell, J. P., 2002 'Review essay: justice and truth in transition', *Global Governance: A Review of Multilateralism and International Organizations*, vol. 8, 119–34.

Shaw, M., 2003 *War and Genocide: Organized Killing in Modern Society*, Malden, MA: Polity Press.

Shiroyama, S. (trans. J. Bester), 1977 *War Criminal: the Life and Death of Hirota Koki*, Tokyo; New York: Kodansha International.

Shklar, J. N., 1964 *Legalism*, Cambridge, MA: Harvard University Press.

Shūsen Gojushūnen Kokumin Iinkai (ed.), 1996 *Sekaiga Sabaku Tōkyō Saiban: 85-ninno Gaikoku Shikishaga Kataru Rengōkoku Saiban* [The Tokyo Trial Judged by the World], Tokyo: Jupita Shuppan.

Simpson, G. J., 1997 'War crimes: a critical introduction', in T. L. H. McCormack and G. J. Simpson (eds), *The Law of War Crimes: National and International Approaches*, Boston, MA: Kluwer Law International.

Sims, N. A. (ed.), 1981 *Explorations in Ethics and International Relations: Essays in Honour of Sydney D. Bailey*, London: Croom Helm London.

Slaughter, A., 1995 'International law in a world of liberal states', *European Journal of International Law*, vol. 6, 503–38.

——, Tulumello, A. S. and Wood, S., 1998 'International law and international relations theory: a new generation of interdisciplinary scholarship', *American Journal of International Law*, vol. 92, 367–97.

Slaughter Burley, A., 1993 'International law and international relations theory: a dual agenda', *American Journal of International Law*, vol. 87, 205–39.

Smith, B. F., 1981 *The Road to Nuremberg*, London: André Deutsch.

—— (ed.), 1982 *The American Road to Nuremberg: The Documentary Record 1944–1945*, Stanford, CA: Hoover Institution Press.

Smith, S., Booth, K. and Zalewski, M. (eds), 1996 *International Theory: Positivism and Beyond*, Cambridge: Cambridge University Press.

Snyder, J., 2004 'One world, rival theories', *Foreign Policy*, no. 145, 52–62.

—— and Vinjamuri, L., 2003/04 'Trials and errors: principle and pragmatism in strategies of international justice', *International Security*, vol. 28, no. 3, 5–44.

Sprecher, D. A., 1999 *Inside the Nuremberg Trial: A Prosecutor's Comprehensive Account*, vol. II, Lanham, MD: University Press of America.

Stedman, S. J., 1992/93 'The new interventionists', *Foreign Affairs*, vol. 72, no. 1, 1–16.

Steiner, H. J. and Alston, P. (eds), 2000 *International Human Rights in Context: Law, Politics, Morals*, 2nd edn, Oxford: Oxford University Press.

Stimson, H. L., 1947 'The Nuremberg Trial: landmark in law', *Foreign Affairs*, vol. 25, 179–89.

Sugawara, Y., 1961 *Tōkyō Saiban no Shōtai* [The Truth of the Tokyo Trial], Tokyo: Jiji Tsūshinsha.

Sumitani, T., 1984 'Sensō hanzai saibanron, sensō sekininronno dōkō: Bunken shōkaiwo chūshinni' [The Trend and Development of the Argument of War Crimes Tribunals and War Responsibility: Literature Review], *Shisō*, no. 719, 123–31.

——, 1995 '"Shōsha no sabaki" ron saikō' [Re-examining the debate on 'victor's justice'], in Ajia Minshūhōtei Junbikai (ed.), *Toinaosu Tōkyō Saiban*, Tokyo: Ryokufū Shuppan.

Suzuki, A., 1973 *'Nankin Daigyakusatsu' no Maboroshi* [The illusion of the Nanjing massacre], Tokyo: Bungei Shunjū.

Takahashi, S., Ōnuma, Y., Andō, N, Hasegawa, M. and Ōhara, Y., 1987 'Shimpojium Tōkyō Saiban' [Symposium: The Tokyo Trial], *Shokun*, vol. 19, no. 8, 44–67.

Takahashi, T., 1999 *Sengo Sekinin-ron* [The Theory of Post-war Responsibility], Tokyo: Kōdansha.

——, 2005 *Yasukuni Mondai* [The Yasukuni Row], Tokyo: Chikuma Shobō.

Takakuwa, K., 1984 *Makkāsā no Shimbunkenetsu* [MacArthur's Newspaper Censorship], Tokyo: Yomiuri Shimbunsha.

Takayanagi, K., 1948 *The Tokio Trials and International Law*, Tokyo: Yuhikaku.

Takeda, K., 1988 *The Dual-Image of the Japanese Emperor*, Basingstoke: Macmillan.

Takemae, E., 2002 *Inside GHQ: The Allied Occupation of Japan and Its Legacy*, New York: Continuum.

Takigawa, M., 1952 *Tōkyō Saiban wo Sabaku* [Judging the Tokyo Trial], vol. 1, Tokyo: Tōwasha.

——, 1978 *Tōkyō Saiban wo Sabaku*, Shinpan [Judging the Tokyo Trial, new edn], 2 vols, Tokyo: Sōtakusha.

Tanaka, A., 2005 'Sensōno gekigenshita sekaide "sensōno rekishi" to dō mukiauka' [How to face 'the history of war' in a war-less world], *Chūōkōron*, September, 32–42.

Tanaka, H., 1994 'Nihonwa sensō sekininni dō taiō shitekitaka' [How has Japan been responding to the issue of war responsibility?], *Sekai*, February, 122–32.

Tanaka, M., 1963 *Pāru Hakase no Nihon Muzai-ron* [Justice Pal's Theory of Japan's Innocence], Tokyo: Keibunsha.

Tanaka, N., 1998 'Rekishi wo kakutoku surutame no teiki' [For acquiring the history], in Ajia Minshū Hōtei Junbikai (ed.), *Jikō naki Sensō Sekinin: Sabakareru Tennō to Nihon jin, Zōhoban*, Tokyo: Ryokufū Shuppan.

Taylor, R. N., 1995 'Inside story: the ghost of Nuremberg', *Guardian*, 28 November.

Taylor, T., 1950 'Preface', in S. Horwitz, 'The Tokyo Trial', *International Conciliation*, No. 465.

——, 1971 *Nuremberg and Vietnam: An American Tragedy*, New York: Bantam Books.

——, 1992 *The Anatomy of the Nuremberg Trials: A Personal Memoir*, New York: Alfred A. Knopf.

Teitel, R. G., 2000 *Transitional Justice*, New York: Oxford University Press.

Terriff, T. and Keeley, J. F., 1995 'The United Nations, conflict management and spheres of interest', *International Peacekeeping*, vol. 2, 510–35.

Téson, F. R., 1988 *Humanitarian Intervention: An Inquiry Into Law And Morality*, Dobbs Ferry: Transnational Publishers.

——, 1998 *A Philosophy of International Law*, Boulder, CO: Westview Press.

Tisdall, S., Pick, H. and Schork, K., 1992 'US edges towards Bosnia force', *Guardian*, 5 August.

Tōkyō Saiban Handobukku Henshū Iinkai (ed.), 1989 *Tōkyō Saiban Handobukku* [The Tokyo Trial Handbook], Tokyo: Aoki Shoten.

Tōkyō Saiban Kenkyūkai (ed.), 1984 *Kyōdō Kenkyū Paru Hanketsu-sho* [Joint Research Pal's Judgment], 2 vols, Tokyo, Kōdansha.

Tōkyō Saiban Shiryō Kankōkai (ed.), 1995 *Tōkyō Saiban Kyakka Miteishutsu Bengogawa Shiryō*, 8 vols, Tokyo: Kokusho Kankōkai.

Tsunoda, J., 1984 'Paru hanketsusho to Shōwashi' [Pal's judgement and the history of the Shōwa era], in Tōkyō Saiban Kenkyūkai (ed.), *Paru Hanketsusho: Kyōdō Kenkyū*, vol. 1, Tokyo, Kōdansha.

Tsurumi, S., 1986 'What the war trials left to the Japanese people', in C. Hosoya, N. Andō, Y. Ōnuma and R. Minear (eds), *The Tokyo War Crimes Trial: An International Symposium*, Tokyo: Kodansha; New York: distributed in the US by Kodansha International through Harper & Row.

——, 1987 *A Cultural History of Postwar Japan: 1945–1980*, London and New York: KPI Limited.

UK Ministry of Defence, 2004 *The Manual of the Law of Armed Conflict*, Oxford, New York: Oxford University Press.

United Nations War Crimes Commission, 1948 *History of the United Nations War Crimes Commission and the Development of the Laws of War*, London: HMSO.

Ushimura, K., 2003 *Beyond the 'Judgment of Civilization': The Intellectual Legacy of the Japanese War Crimes Trials, 1946–1949*, Tokyo: The International House of Japan.

——, 2004 *'Shōsha no Sabaki' ni Mukiatte: Tōkyō Saiban wo Yominaosu* [Facing 'Victor's Justice': Re-reading the Tokyo Trial], Tokyo: Chikuma Shobō.

——, 2005 'Rekishininshiki ronsōwo "bunkano sabaki" to surunakare: Tokyō saiban saikō' [Controversy over the view of history and the re-examination of the Tokyo Trial], *Chūōkōron*, September, 44–51.

Ushiomi, T. (ed.), 1977 *Kainō Michitaka Chosakushū*, vol. 3, Tokyo: Nihon Hyōronsha.

Utsumi, A., 1982 *Chōsenjin BC-kyū Senpan no Kiroku* [The record of Korean Class B and C war criminals], Tokyo: Keisōshobō.

——, 1995 'Toinaosu Tōkyō Saiban no kankōni atete' [Preface], in Ajia Minshūhōtei Junbikai (ed.), *Toinaosu Tōkyō Saiban*, Tokyo: Ryokufū Shuppan.

——, 1997 'Changing Japanese views of the Allied occupation of Japan and the war crimes trials', *Journal of the Australian War Memorial*, Issue 30. Available online at: www.awm.gov.au/journal/j30/utsumi.htm (accessed 2 May 2003).

Van Zyl, P., 2005 'Promoting transitional justice in post-conflict societies', in A. Bryden and H. Hänggi (eds.), *Security Governance in Post-Conflict Peacebuilding*, LIT Verlag: Geneva Centre for the Democratic Control of Armed Forces.

Vincent, R. J., 1986 *Human Rights and International Relations*, Cambridge: Cambridge University Press.

Vinjamuri, L. and Snyder, J., 2004 'Advocacy and scholarship in the study of international war crime tribunals and transitional justice', *Annual Review of Political Science*, vol. 7, 345–62.

Walliman, I. and Dobkowski, M. N. (eds), 1987 *Genocide and the Modern Age: Etiology and Case studies of Mass Death*, Westport, CT: Greenwood Press.

Waltz, K. N., 1959 *Man, the State and War: A Theoretical Analysis*, New York: Columbia University Press.

Walzer, M., 1992 *Just and Unjust Wars: A Moral Argument with Historical Illustrations*, 2nd edn, New York: Basic Books.

——, 1994 *Thick and Thin: Moral Argument at Home and Abroad*, Notre Dame: University of Notre Dame Press.

Watt, D. C., 1981 'Historical introduction', in R. J. Pritchard and S. M. Zaide (eds) and Project Director: D. C. Watt, *The Tokyo War Crimes Trial: Index and Guide in Five Volumes*, vol. I, New York and London: Garland Publishing Inc.

Weiss, T. G., 1999 *Military–Civilian Interactions: Intervening in Humanitarian Crises*, Lanham, MD: Rowman & Littlefield.

Welch, J. M., 2001 *The Tokyo Trial: A Bibliographic Guide to English-Language Sources*, Westport, CT: Greenwood Press.

Weller, M., 1999 'On the hazards of foreign travel for dictators and other international criminals', *International Affairs*, vol. 75, 599–617.

Wells, D. A., 1984 *War Crimes and Laws of War*, Lanham, MD: University Press of America.

Wendt, A., 1992 'Anarchy is what states make of it: the social construction of power politics', *International Organization*, vol. 46, 391–425.

——, 1999 *Social Theory of International Politics*, Cambridge: Cambridge University Press.

Wheeler, N. J., 2000 *Saving Strangers: Humanitarian Intervention in International Society*, Oxford: Oxford University Press.

White, N. D., 1997 *Keeping the Peace: The United Nations and the Maintenance of*

International Peace and Security, 2nd edn, Manchester: Manchester University Press.

Whitman, J., 1994 '"If it's right, it's gotta be done": a cautionary note on UN humanitarian intervention', *Cambridge Review of International Affairs*, vol. 8, 40–54.

Wiessner, S. and Willard, A. R., 1999 'Policy-oriented jurisprudence and human rights abuses in internal conflict: toward a world public order of human dignity', *American Journal of International Law*, vol. 93, 316–34.

Wight, M., 1991 *International Theory: The Three Traditions*, London: Leicester University Press.

Williams, J., 1999 'The ethical basis of humanitarian intervention, the Security Council and Yugoslavia', *International Peacekeeping*, vol. 6, no. 2, 1–23.

Williams, P. R. and Scharf, M. P., 2002 *Peace with Justice? War Crimes and Accountability in the Former Yugoslavia*, Lanham, MD: Rowman & Littlefield.

Willis, J. F., 1982 *Prologue to Nuremberg: The Politics and Diplomacy of Punishing War Criminals of the First World War*, Westport, CT; London: Greenwood Press.

Yang, D., 2003 'Reconciliation between Japan and China: problems and prospects', in Y. Funabashi (ed.), *Reconciliation in the Asia-Pacific*, Washington, DC: United States Institute of Peace Press.

Yokota, K., 1947 *Sensō Hanzai Ron* [On War Crimes], Tokyo: Yūhikaku.

Yomiuri Shimbun Sensō Seekinin Kenshō Iinkai (ed.), 2006 *Kenshō Sensō Seknin I* [Examining War Responsibility 1], Tokyo: Chuōkōronsha.

Yoshida, Y., 1991 'Senryōki ni okeru sensō skininron' [The argument of war responsibility during the occupation], *Hitotsubashi Ronsō*, vol. 105, no. 2, 121–38.

——, 1995a 'Senryōki no sensō sekininron' [The debate on war responsibility during the occupation], in Ajia Minshūhōtei Junbikai (ed.), *Toinaosu Tōkyō Saiban*, Tokyo: Ryokufū Shuppan.

——, 1995b 'Sensō sekinin to Kyokutō Kokusai Gunji Saiban' [War crimes and the International Military Tribunal for the Far East] in M. Nakamura, A. Amakawa, K. Yun and T. Igarashi (eds), *Sengo Nihon: Senryō to Sengokaikaku,* Tokyo: Iwanamishoten, vol. 5.

Yoshimi, Y., 1992 'Senryōki nihon no minshūishiki: Sensōsekininron wo megutte' [Japanese public perception during the occupation: regarding the argument of war responsibility], *Shisō*, no. 811, 73–99.

——, 2001 (trans. S. O'Brien) *Comfort Women: Sexual Slavery in the Japanese Military During Second World War*, New York: Columbia University Press.

Yui, D., 1997 'Komento' [Comment], in T. Igarashi and S. Kitaoka (eds), *'Sōron' Tōkyō Saiban towa Nandattanoka*, Tokyo: Tsukijishokan.

Zalaquett, J., 1995a 'Balancing ethical imperatives and political constraints: the dilemma of new democracies confronting past human rights violations', reprinted in N. J. Kritz (ed.), *Transitional Justice: How Emerging Democracies Reckon with Former Regimes, Vol. I, General Considerations*, Washington, DC: United States Institute of Peace Press.

——, 1995b 'Confronting human rights violations committed by former governments: principles applicable and political constraints', reprinted in N. J. Kritz (ed.), *Transitional Justice: How Emerging Democracies Reckon with Former Regimes, Vol. I, General Considerations*, Washington, DC: United States Institute of Peace Press.

Zolo, D., 1998 'Hans Kelsen: international peace through international law', *European Journal of International Law*, vol. 9, 306–24.

Index